3 0012 00124771 6

KU-237-055

Leabharlann Chor   Luim

WITHDRAWN FROM STOCK

Patrick J. O'Connor

H97179

LIMERICK
COUNTY LIBRARY

FAIRS AND MARKETS OF IRELAND
A CULTURAL GEOGRAPHY

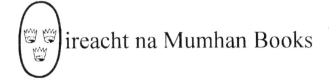

ireacht na Mumhan Books

Published in Ireland by
Oireacht na Mumhan Books
Coolanoran
Newcastle West
Co. Limerick

Copyright © Patrick J. O'Connor
All rights reserved
ISBN 09533896 3 4

Printed by Litho Press, Midleton, Co. Cork

i.m.
Jim and Florrie McKeon

CONTENTS

List of illustrations

2. *Plates*

Preface

The genesis of this book is simple and clear-cut. It stems from an invitation to contribute an item on fairs and markets in eighteenth and nineteenth-century Ireland to the *Encyclopaedia of Ireland*, New York: MacMillan Reference, 2003. Having perused the field, some landmark contributions stood out, spanning the spectrum from origins to ends. Historians such as Doherty and Ó Corráin have made a significant contribution to the elucidation of fair and market origins from their studies of early documentation. In the field of popular history, Patrick Logan blazed a trail with his wide-ranging survey of fair and market day in 1985. That same year Patrick O'Flanagan sought some theoretical underpinnings for the idea of fairs and markets as an index of economic development and regional growth. Then, quite adventitiously, as I was preparing my entry for the encyclopaedia, in 2001 a group of local historians came together to publish a collection of essays on Irish fairs and markets. The time may have been ripe for synthesis. In any event, it is a challenge that I have taken up, and answer with a cultural geography.

The timing may also be significant, especially since the freshness of fair and market day is fast fading from memory. Moreover, in writing this book, I am reminded that one should never throw away the chance of an *aide-mémoire*. My late mother, a dress-maker, was a great hoarder of odds and ends. I have clung to her hoarding instincts, and in gathering up my senses of fair day, I was charmed to come across jottings of trips to the fairs of Castlegregory and Dingle from September 1968. At the time I was pursuing the interests of fieldwork in the good company of Lukie Doherty, cattle-dealer, and John Coleman, tangler. Thus I have been gifted as rounded an ending as I could wish for, right at the death of the fairs as gathering days. The dialogue, portraiture and images all came bouncing back to me from cherished country of the mind.

On my way to *finis*, I have been helped by a number of people. For constancy, goodness and kindness, I gratefully acknowledge the support of my wife, Esther. I wish to thank Patrick O'Flanagan for furnishing me with a copy of the one great source for re-construction: *Report of the Fairs and Market Commission*, 1852-3. Always helpful, inquisitive and constructive, I extend my warm thanks to Brian Keary for his sagacity about fairs and unrelated matters, and for presenting me with a copy of *Old Moore's Almanac*, 2003. Others to help or encourage, and merit my thanks, include the current editor of *Old Moore's* Almanac, along with Ken Bergin, Pádraig de Brún, Eoin Devereux, Tommy McKeon, Michael Maguire, John O'Connor, and John Power. I wish to thank the University of Limerick for funding which enabled me to present a paper on the subject of Irish fairs and markets at the International Conference of the Social Sciences, Honolulu, Hawaii, June 2002. Thanks to the trustees of the National Library of

Ireland for permission to reproduce twelve photographs of fairs and markets from its photographic collections. The usual conditions of authorship apply to this work. In the explanatory narrative, which follows, faults and flaws are strictly my own.

CHAPTER ONE

Origins

Fairs and markets are an old story in Ireland, reaching back in the Gaelic tradition to the *óenach* or *aonach* ("fair") and to *margad[h]* ("market"), a late loan word from the Latin *mercatus* as mediated by Old Norse *markadr*.[1] Like many an old story, fairs and markets underwent mutation in the course of history, but stayed as gathering days. And so *óenach*, an old word written down in the ninth century, was used for a provincial or tribal assembly held at Lughnasa (*circa* 1st August) to celebrate the harvest. It may also have signified borderland assemblies of a generally earlier date where gifts were exchanged between kings and trade took place among followers. As with the fair, there was a slow emergence of the market. By the late eight-century many of the greater monasteries had grown into trading centres and functioned as *óenach* (assembly and exchange) sites in their own right. However, the concept of the *margad* ("market") as a permanent institution appears to have been introduced by the Norse.[2] From the ninth century onwards it took root in their trading stations as part of an urban civilisation.

1

Among the earliest known places of assembly and exchange were the *óenach* sites associated with the festival of Lughnasa. The most famous was Óenach Tailten, resort of the provincial king of Meath and the high king of Ireland. Located on a loop of the River Blackwater in the townland and parish of Teltown, Co. Meath, it is a place imbued with majestic aura. Here the idea of the sovereignty of Ireland arose and was fostered. Tailtiu[3] may have originated as the sacred place of a small community, but by the early historic period it had become vested in the high king, whose right it was to preside over the Óenach. By then Tailtiu had gathered a raft of meanings as an afterlife landscape, a site of legendary battles, and a place of annual assembly.

It is well documented.[4] The Annals accord it contemporary and significant reference. Its origin stories and legendary connections are well preserved in literature. Two long poems were specially composed for it, one for the Óenach of 885, and the other for the Óenach of 1007. Even incidental passages confer upon it the measure of due significance. Topographical features still resonate its fame, most notably *Lag an Aonaigh* ("the hollow of the fair"). Here according to tradition marriages were celebrated in the rites of Elder Faiths. Gaiety and gathering is a leading *leitmotiv*. The cult of personality is vented. In a poem lamenting the death of the high king Aedh Finnliath in 876, for example, he is accorded the accolade of *graifnidh Tailten telglaine* ("master of the horse-races of fair-hilled Tailtiu").[5] All this is congruent with Tailtiu of the high kings, site of the most famous assembly in Ireland and adapted successfully into a Gaelic Christian polity.

Óenaighe to celebrate Lughnasa were also held at the foci of provincial kingdoms. Accordingly Cruachan in Connacht, Emain Macha in Ulster, and probably Cashel in Munster come into reckoning. The evidence for Cruachan and Emain Macha is scant and scattered, while that for Cashel may best be adduced by reading backwards from the seventeenth century. Then there were two fairs annually in Cashel under the patronage of the archbishop, which still upheld the dual motif of Christianity and Elder Faiths. The first had traditionally preceded St. Patrick's Day (17 March); the second foregrounded Domhnach Chrom Dubh (Harvest Sunday), which is inextricably linked to the festival of Lughnasa. It is commemorative of Crom Dubh, the old pagan deity and tenacious opponent of St. Patrick. A common saying of Cashel fair held currency well into the nineteenth century: 'Things were not so dear (or so cheap!) since the days of Cromdu'.[6] It leads to the conclusion that an assembly was held at the Rock (of Cashel) at the beginning of harvest and that the modern fair is a partial survival of the ancient assembly.[7]

Óenach Carmain, the provincial assembly of Leinster, presents a different problem. Like Tailtiu, it was held on the site of a cemetery, the ostensible burial place of kings, but we do not know where it was. A setting on the middle stretch of the River Barrow in south Kildare-Carlow is one distinct possibility.[8] But whatever about its location, Óenach Carmain finds the fullest coverage of any Irish assembly in an eleventh-century poem.[9] The Óenach begins on the Calends of August, i.e. the 1st of the month. The king of Leinster presides, flanked by the king of Ossory and the king of Offaly. Legal enactments and taxes are settled. There is no suing for debt. Mass is recited. It yields to amusements and diversion. Trade is conducted, far-flung commerce and exotic links invoked, and space allocated:

> Three busy markets on the ground,
> A market of food, a market of live stock,
> The great market of the Greek strangers
> Where there is gold and fine raiment.
> The slope of the horses, the slope of the cooking,
> The slope of the women met for embroidery.

All in all, the Óenach is rendered as a great occasion for acclaim and patronage, blessing and pleasure, trade and commerce, and even as a piece of antiquarian lore the poem has the aura of power and persuasiveness.

It seems clear that the óenaighe of Lughnasa formed the most powerful link to the assembly and exchange sites of antiquity. However, it is extremely difficult to reconstruct the network of such sites. Conventional history fails to serve and few additional sites may be added with the aid of tradition. Which of the Lammas fairs (the English equivalent of the Lughnasa fair), for instance, might merit consideration? Of these MacNeill enumerates 30 countrywide, but is drawn only circumstantially to two: the patron Fair of Muff, Co. Cavan, and Old Clogher Fair, Co. Tyrone.[10]

The first she claims without doubt as a Lughnasa survival linked to a horse fair at the Rock of Muff and a festive gathering on the nearby hill of Loughinlay. The two events are recognized in local tradition as related and certainly furnish an old motif. Moreover, in the past, the gathering on the hill lasted for a week before the fair, which itself kept to the rhythms of rural festivity. Assembly and exchange remain the order of the day (12th August). Trade in horses is brisk and earnest. Others are drawn for amusement. Drink is dispensed in a converted shed, which serves as a refreshment tent and a marquee for dancing.[11] The fair upholds its rurality on a bye-road in the open countryside, having resisted the overtures of the shopkeepers of the nearby town of Kingscourt to move it there. A snatch from an old song signifies its immemorial draw on harvest-men:[12]

> First the fair of Muff and then the holiday:
> We'll meet him on the road and well he knows the way.

The harvest fair of Clogher (26th July) is also suggestive of links with antiquity. It was a day of high festivity with all the amusements of a country fair. Two alternative names for it were Spóilín Fair and Gooseberry Fair. The first evokes joints of beef roasted on spits and cooked in bothies for frequenters of the fair; the second refers to gooseberries as the earliest of the cultivated fruits to ripen, just as blaeberries were the earliest of the wild fruits. A rather fetching custom connected with the fair was the Clogher Mountain Hunt, when men met on the Monaghan-Tyrone borderland and hunted hares with their dogs on the slopes of Sliabh Beagh. Towards evening the huntsmen arrived in Clogher and rounded off the day with the patrons of the fair. Hunting on foot with dogs is one of the oldest themes in Irish literature and to find it in connection with an old fair is particularly intriguing. Clogher was an old royal seat. It was therefore a likely place of assembly and a likely setting for a Lughnasa fair.

One other feature of early óenaighe is worthy of note. This is their naming and putative origin. A distinct pattern emerges.[13] Óenach Tailten, Óenach Carmain and Óenach Macha all took their names from mythological women. Cruachan too falls into line. Both Óenach Tailten and Óenach Macha are linked to the death-place and grave of a female deity. The story of Carman similarly makes the death and burial of an otherworld woman the starting-point of the assembly. Each of the women was a captive. The net stretches wider. There is, for instance, Óenach Áine at Knockainy, Co. Limerick, where fairs were held on 11th August (which corresponds with Old Lughnasa). Moreover, until the late nineteenth-century flaming sheafs of hay and straw were carried to the hill of Áine in harvest-time obeisance. Then there is Óenach Téite, which in time mutated to Nenagh (*An tAonach*, "the fair"), Co. Tipperary, and which is named from a mythological woman. This óenach setting was burned in 995 and again in 1056/9,[14] and it offers the prospect of a pre-urban node of secular origin to grace the land of Ireland.

II

Such nodes developed for certain around Early Christian monasteries. These were able to generate surpluses and grow into incipient towns. By the eight and ninth centuries, monastic towns with streets of wooden houses had come to accommodate the development of workshops and crafts.[15] They were set amid extensive farmlands where grain growing was a marker of civility and productivity. Their very success attracted an increasing measure of secular influence. As early as the eight century concern was registered about the behaviour of lay elements within the monastic precincts. Reference is made to theft and, in particular, to *precones* ("criers", "heralds") which has been translated as "hawkers".[16] Commercial activity had begun.

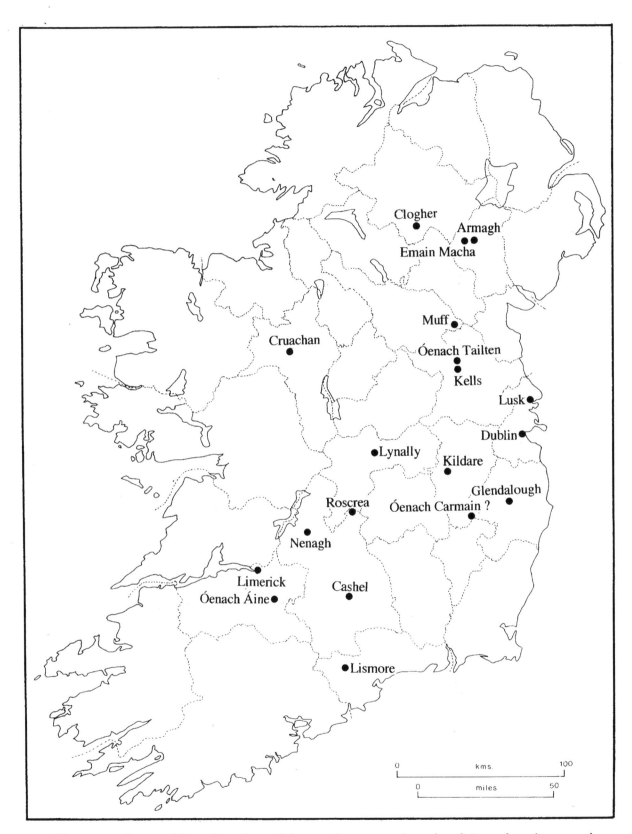

Fig. 1.1. points to fair and market origins, and conveys the mix of *óenach* and *margad* sites, which are referenced in early documentation and cited in the accompanying commentary

Monasteries declare as *óenach* sites *c.* 800 AD, and the earliest known case perfectly exemplifies the interplay of lay and monastic interests. It records the death of a local king at the "fair" of Mac Cuilinn (*in circio ferie filii Cuilinn Luscan*) at Lusk in Co. Dublin.[17] Lusk was the site of an Early Christian monastery; *circus* or *circius* is one of the Latin words used to gloss *óenach*. Adoption of the *óenach* by the monastery points to a local surplus and the need for local exchange. Later the monastic *óenach* came into prominence. That of Lynally, Co. Offaly, for example, is celebrated alongside the illustrious venues of Tailtiu and Cruachan.[18] Keen appraisal by secular rulers is also symptomatic, as they sought increasingly to dominate and lay under tribute the economic resources of the monastic town.

Such towns were possessed of large populations by medieval standards. Indeed, it was their populous nature, together with their role as *civitates refugii* ("*cities of refuge*") that made them so important to the economic exchanges of slavery. Both the Norse and the Irish exploited them from the ninth century onwards. The resultant trade, augmented by raids in England and continental Europe, brought the *margad* as mechanism of exchange and an influx of gold and silver. Much innovation had become manifest by the tenth century, including the introduction of coinage, increase in production, expansion of trade, and the clear-cut trappings of urbanisation. The development of local buying and selling was greatly facilitated by coinage as a medium of exchange. It was also facilitated by the transition from gold to silver.

The vocabulary of trade forthrightly entered the language of the day.[19] Irish literature has many references to buying and selling. In particular, the verb *ceannaigid*, to buy or purchase, is laden with meaning. *Cennach* is a bargain, transaction, traffic, commerce. Moreover, the Latin terms glossed by the word *cennaige* (merchant, pedlar, trader) give an indication of the breadth of meaning in the literature. Linguistic evidence for Norse trade is equally convincing. The Irish words for *margad* (a market), *mangaire* (a dealer) *marg* (a mark) and *pingin* (a penny), as well as host of other terms connected with trade and shipping, derive from Old Norse. The haggling of the merchants finds expression as *gioc-goc* or broken speech of the Norse dealers.

In an expansive era the most successful of the Norse trading stations forged links with the most prestigious of the monastic towns. This makes it easier to understand references in the eleventh and twelfth centuries to the use of coinage in local exchange. An example is provided by the monastic town of Armagh, where the price of a *sesedach* of mast doubled from one penny (*co fagaibthi sesedach cnó ar aon pinginn*) to two in the local market between 1031 and 1097. In addition coins from the Dublin mint of the Vikings have been found at the major monastic sites of Armagh, Glendalough and Kildare, while a native bracteate coinage, not associated with Dublin, may have been minted at Clonmacnoise, Ferns and Cashel.[20] There is also reference to industrial activity in Kildare, to the *margad* within Kells and the buying and selling of private property there, and to Lismore as an important port of call for foreign trading vessels. By the eleventh century it is clear that the major monasteries had well-defined markets and carefully ordained sacred and secular sectors.

Whether in these mostly inland situations or the estuarine towns of the Norse, the *óenach* or *margad* registered the functions of buying and selling, getting and spending, at a fixed location.[21] The *óenach* or *margad* at Limerick was located outside the tight walled circuit of the Viking town as recorded in the *Annals of Inisfallen c.* 1108. In Dublin the market-place was also outside the walls in the direction of Kilmainham. It lay within the *faithche* (the area of guaranteed peace in front of a dwelling, church or town), in which continuity-of- site was later upheld by the Cornmarket. At monastic towns the market-place claimed an elongated open space as in Kells; or was marked by a northern and southern cross as in the *Óenach Macha* of Armagh; or was located outside the walls of the monastery as in Glendalough.

In keeping with the church calendar, saints' days were the favoured trading days and in Roscrea, for instance, there is mention of the *óenach* held on the feast of Saints Peter and Paul in an early twelfth-century text. The *óenach* of Glendalough too finds mention in the twelfth-century *Life* of Kevin: 'No fight may be dared at his fair, nor challenge of wrongs, nor of rights, no quarrel, nor theft, nor rapine, but coming and going in security'.[23] The monastic town of Cashel on the other hand offers a clear reference to its *margad c.* 1130, when hailstones fell with ferocity upon the market place. The early *óenach* was usually held once a year. When taken over by the church it was held on a feast-day. The *margad*, in contrast, appears to have catered for the more routine pulses of supply and demand, and may have been held on a fixed day, possibly once a week, in a fixed location. Between the tenth and early twelfth century the pace of transactional activity quickened in Norse town and monastic town,[24] a point well appreciated by Irish secular rulers, who took up residences in both.

CHAPTER TWO

Charters, Patrons, Patterns

Whatever about a possible blurring of distinction between markets and fairs in the early medieval period (as chapter one suggests), there was none by the high Middle Ages. Anglo-Norman colonisation and settlement made the decisive difference. A fair may be best characterised as a lavish market usually held once a year, but running for several days at a time. Markets on the other hand were typically held on a particular day once weekly. The Anglo-Normans formalised pre-existing arrangements and greatly added to them by creating a fresh network of points of exchange. Thus they gave signal expression to the needs of their expansive economy.

Most markets and fairs were founded anew in the thirteenth century and confirmed by charter of the king or local lord. This was the critical innovation. It prescribed the legal basis of the fair and/or market, and gave the founder the right to levy tolls. In return the grantee was obliged to provide the ground and facilities, install a working system of weights and measures, and see to the maintenance of law and order. The mechanisms were set within the feudal regime so as to propagate new patterns of trade. However, the evidence for medieval markets and fairs in Ireland is thinly spread. It is therefore necessary to avail of a range of source materials in attempting to reconstruct the patterns that prevailed.

I

Throughout much of Western Europe the thirteenth century was a period of unparalleled population growth and economic expansion. That same century in Ireland came to represent the heyday of the Norman achievement. Improvements in farming practices and output were such as to merit the tag of 'agricultural revolution'.[1] The rapid development of trade and commerce drove a market-oriented economy in the favoured east and south of the island. In response the occupational profile became more diversified as the numbers of merchants, artisans and craftsmen grew. Lords and their feudal tenants had the benefits of discretionary spending to enjoy on everyday commodities and luxuries. Peasants too were drawn into cash exchanges by payment of rents, fines and taxes. All these factors contributed to the need for points of contact, exchange and sale throughout the developed countryside, culminating in the fixing of organised fairs and markets. The growth of towns and the concomitant growth of fairs and markets became the hallmark of the most advanced regions of England in the thirteenth century.[2] A similar pattern developed in those parts of Ireland successfully colonised by the Normans.

Given their usual extravagance and their once yearly occurrence, the aim of fairs was to draw a clientele from well beyond the normal tributary area of a market town or village. Merchants were prepared to travel considerable distances to purchase local surpluses and to supply items not readily available in a particular locality. Fairs also upheld the festivity, amusement and celebrity of the ancient *óenaighe*. To further the attraction, touches of exotica may occasionally have been introduced by way of circus ensembles and carnivalesque. Thus the medieval fair of several days duration brought welcome elements of the wider world to small communities intent on a break from their usual workaday existence.

Charters of rights to hold fairs from the king to local lords were spread throughout the thirteenth century, with peaks being recorded in the 1226 and 1252.[3] The purpose of these formal grants was to ensure an income to the holder in the form of tolls on sales, and doubtless such grants formed part of the bait to the colonisation and settlement of medieval Ireland. Several temporal and spatial patterns are apparent. Firstly, most of the fairs that were established by grant upheld older patterns of association with religious festivals. Many began on the eve of the saint's feast day and continued for several days, including the religious festival itself and the following day. The vast majority of the fairs were held in the period May-September, with the median month of July proving the most popular. In contrast, the only deep winter fair to be documented in the thirteenth century is Tuam, Co. Galway. The right to hold it was granted in 1260, and it suggests a good measure of post-Christmas prandial activity by running from 29th December to the 5th January.[4]

By far the greatest number of fairs lasted for eight days, including the four ordained by the charter of King John in 1204. According to the relevant section it was proposed that:[5]

> There be a fair at Donnyburn [Donnybrook, Co. Dublin] annually to continue for eight days on the feast of the Invention of the Holy Cross; another at the Bridge of St. John the Baptist,[6] likewise for eight days, allowing them the like stallages and tolls; and another at Waterford on the Feast of St. Peter in Chains; another at Limerick, on the Feast of St. Martin, for eight days, and we command that you cause it to be thus done, and proclamations made, that all merchants should come thither willingly.

Some continued for a mammoth fifteen days, such as those in metropolitan Dublin, Drogheda, Dundalk and Youghal. Fairs granted to Hugh de Lacy in 1227 at Nobber, Co. Meath, and Carlingford, Co. Louth, also lasted for fifteen days.[7] Indeed a consistent pattern emerges in respect of the host towns of fifteen-day fairs. Most were located in the east and south with ready access to ports, from which they were likely supplied with goods. In smaller inland settlements on the other hand fairs generally ran for three to six days.

In addition to the infrequent fairs, which gave a leavening to local life, there was also the need to cater for the routine requirements of local populations. The marketplace fulfilled such requirements. Once a week the market served as an exchange centre for the surrounding tributary area in the buying and selling of staple food items and other necessaries such as salt. Market grants were issued steadily throughout the thirteenth century, mostly in association with annual fair grants, but sometimes not. The mechanism was simple. A market was licensed at a named place on a specified day of the week, from which the holder was entitled to collect tolls. By this means a network of smaller markets and market towns sprang up, which constituted an important part of the growing agrarian and mercantile economy, and generated local patterns of circulation together with prongs of commercial traffic.

As with fairs, the 1220s and the 1250s marked the peak decades of the award of market charters in thirteenth-century Ireland. In the earlier decade Co. Limerick alone laid claim to grants for the settlements of Kilmallock (1221), Mungret (1224), Adare (1226) and Knockainy (1226).[8] In the same decade Leinster settlements as diverse as Enniscorthy, Co. Wexford; St. Kevin (Glendalough), Co. Wicklow; Dunboyne, Co. Meath; and Collon, Co. Louth, were all awarded market charters. Assimilation of old monastic towns and old secular foci within the feudal order is well in evidence. In contrast, locational conservatism is less conspicuous in the later decade, when the network of designated market towns included Dunleer, Co. Louth; Corofin and Clare[castle], Co. Clare; and Innishannon, Co. Cork. All through the thirteenth century the staunchest areas of Anglo-Norman settlement and preferment came to carry the stamp of the incipient market town as illustrated further by Carrigtohill, Co. Cork in 1234; Cahir, Co. Tipperary in 1285; Maynooth, Co. Kildare in 1286; and Tallow, Co. Waterford in 1299. In all these places the market was a once-a-week affair, and Thursday was the favoured day.

Fig. 2.1. may offer an accurate representation of the mature pattern.[9] It is based on a composite of two categories of evidence. Firstly, there is the grant of borough status[10] to a local lord, which must also have been linked with, or preceded by, the grant of a weekly market at the designated location. Secondly, there is direct evidence of the grant of a market charter. The contiguous counties of Louth, Meath, Dublin and Kildare show the primacy of East Leinster in urban genesis and market emplacement. Significantly it formed the most stable and intensively settled zone of Anglo-Norman Ireland. The transitional belt across the south of Ireland extending from Co. Wexford to Co. Limerick shows up strongly as a zone of intermediate density. In this hybrid country of Norman and Gael as it came to evolve, market towns established durable credentials amid productive hinterlands. The fringelands of Norman influence and the frontier regions came to feature a low density of market towns in Westmeath, Connacht and north Kerry. Everywhere there was a high rate of attrition and only the fittest markets survived in settlements that attained and kept the status of market town. This occurred mainly in the fertile east and south.

II

One of the most remarkable features of medieval fair and market settings was the continuing draw to the precincts of churches. This was an old practice hallowed by tradition not only in Ireland, but also in Britain and continental Europe. In France the medieval cemetery alongside the church has been characterised as a *piazzo del popolo* – a public square, a marketplace, the scene of community gatherings, an athletic field, even a haven of illicit resort and dubious encounter.[11] The sacred, secular and profane could scarcely have been better intertwined. In Ireland too it is evident that the sanctified ground around the church was the focus for a wide range of secular activity, which continued well into the Middle Ages.[12] However, practices came into so much disrepute as to require royal ordinance. In 1308 Edward II was moved to forbid the holding of

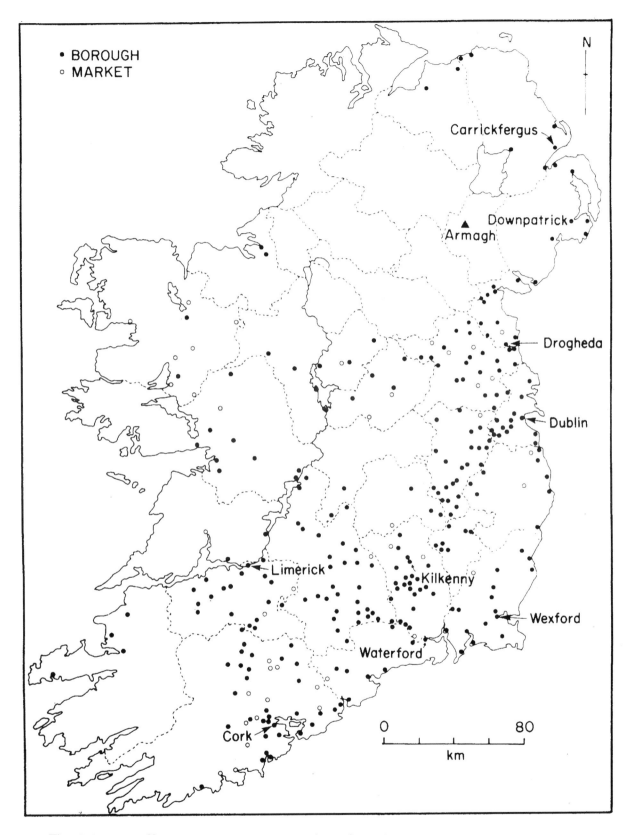

Fig. 2.1. may offer an accurate representation of medieval markets in mature form. It is based upon the composite evidence of 1) the grant of borough status and 2) direct evidence of the grant of a market charter

markets and fairs in churchyards to defend 'the honour of Holy Church'.[13] There was also the pragmatic consideration that the royal writ did not run within church property and no taxes could be collected there.

Links with the Church were bound in time and space. Grants for fairs and markets continued to be based on the feast days and religious festivals of the Christian calendar. St. Colmcille, for example, is inextricably linked with Swords in Co. Dublin, so much so that the town of Swords is often referred to as Sord Colmcille. Moreover, the annual eight-day fair, which was granted to the Archbishop of Dublin, John Comyn, in 1193, commenced on the vigil of the feast of St. Colmcille (8th June).[14] Its commencement, like all other fairs of the period, was marked with solemn church devotions, and with the dictum that all trade should be conducted in good faith. Based on a charter of 1226, the fair of Naas, Co. Kildare was set to run for eight days from the vigil of the feast of SS Simon and Jude [28th October].[15] A later charter, dated 30th September 1234, upheld the familiar cult of Mary, when Luke, Archbishop of Dublin, was granted a yearly fair at his manor of Ballymore Eustace, Co. Kildare, beginning on the vigil of the Assumption, and continuing for eight days.[16]

In spatial arrangements proximity between church and market or fair setting is one of the persistent motifs of medieval settlement. It is well seen in the case of Donnybrook (*Domhnach Broc*, 'the church of Broc'), scene of the celebrated fair, where dancing on graves may have been literal as well as metaphorical. Church site and marketplace claim frequent juxtaposition. This may indicate that when trading was no longer permitted within church grounds, following on from the statute of 1308, traders moved outside the bounded world of the church, and continued to trade as before. In medieval New Ross, market stalls took up vantage opposite St. Saviour's Church; in Naas, Co. Kildare, the marketplace abutted onto St. David's Church; and in Nobber, Co. Meath, the market cross may have claimed the open space at the junction of Church Lane with Main Street. Similar juxtapositions are conspicuous in Kilkenny city, Kildare town, medieval Wexford, and Kells, Co. Meath. A fine example in mature form is furnished by the walled town of Carrickfergus, Co. Antrim, where the market cross mediates centrally between church and castle, and symbolises the interplay of lay and ecclesiastical interests.

III

The grantees of fairs and markets were those who had successfully petitioned the king for a charter. Successful petitioners fell into several categories, as a recent study shows.[17] Lay lords bulk by far the largest, and account for 61 per cent of the fair licences and 65 per cent of the market licences granted during the thirteenth century. Bishops came next, and with 17 per cent of the fairs and 29 per cent of the markets lent weight to the substantial temporalities of the medieval secular church. In contrast, the abbots of monastic orders accounted for only one per cent of the fairs and 2 per cent of the markets. Other miscellaneous sources, including corporations and burgesses, accounted for the remaining 21 per cent of the fairs and 4 per cent of the markets.

In particular, the Anglo-Norman lay elite sought fair and market licences to promote the fortunes of their settlements, formalise trade and enhance their revenues. This is seen to conspicuous effect within Co. Cork. An early mark is posited in 1226, when Andrew Blundes secured the grant of a weekly market and yearly fair at the centre of his manor of Kinsale.[18] Enhancement of another nascent port town's prospects followed in 1234, when Maurice Fitzgerald was granted a royal licence to hold a weekly market every Saturday at his town of Youghal and a yearly fair there from 28th September to 12th October.[19] Inland locations declared in the same year. On 25th September 1234 David de Barry obtained licences to establish a weekly market, to be held every Saturday, and a yearly fair to be held from 17th to 24th October, at his town of Buttevant and a weekly market, to be held on Tuesday, at Carrigtohill.[20]

Disputes due to competition between the fairs and markets of rival settlements and their holders often arose.[21] In 1256, for example, the market and fair at Philip de Barry's borough of Innishannon, Co. Cork, became a matter of contention in the king's court with the burgesses of the city of Cork. Contention and competition between the markets of Cork and Youghal appears to have been a protracted feature of the thirteenth century. Likewise in 1290 the burgesses of Shandon, which belonged to John de Cogan and Maurice de Rochford, sought royal intervention to prevent the citizens of Cork from impeding the free flow of their trade. Clearly because Shandon lay in close proximity to Cork, it was destined to be dominated by the mercantile interests of the city. Elsewhere, wherever patrons such as de Lacy in Meath, succeeded in establishing several fairs and markets on their lands, trade rivalries were obviated by grants for different days and periods. Thus toll collectors and traders could travel from place to place within the lordship.

Bishops also commanded multiple grants. John de St. John, treasurer of Ireland and first Anglo-Norman bishop of Ferns, furnishes a notable example. Obviously intent on generating revenue for self, he may have seen virtue too in the economic development of his estates. In 1226 he secured grants of weekly markets and annual fairs at his manorial centres of Ferns, Enniscorthy and Templeshanbo,[22] and at best the consequences may have vivified the Wexford countryside. The same may have occurred within the adjacent diocese of Ossory following on from bishop Geoffrey de Turville's establishment of fairs and markets at five different locations in 1245. These included the fair at the Irishtown of Kilkenny - the native precinct of the city - and a weekly market there on Wednesday. The fair continued and was known as St. Canice Fair and the market was still able to invoke exemption from lay interference in the seventeenth century.[23]

With the patronage of the earl of Norfolk, New Ross in Co. Wexford furnished one of the most renowned fair and market settings of medieval Ireland. This followed on from the town's first charter in 1283-6, and a measure of the town's exuberance is indicated *circa* 1307, when it may have ranked second only to Dublin in terms of population size.[24] The great annual fair began on the feast of the Immaculate Conception, 8th December, continued for several days, and stayed fixed in the New Ross cycle of events until 1899. According to tradition the fair was located where the Tholsel now stands in line of site continuity with the old market cross of the town.[25]

In New Ross patronage extended well to the provision of infrastructure for its fairs and markets. During the great annual fair the Earl Marshall, descendant of the town's founder, had stalls erected opposite St. Saviour's Church (fig 2.2.). Other stalls were leased to one Gallard Maubin, who had responsibility for their upkeep. As an indication of concourse and commerce, houses were hired for the duration of the fair. Further houses were hired in which court sittings could be held. House values also responded sensitively to market location. In 1289, for instance, the community of Market Street paid forty shillings for permission to hold a market at the corner of their street. House hire followed directly and rentals doubled at the optimal locations.[26] By 1307, an apparent climax year, the perquisites of the market together with the rent of stalls were valued at 60s. yearly.[27] New Ross had attained premier standing for the vibrancy of its trade and marketing. It easily saw off the competition of Rosbercon, established optimistically across the River Barrow, where a four-day fair had been granted in 1286, together with a weekly market on Wednesday.[28]

IV

For evidence of the patterns underpinning the fairs and markets of the period, we may look primarily to the walled towns of medieval Ireland. Murage grants had a direct basis in the tolls raised from the movement of goods,[29] and by implication from the transactions of the fair and marketplace. Walling a town was expensive, often requiring repeated levies on goods passing through the town. Drogheda offers a notable example, with at least thirteen murage grants spanning the period 1234-1424, but little specific detail for the most part.[30] More revealing is the small town example of Fethard, Co. Tipperary, which lists the commodities that attracted tolls of murage in a grant of 1292. Here we are given detailed inventory of the range of goods that made for trade in a small Irish town *circa* 1300.[31] These included horses, mares, oxen, cows, sheep, goats and hogs; hides, salt, meat, butter, cheese, onions, and garlic; sea fish, salmon, lampreys and herring; skins wool, hides, linen, and other cloth; salt, wine, honey, soap, alum, and wood; coal, firewood, lead, iron, nails, and horseshoes. As gathered from the murage grants to various towns, the commodities of internal trade may be divided roughly into the produce of the country and imported goods brought in from the ports. Livestock, cereals and other foodstuffs, hides and skins, wool and cloth, utensils and timber featured in the first group, while wine, salt metals, fine cloths, dyes, spices, and a variety of luxury goods counted among the second.

Ireland's peripheral location proved no impediment to the pulses of trade and commerce. On the contrary, throughout the medieval period foreign merchants were traversing Ireland and selling their wares. Goods came from as far as Byzantium and the Orient. Traders from Florence were attracted to New Ross as early as 1217.[32] Merchants from a diversity of countries and regions such as France, Germany, Spain, Portugal, Navarre, Lombardy, Tuscany, Provence, Aquitaine, Flanders and Brabant plied their trade in the shops, fairs and marketplaces of Ireland. They chartered ships to bring in wine and luxury goods. Latin was the enabling language of trade and it allowed them to travel far afield. Many were pedlars who hawked their goods from town to town, often specialising in small luxury items such as spices, gems, silks and fine cloths. Robbery was an occupational hazard. In 1306, for instance, a merchant on his way to market was robbed of his horse and its accoutrements, together with cloth of Laghton, a *fallaing* (Irish mantle), a piece of silver, a robe, shirt, girdle, hat and primer, skins, shearing cloth, copper and a sword.[33] That same year a ship wrecked off the coast of Portmarnock, Co. Dublin, gives an idea of the goods being imported for sale. Counted among the cargo were wax, jewels, wine, copper pots, and barrels of spices and cloth.

All the evidence suggests the availability of a rich array of commodities in the town markets and fairs of medieval Ireland.[35] There was meat and fish in abundance and variety. More exotic foods such as rice, almonds, figs, raisins, dried fruits, garlic and olive oil were also for sale. Household items such as cauldrons, griddles, platters, dishes and kitchen utensils commanded display. Heavier metal objects made of iron, brass, copper, lead and tin were also presented to buyers, together with horse trappings, horse irons and saddles. Imports such as French and English grinding stones, coal boards, tiles, clear and coloured glass, hemp, wood, sumac, alum, copperas, madder, pitch, tar, oils and resin met with steady custom. Silks from China, cloth of silk and gold, samite (a heavy silk fabric), diaper (cloth with patterns or repeated figures), carpets, embroidered cloths and covers, and woolen cloths of Galloway and Worsted, canvas, linen, cordwain and the Irish mantle were much in demand.

The sale of cloth was a recurrent feature of every fair and market in Ireland, and a number of incidental references infer that both native and foreign merchants participated in the trade.[36] In 1284 a prominent Italian merchant was captured by the Powers of Waterford and he forfeited cloth to the value of twelve marks; in a similar incident near Wexford in 1334, Nicholas de Pickering was robbed of 40s. in money, and linen and woollen cloth worth 60s. Clearly going to market was a hazardous exercise for the merchant, but one to make it successfully was a certain Henry de Norwych. He came to Cashel in 1303 with a cartload of merchandise that included seven ells of russet cloth worth 15s.[37]

Many of the English merchants who brought cloth to Ireland through Chester had trading links with the inland towns of the Pale. Whether they travelled to market from town to town is uncertain; they may have conducted their business from the ports of Dublin and Drogheda. But they certainly forged business links with such towns as Ardee, Athboy, Kells, Navan and Trim, as well as with Dublin and Drogheda. Good quality cloth was a highly valued commodity all over medieval Ireland. Trading in cloth was therefore particularly valuable and merchants prospered in all branches of the trade. It was a lightweight, portable, sometimes expensive, and always essential commodity. An Anglo-Irish satirical poem of *c.* 1308 points to the wealth that merchants gained from sales of cloth and wool:[38]

> Hail be yer marchans with yur gret packes
> Of draperie auour de peise and yur wol sackes,
> Gold siluer stones riche markes and ek pundes
> Litil giue ye thereof to the wrech pouer.

As the poem suggests, wool as well as cloth played the part of indispensability in the marketplaces of medieval Ireland. Sheep were kept mainly for their wool. Moreover, one of the hallmarks of the rural economy was the extraordinary development of sheep farming.[39] The effects were transmitted to central places. The market at Naas, Co.

Kildare, for example, was a centre for the purchase of wool. This is neatly synopsised in 1305, when one man purchased nine sacks of wool at the market there, and another came to the market of Naas to sell lambs.[40] By that time wool production had spread to south Co. Kildare, where the manor of Ballysax proved the key to restocking, and the navigable River Barrow allowed the wool trade to burgeon all the way to New Ross.

Available evidence suggests that southeast Ireland, commanded by the ports of Waterford and New Ross, was the great wool producing area of medieval Ireland. This was the land of the great monastic granges, renowned for their wool crop, and of the navigable Sister Rivers, which facilitated movement to port. It was also the land of the lesser farmers and peasants, who as in England produced a great amount of the wool, and sold it in the nearest town. The local wool merchants in turn sold it direct to exporters, since foreign merchants were forbidden, in New Ross and in other towns, to buy goods directly from producers. All this was calculated to prime the part of wool at marketplaces, and sufficient evidence may be adduced of such priming in Kilkenny, Callan, Thomastown, Clonmel, New Ross and Waterford in the period 1295-1355.[41] Thomastown, on the River Nore, nearly midway between Kilkenny and New Ross, was an important market and depot for wool and hides, all the more so since shallow draught barges could float from Kilkenny to New Ross with facility. New Ross on its own account drew on the wool trade generated by the Nore and Barrow navigation system and also on local sources, such as the manor of Old Ross, where sheep numbers rose spectacularly in the period 1281-88.[42]

Just below the confluence of the rivers Nore and Barrow, New Ross in its heyday may be taken to mark the apogee of the medieval market town. Its locational attributes were such as to attract merchants and traders from afar, since rivers were the main commercial highways of the age and its head of estuary setting befitted it for port. Its early names are instructive: *Villa Nova Pontis Willielmi Marescalli* ('The new town of the bridge of William Marshal'), or *Nova Villa de Ponte de Ross* ('The new town of the bridge of Ross'), or plain *Ros Ponte* ('Ross bridge'). The great bridge was the common element and it first gave the town its importance. In the course of time it was enclosed by a wall, like all the leading medieval towns, to protect its inhabitants and offer the assurance of safety that would draw buyers and sellers to market.

A well-known poem of the thirteenth century has for its theme the walling of New Ross.[43] It tells how the burgesses began to mark out the fosse on 2nd February 1265. They passed a bye law (such as the poet never heard of in France or England) that all the people of the town, grouped by trade or craft, were to work on the wall: the vintners, mercers, merchants and drapers on Monday; the tailors, cloth workers, fullers and saddlers on Tuesday; the cordwainers, tanners and butchers on Wednesday; and so on to baker, dyers, leatherworkers etc. They dug a fosse, the poet tells us, '20 feet in depth and its length extended over a league'. Thus, even if the accomplishment is exaggerated, we are given an insight into the diversity of life and occupational profile of an important market town. Clearly New Ross was well insulated for trade and secure from attack. The circuit of the wall extended for 1 mile (1.6 km), enclosing an area of *c*. 105 statute acres which was divided into a grid pattern of medieval streets. Within the walls the marketplace occupied a rectilinear open space in close proximity to St. Mary's parish church.[44] Access was afforded by the Market (also known as Fair) Gate from the suburb of Irishtown, which

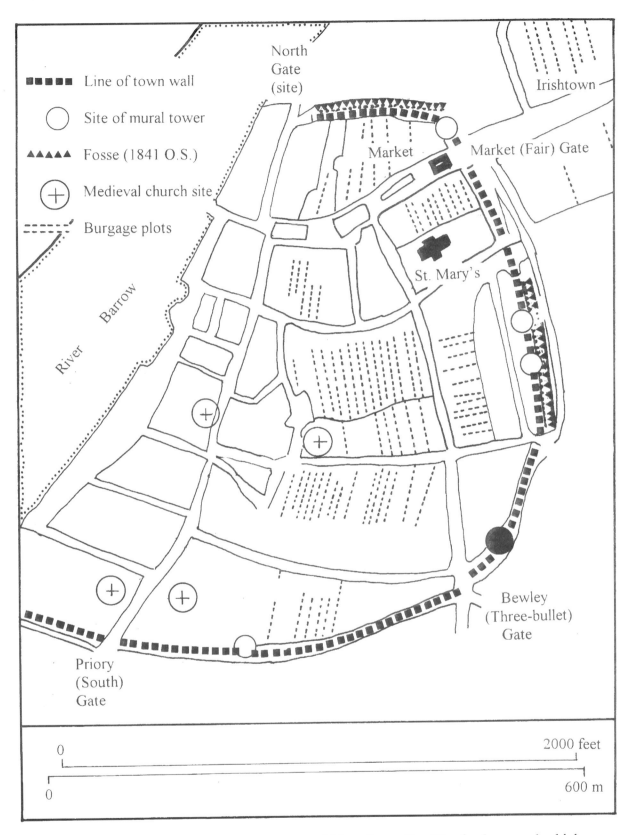

Legend:
- ▬ ▬ ▬ ▬ Line of town wall
- ◯ Site of mural tower
- ▲▲▲▲▲ Fosse (1841 O.S.)
- ⊕ Medieval church site
- - - - - Burgage plots

North Gate (site)

Irishtown

Market

Market (Fair) Gate

St. Mary's

River Barrow

Bewley (Three-bullet) Gate

Priory (South) Gate

0   2000 feet

0   600 m

Fig. 2.2. shows the medieval market town of New Ross, Co. Wexford, around which mural fortifications extended for 1.6 km. and enclosed an area of *c.* 105 statute acres. Access was afforded by the Market (aka Fair) Gate from the suburb of Irishtown lay, as usual, outside the walls. To-day the Market Gate alone remains as relict feature of the walled circuit to attest to medieval accessibility to the trading places of New Ross.

V

In medieval England the median distance travelled by customers to market has been estimated at 6.66 miles, or what thirteenth-century lawyers would have regarded as a normal day's journey.[45] Irish buyers and sellers certainly travelled farther, although in the one case study open to scrutiny, some interesting results emerge. This relates to Co. Cork, where according to the sheriff's report of June 1299, 38 market towns were listed for the county.[46] All are amenable to identification. Using only half the median distance of England (i.e. 3.3 miles, or easy walking distance), findings show a considerable degree of overlapping spheres in the markets of the east of the county and clear gaps in the west (figs. 2.3 and 2.4.). Overlap is marked, for example, within the compact cantred of Fermoy, where Athoul (Ballyhooly), Brigown (Mitchelstown), Bridgetown, Carrig, Castletownroche, Doneraile, Glanworth, Kilworth and Mallow all competed for custom in strongly manorial country. There was also competition with nearest neighbours outside the cantred. The clusters of market towns diffused over north, mid and east Cork constituted an extensive network of commercial traffic, powerfully reinforced by the major ports of Cork, Kinsale and Youghal. In contrast, the Gaelic west was profoundly deficient in markets. Only Timoleague and Dunnamark near Bantry stood their weekly turn.

It appears unlikely that Co. Cork's closest patterns of market location were replicated to any great extent and that buyers and sellers, merchants and goods, travelled further to market in Ireland than in England. In 1395, for instance, William Ilger travelled over ten miles from Ballyhack, Co. Wexford, to sell a consignment of salt, iron, hides, skins, leather and cloth at New Ross; at another time oats was brought all the way by boat on the River Barrow from Ballysax, Co. Kildare to a 'certain stall' in the same town.[47] Location on a navigable river greatly extended the trading hinterland of a town, a point well attested by the bead of settlements along the Barrow stretching from Athy to New Ross. Making the same point on the River Nore, Kilkenny city was able to capitalise on its rich agricultural hinterland, and attract merchants from distant places. It is recorded, for example, that a citizen of Dublin regularly sent a packhorse load of merchandise to be sold at the great fair there.[48]

Taking goods to and from market often proved dangerous. Accordingly, watchmen were apt to find employment both day and night to protect the merchandise. In 1303, for instance, Michael de Fernden, on his way home from market at Cashel, Co. Tipperary, felt obliged to hire a watchman to protect his cart loaded with merchandise, while he slept in a nearby lodging house.[49] In another colourful incident which occurred in 1306, William Douce, a Dublin merchant, on his way through Co. Kildare to the fair in Kilkenny, was robbed at Naas of a box of 'small things', a pair of linen webs, a pair of shoes and a pair of hose. The thief was Cristiana la Sadelhackere, who had colluded with William's servingman and promised to 'lie' with him. She was subsequently found guilty at a court in Kildare.[50] Penalties were often extreme. In the case of Thomas Fwelewrygth a sentence of hanging was handed down in 1306 for robbing a merchant of Dublin, Henry de Kilbeworth, of a horse, cloth and other goods.[51] Occupational hazards were all the

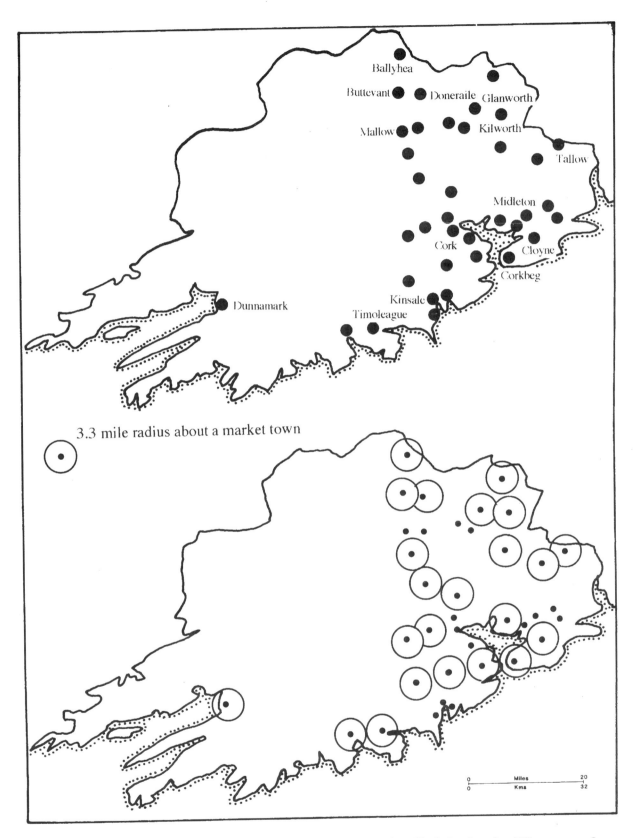

3.3 mile radius about a market town

Fig. 2.3. shows the 38 market towns enumerated for Co. Cork in the sheriff's report of 1299, while fig. 2.4. shows a considerable degree of overlap in the market spheres of east Co. Cork and great gaps in the west

LIMERICK COUNTY LIBRARY

more heightened in times of war and instability, when piracy and plundering prevailed along rivers and main roads.

Nor were goods safe on open display at the point of sale in fair and marketplace. Watchmen had to be hired in New Ross for the duration of the great December fair. Still theft could never be quite precluded. Indeed, it could occur spectacularly wherever security was lax. Such a case presented in 1298 when the former servingman of Thomas Maunsel stole eighty horses from the market of Cloncurry in Co. Kildare.[52] The market must therefore have been quite a substantial one and Cloncurry c. 1300 must have made a sizeable manorial centre. In Kilkenny night-watchmen were hired from the feast of All Saints until the following Ash Wednesday to stand sentinel over the market stalls from curfew to cockcrow.[53] Concerns about security extended up to royal ordinance.[54] In 1285, Edward 1 commanded that the gates of towns should remain shut from dusk till dawn, and that no lodgers should be kept in town overnight. Highways from one market town to another were to be levelled and widened. Clearances were to be made on either side of the road. Bridges were to be repaired or rebuilt.

VI

The conquest of Ireland by the Anglo-Normans, in which the mechanisms of trade – towns, markets, fairs – flourished in the favoured regions, had begun to collapse by the early fourteenth century. By then, as it was later expressed, 'the quiet estate wherein the land had long remained began to decay'.[55] Invasion, disease, pestilence, lawlessness and disorder all stamped the face of later medieval Ireland; the common law area shrank and Gaelic lords recovered their lordships. All this had severe implications for demography. Falling population numbers led the decline of marketing activity and to the failure or demise of many fairs and markets. Earlier speculative grants of market charters withered away in the face of newer and harsher realities. By the start of the fifteenth century, even staunch Anglo-Norman towns had felt the slump in commerce.[56] In 1402, the burgesses of Kilkenny, were obliged to obtain the king's permission to sell at market victuals or merchandise to their enemies in times of peace or truce. In 1403 the townspeople of New Ross were forced to follow suit. The king, in reply to their petition, granted them permission to trade with their Irish enemies in such goods as victuals and other necessaries. Horses and arms were excluded.

Soon afterwards there is explicit reference to the establishment of markets and fairs in the territories of the native Irish lords. In 1429 the Irish parliament declared:[57]

> Likewise, forasmuch as diverse Irish enemies of our lord the king, levy, raise, and hold among them different fairs and markets, and sundry merchants, English lieges go and repair to the said fairs and markets, and some send their merchandise to the said enemies by their servants or people called "laxmen", and there sell and buy divers merchandises, and goods for sale, whereout the said enemies take great customs and benefits, to their great profit, and the injury of all the burghs [boroughs] and market-towns of this land, and of the lieges of the same land. It is agreed, ordained and established that henceforth, no manner of merchant, nor any other liege person shall go or resort in time of peace or of war to any manner of fair, market or other place among the said enemies with merchandises or goods for sale, or send the same to them --------

The likeliest location of such fairs and markets was outside the Pale or on the marches, in which case the impact on the towns of the old lordship of Meath may have been deep and negative. The Irish had been inured for centuries to come to trade with the market towns of Meath. Role reversal for the 'Old English' of the Pale appears to have been set in place.

Such was certainly the case by 1480, when the Irish parliament observed and pronounced as follows:[58]

> That whereas divers Irish merchants, lately supplied with stock of good, by concourse of English merchants, in Irish country, have lately found great means of destroying and injuring the markets of Athboy, Kells, Fore, Mullingar, the Oldcastle, and other ancient English market towns, by means, namely [that] they have commenced markets in Orailly's country and in Offerroll's country at Cavan, Granard, Longford and other places, which if they are long continued will bring great riches to the king's enemies, and great poverty to the king's subjects. Whereupon it is ordained by authority of the said Parliament that no English merchant, shall take any good or merchandise to any of the said markets of Cavan, Granard, Longford, or to any Irish country out of English country or carry any goods from the said markets, or make any concourse, or resort to them, on pain of forfeiture of the said goods and merchandise, and their bodies to the king's will.

From at least the beginning of the fifteenth century, towns had developed at Longford and Granard, both centred on O'Farrell castles, and at the O'Reilly town of Cavan. Enterprising merchants, Irish and Old English, needed the protection of these local lords, for which they were prepared to pay. The Irish of the north midlands were well prepared to pay too for salt and wine and luxury goods.

Urban development, complete with markets and fairs, was not the norm in Gaelic Ireland. Usually the surpluses generated in the economy were redistributed not through the market but rather as obligations to an overlord in return for protection and other services. However, markets and fairs appear to have been held at some ecclesiastical sites well within the ambit of a Gaelic realm. Such a case is Estersnow (*Díseart Nuadhan*, 'the hermitage of St. Nuadha') set amid the plains country of north Roscommon. For here it is recorded in 1590 that a Saturday market had traditionally been held beside the church 'when there is peace'.[59] There is little further information. It seems to have been a practice for merchants to purchase from a lord the exclusive right of trading within his territory. In the 1560s, native Gaelic merchants at Armagh travelled on business through the O'Neill territories of *Tír Eoghain*, and their pattern of movement is unlikely to have been of recent provenance. At the other end of their sphere the O'Neills were able to extract tribute from the merchants of Dundalk since at least 1430.

Old trading patterns were well and truly shattered by the sixteenth century. To return again to the Pale and the marches, the towns of Ardee, Trim, Navan, Athboy, Kells and Mullingar, which once waxed rich from trade with the Irish, were recorded in the 1560s as 'sore decayed and in manner desolate'.[60] Other towns within the old Norman sphere of preferment might make only the most hapless of outposts of a fair day. Such a case is presented in 1569, when the lord deputy, Sir Henry Sidney, wrote of the spoliation of the great fair of Enniscorthy, Co. Wexford. Rape, murder and rapine were the order of the day in an assembly full of country people and most of the merchants of the town of Wexford.[61]

The same author was in a more subdued mood that same year in the town of Carrickfergus, Co. Antrim, which too was an outpost, and which from its early days must have worked out a *modus vivendi* with the native Irish. A fat cow could be had at market for *6s.8d* and two dozen eggs for a single penny. Carrickfergus was the possessor of a

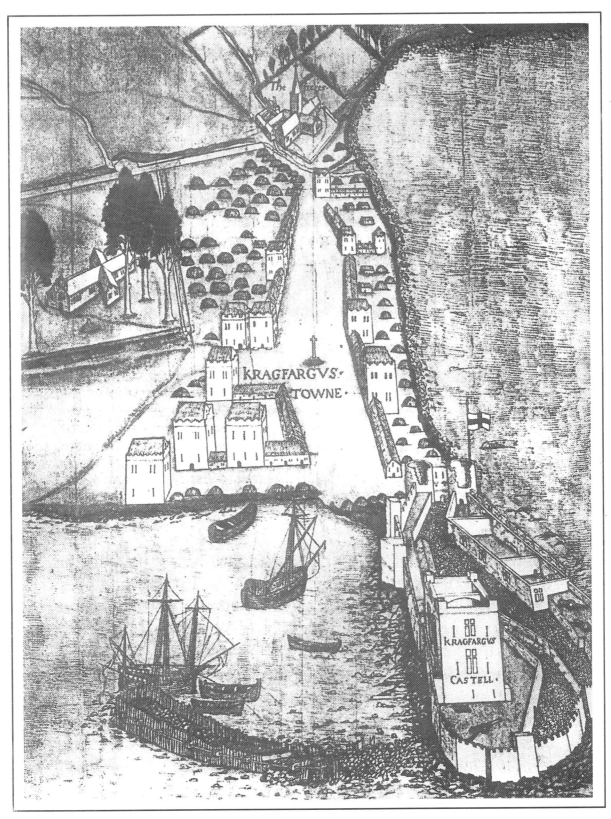

Fig. 2.5. shows Carrickfergus, Co. Antrim, *circa* 1560, where the market cross mediates centrally between church and castle, and where in 1569 a fat cow could be had at market for 6s. *8d.* and two dozen eggs for a single penny

good market twice a week, and had forged an extensive network of trading inter-connections:[62]

> Not only all kinds of things of that country breed were to be sold, but out of the English Pale, the Isle of Man and Scotland came much merchandise, victuals and other commodities, and out of France in one summer three barks of forty tonnes apiece discharged their loading of excellent good Gascoigne wine, the which they sold for nineteen cow skins the hogshead [fifty gallons].

Yet for all its trading connections, Carrickfergus took on an embattled appearance on a contemporary town plan (fig. 2.5.), with its strong thirteenth-century castle and linear arrangements of late medieval tower houses.

In Gaelicised Ireland the impositions of territorial rulers upon the normal business of the fair and marketplace could be severe, if not penal. This is well seen in Munster, where the earl of Desmond held sway over a swathe of country which the lord deputy, Sir Henry Sidney, adjudged to be greater than Yorkshire. As Sidney commented, it was all under the 'rule, or rather tyranny' of the Earl (1559-83).[63] Tralee, Co. Kerry, was one of his chief residences, and his visits to the town were timed to coincide with the fair, when he collected his rents and tolls. These were onerous, a point made explicit elsewhere by his levying of every cart and beast brought to market at the Co. Limerick towns of Kilmallock and Rathkeale. In Rathkeale, according to a survey of 1584-6, fairs were held annually for two days based upon the feast of the Blessed Virgin in autumn (15th August). Additional tolls levied by the Earl were as follows:[64]

> For every cow or garron[horse] coming into and being in the fair 4d. half-face; for every barrel of wine or beer and whiskey [aqua vita] three quarts; and the tenth part of all merchandise sold there, unless the seller hired a shop or paid for some other place where he sold merchandise and goods.

In Rathkeale, as in much of Ireland, the impositions on trade were severe at a time when lawlessness and political instability prevailed. It was also a time when English colonial theory came to be applied to Ireland,[65] and in the practical application of that theory the provision of fairs and markets at central places was to form a key component.

VII

Not that charters for markets and fairs fell away altogether during the late medieval and early modern period, having proliferated in the thirteenth century.[66] In the fourteenth century there was a minor flurry of charter confirmation within the Pale or on the marches beyond. On 15th September 1338, Theobald de Verdon was confirmed in a weekly market in Dundalk, Co. Louth, and in a fifteen-day fair there annually. On the same day he was granted an eight-day fair at Duleek, Co. Meath, another eight-day fair at the manorial centre of Empor in Co. Westmeath, and a market there on Thursdays (fig 2. 6.). All these proved their staying power in the straightened circumstances of later medieval Ireland. However, there was clearly a speculative element in the de Verdon charters, as three others to little known manorial centres in Co. Westmeath failed, along with another in Co. Meath. Still within the same general area of preferment the earl of Kildare was confirmed in a three-day fair at Maynooth, Co. Kildare, in 1340; William Fleming received a charter for a Sunday market at Sydan, Co. Meath, in 1345; and to lend an unambiguous touch of nepotism in 1358, Edward III's son, Lionel, earl of Ulster, was granted an annual five-day fair at Carlingford and a weekly market there on Thursday. Such a grant may also have signified the prestige with which Carlingford was

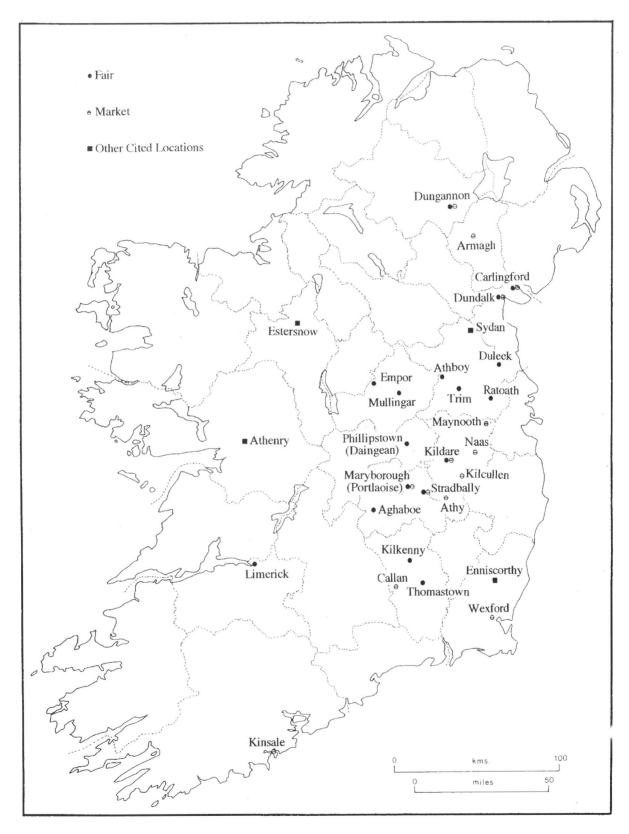

Fig. 2.6. Patent confirmation for fairs and markets from the fourteenth century to 1600 was generally sparse and went through several mutations. Throughout the period, the east of Ireland was heavily favoured

invested at this time.[67] Outside of north Leinster, the corporation of the town of Wexford was confirmed in a weekly market on a Saturday in 1317, and the bishop of Ossory was confirmed in a market on a Wednesday at Irishtown, Kilkenny, in 1376.

Reflecting increasing instability, charters tailed away in the fifteenth century. The level plains country of Leinster remained the preferred sphere – largely co-terminous with the fine-set distribution of the element *town* in townland names[68] – and thus betokening close and durable settlement on the part of the 'Old English' descendants of the Anglo-Normans. In 1403 the corporation of Kilcullen, Co. Kildare, was confirmed in a weekly market on Tuesday, while the corporation of Athboy, Co. Meath, received the annual grant of an extravagant fifteen-day fair in 1407. The corporation of Trim followed with the charter of King Henry VI in 1429. It 'confirmed the licence to hold the fair which the corporation had held time out of mind within the liberties'.[69] Amplifying further in Co. Meath, charters were awarded to Sir Edward Perers and Sir T. Fleming, baron of Slane, of a market and fair in the first instance, and a market in the second, at little known locations in 1410 and 1411 respectively.[70] Neither proved productive or enduring. Better fortune attended the granting of two annual fairs at Ratoath, Co. Meath, to the duke of York in 1450, though the Monday market failed. Kildare town came to undergo a change in its market day in 1458, so as to obviate competition with Naas, while at the same time the earl of Kildare was granted an annual three-day fair in the town. Appropriately, the fair commenced on the feastday of St. Brighid (1st February), the founder of Kildare and patroness of the crops and the farm animals.

The much disturbed sixteenth century brought a mix of old and new elements to charter confirmation, but no great pick-up in activity. Old town corporations were favoured with fresh market charters, led by Athy (1515), Kildare (1515), Callan (1568), Naas (1569), and Kilkenny (1574). Charters for fairs were similarly awarded to the corporations to Thomastown (1553), Trim (1570), Athenry (1574), Kilkenny (1574), Mullingar (1583), and Kinsale (1589). English colonial policy was also directed at centres set amid new plantation country, as in Phillipstown, Co. Offaly, and Maryborough, Co. Laois, in 1570. In the same country the new English proprietor, John Isham, was confirmed in a charter for a market and fair at Stradbally, and a fair at Aghaboe, in 1597. Another novel feature at a time of flux in Elizabethan state policy was for Gaelic patrons to secure the favour of fair and market charters at central places on their lordships. Hugh O'Neill, earl of Tyrone, succeeded in a weekly market charter for Armagh, and a charter for a Thursday market and annual fair at Dungannon, in 1587. Confirmation by charter of the weekly market at Temple Isertnoune, Co. Roscommon (Estersnow, *Diseart Nuadhan*), in the hands of its Gaelic patron, Terence Beirne, came in 1593.

Change from Old English or Gaelic patron to New English proprietor was already under way. The mutation is well attested in the case of Enniscorthy in the Elizabethan period. We have already learned of the wanton excesses witnessed by Sir Henry Sidney at the fair of 1569, and its outpost standing is confirmed by being designated 'Duffer country' (*Dubh Thire*, 'the black country') in 1576, when a charter 'of certain customs' was granted to the earl of Ormond.[71] All this changed decisively in the 1580s, as Sir Henry Wallop gained control of Enniscorthy, the key to Duffrey country, for one suffused with proprietorial and entrepreneurial drive. He sought to break the back of the Gaels of Wexford and 'plant better in their places'.[72] He remodelled Enniscorthy as a base for exploiting the timber trade and he got the grant of a weekly market in 1586. By the time of confirmation in 1611, a new order had been brokered, imbued with ideas of rapid and continuous change. In that new order the fresh provision of fairs and markets was to play a critical role.

CHAPTER THREE

Patents, Proprietors, Patterns

The process of imperial expansion is one of the great themes of history.[1] So it proved in Ireland, and from 1600 to the early nineteenth century the country grew with remarkable rapidity. Shaped by the process, a social and cultural transformation occurred in what a leading historian has described as 'the last western European country to abandon the medieval world'.[2] The transition was sharp. In driving it, one of the motor forces was the growth in trade. This entailed treating the whole island as an entity, as well as putting in place the necessary mechanisms – markets, fairs and towns. It all commenced with alacrity when peace prevailed after 1603, and in the case of patent confirmation for markets and fairs, the entire chronology is traceable from 1600 to 1852-3. The proprietors of patented markets and fairs duly declare and an index of economic development and regional growth patterns becomes available.[3]

For the underpinning evidence, an almost complete inventory of patented markets and fairs may be compiled from a parliamentary report of 1853.[4] This report records the name and location of each market and fair by county. Nearly all the patented fairs and markets are identifiable and 98 per cent of active non-patented markets and fairs in 1852-3 may similarly be identified, despite many corrupt renderings of the place-names. Wherever relevant, the 1853 report specifies the date of the first, and any subsequent patent(s).[5] Then follows the name or names of the grantee(s), the day(s) recorded in the first and any later patent(s), and finally, the day(s) on which the market or fair was held in 1852-3. The report is not without its defects and ambiguities (for example, it omits a list of failed centres for Co. Derry, and errors occur in place-name rendering and assignment). It remains unrivalled, however, as the nearest approach to a standard source affording countrywide coverage for fairs and markets provision in the period 1600-*c*.1850.

That the data is also amenable to mapping, has already been established by the geographer, Patrick O'Flanagan, in his pioneering paper on markets and fairs 1600-1800.[6] In this instance simple distribution maps are used to plot the incidence of markets and fairs at each location identified in a particular time period. The time periods are each of fifty-years duration from 1600-*c*.1850, and the patent date used is that of first patent. It is assumed that no extended break occurred in the holding of fairs and markets between the date of first patent and still active marketing centres in 1852-3. The maps that are generated will form the basis for commentary and for engagement with a wide range of documentary sources.

From 1600-1650, the first phase saw the vigorous diffusion of patented markets and fairs throughout Ireland, which was linked to a new proprietorial order, intrusive colonisation, plantation and settlement, the creation of new towns and villages, and the regeneration of older centres. There was also a strong speculative in the patenting, given the high rate of attrition and failure. The 1641 rebellion and the Cromwellian campaign of the 1650s set the scene for spatial contraction and reorientation in the next phase, 1651-1700. In the first half of the eighteenth century, mid Munster takes the part of prominence in fairs patenting, along with a more diffuse pattern for markets. Sustained economic improvement in the second half of the century saw the widespread adoption of first-time fair patents, as well as the further consolidation of patented markets in Ulster and the north midlands. Then to complete the sequence to mid nineteenth century (1801-50), there was a thin dispersion of first-time fair patents, along with a scatter of market patents favouring new towns and villages in the far west.

I

In the period 1600-1650, English colonial policy in Ireland really struck home with power in the delivery. Such potency is all the more apparent, given that the constructive phase only extended from 1603-41, with war prevailing at either end. There was a significant influx of sponsored settlement from Britain, most notably in the case of the Munster and Ulster plantations, together with more selectively implemented plantations in Leitrim and Longford, in King's county (Offaly), in parts of Westmeath and Queen's county (Laois), and in north Wexford. This thrust was supported by isolated grants of land elsewhere and by private acquisitions in Munster, Connacht and Wicklow. A new proprietorial order was established in the land, and settled an agricultural population on it. That same order assiduously promoted village and town settlement to seek to ensure the rapid advancement of trade in an undeveloped countryside. As guiding index to all this, fair and market patents were granted at a rate never remotely matched in any other fifty-year period in Irish history.

Befitting a period of unabashed optimism, there was a strong speculative element in the patents granted in 1603-41. This came to be marked in the high rates of failure experienced by 1852-3 in respect of fairs, markets, or both. It is possible, that in the case of some of the more obscure locations, fairs and markets may have never actually commenced. Others may have represented continuity *in situ* since the medieval period, only to find an optimistic projection in the early modern. Such a case occurs at Louth, Co. Louth,[7] where in 1608 the Old English proprietor, Sir John Talbot was granted a licence as follows:

> To hold a Tuesday market and a fair on 13 Jun. to continue for three days, at the town of Louthe, with a court of pye-powder and the usual tolls, &c. and to build houses there for tanning hides and skins, the King appointing the said town a convenient and fit place for that purpose, and for the benefit of his subjects in Ulster.

In the event, Louth never lived up to its name and its market and fairs subsequently lapsed. Breakdowns and disruptions to trade had also occurred. The case of Ballymore Eustace, Co. Kildare, furnishes such an indication in 1609, when Thomas, archbishop of Dublin, was granted a 'revival of the market, formerly held at Ballymore', and a licence to hold a three-day fair there commencing on the feast of the Assumption.[8]

The real driving force, however, came in close synchronicity with new town and village foundations. None could be more explicit than that for Bandon, Co. Cork,[9] when in 1610, the New English proprietor, Henry Beecher, was granted the following patent:

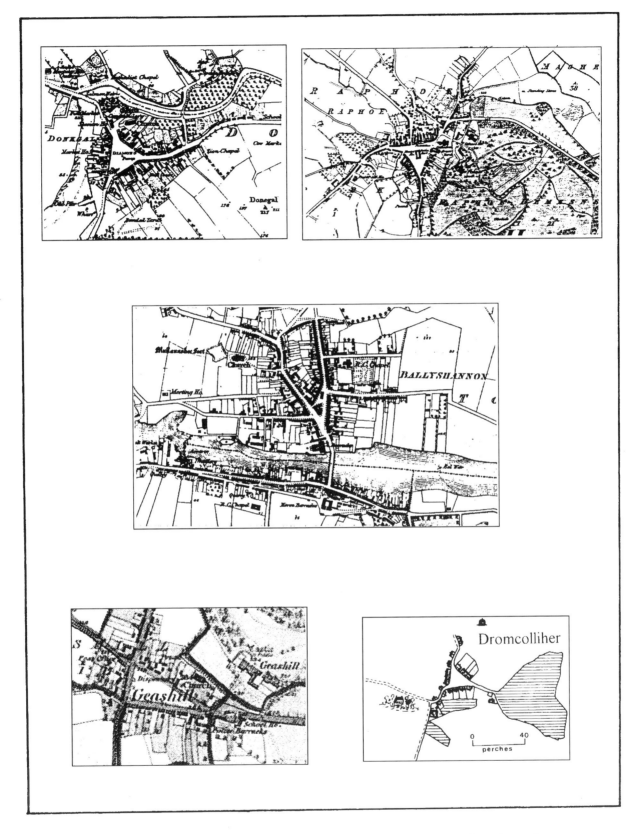

Fig. 3.1. A common motif in pre-1641 towns and villages was the triangular green, the marketplace of the newly germinated settlement, as in Donegal town, Raphoe, and Ballyshannon, Co. Donegal; Geashill, Co. Offaly; and Dromcolliher, Co. Limerick

> To hold a Saturday market, and two fairs on the feasts of St. Mark the evangelist, and SS. Simon and Jude the apostles, and the day after each, at the town lately built on the S. side of the River Bandon near the bridge.

The same process of instituting fairs and markets at new settlement foundations may be seen at regional level. In Inishowen, Co. Donegal, in 1610, the lord deputy, Sir Arthur Chichester was granted patents as follows:[10]

> A Friday market and two fairs on 31 Aug. and 30 Apr. and the day after each at Boncranoche [Buncrana]; a Monday market, and 2 fairs on 30 Sep. and 1 Apr. and the day after each at Greenecastle [Greencastle]; a fair on 30 Oct. and the day after at Dronge otherwise Caronvleugh in Malyne island [Malin].

Chichester was a key player in the regional planning of the Ulster plantation, as well as an influential proprietor on his own account. The latter finds further expression upon take-over of the old O'Neill stronghold of Dungannon, Co. Tyrone, where the following stipulations were to apply by a grant of 1612:[11]

> To hold a Thursday market at Dungannon, and two fairs there yearly viz. one on the Monday next after the feast of St. Philip and St. James and the day after, and the other on the Monday next after Michaelmas Day and the day after ------------ A prohibition from selling goods by retail, within 4 miles of the castle of Dungannon, to all except the inhabitants or those planted there by Sir Arthur. –Sir Arthur to set apart a convenient place --- for the site of the town, to be built streetways; another part for a market place; and another for a church and church-yard.

The same stipulations relating to new town foundations and the provision of market-places, markets and fairs had widespread application in Ulster, and pertained, for example, to the Brooke town of Donegal; the Cole town of Enniskillen, Co. Fermanagh; and the Ridgeway town of Virginia, Co. Cavan.

Widespread evidence may be adduced of the link between markets and fairs provision and the germination of new settlements, especially during the reign of James I (1603-25). An obvious location comes by way of Newmarket, Co. Cork, where the pre-urban nucleus of the MacAuliffes' came to be invested with a Thursday market and two annual fairs in the hands of its new proprietor, Sir Richard Aldworth. Sometimes a new village settlement took its name from its New English or Scottish proprietor in synchronicity with the grant of a patent for a weekly market and annual fair(s). Such a case is furnished at Lowtherstown (later Irvinestown), Co. Fermanagh, where Gerald Lowther, one of the justices of the common pleas, received patent confirmation in 1618.[12] Others to merit early recognition include Castlecaulfield, Co. Tyrone (Sir Toby Caulfield); Cookstown, Co. Tyrone (Allan Cooke); Manorhamilton, Co. Leitrim (Sir F. Hamilton); Newtown-stewart, Co. Tyrone (Sir William Stewart); and Parsonstown (later Birr), Co. Offaly (Sir Lawrence Parsons).

A common motif in pre-1641 towns and villages was the triangular green at centre, the marketplace of the newly germinated settlement.[13] Such greens were by no means exclusive to the period, but the motif may betray a common cultural origin and a sense of huddled insecurity in early colonising days (fig. 3.1.). Moreover, this distinctive morphology enjoys a widespread distribution throughout Ireland, especially in areas that experienced appreciable colonisation in the period 1603-41. Linkage between nascent settlements and the provision of markets and fairs may also be made. In Ulster, Co. Donegal furnishes the superb examples of Malin and Donegal town, which attracted fair and market patents in 1610 and 1611 respectively. Success for the latter appears assured by continuity of the Brooke lineage and by additional patents for fairs in 1623 and 1640. In well planted country outside Ulster, Leinster offers the examples of Killeigh, Co.

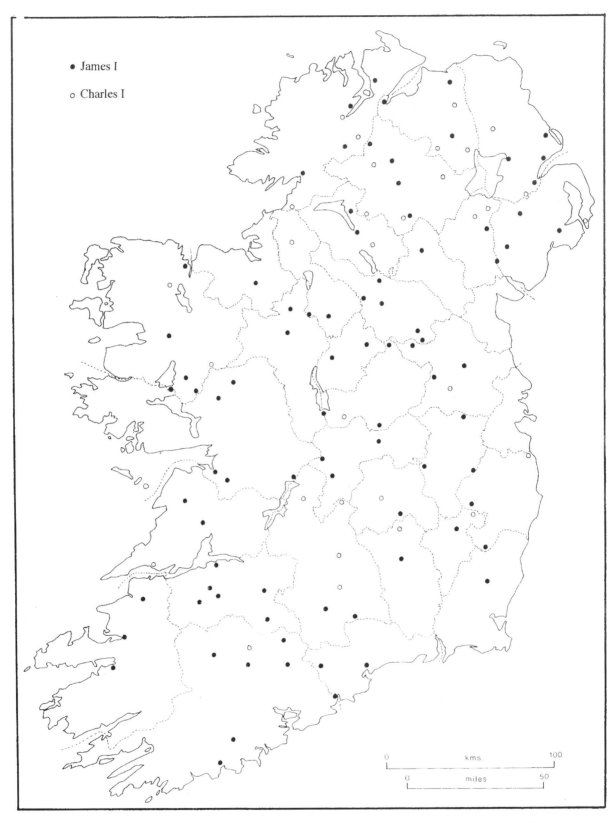

Fig. 3.2. shows markets patented in the period 1600-1650, which were still going concerns by mid nineteenth century, without, it is postulated, any prolonged breaks in trading

Offaly, and Carysfort or Macreddin, Co. Wicklow. The former was suitably situated in a county of villages of triangular form,[14] and its proprietor, Lady Ossaly, received patent confirmation for two annual fairs in 1620. Much greater ambition than delivery attended Carysfort in Ballinacor South barony, Co. Wicklow, where its corporation was the recipient of a patent for a Thursday market and two annual fairs in 1628. It withered away for want of patronage, and its fairs and market lapsed. In Munster, Co. Limerick attracted substantial colonisation in the post-plantation phase 1603-41, and it too lays claim to settlements with triangular greens. Dromcolliher, on Sir William Courtenay's estate in west county, furnishes the early grant of a fair to Courtenay's son, George, and the finest triangular green in the county.

Land transfer to new proprietors and a strong measure of intrusive colonisation was an undoubted catalyst in the promotion of new settlements and endowing them with the mechanisms of trade. It was, however, only part of the story. Figs 3.2. and 3.3. show the virtual ubiquity of patent confirmation for markets and fairs throughout the island as a whole from 1600-1650. In addition, it should be noted that active trading, either for the purpose of fairs or markets, or both, had ceased at another 446 sites by 1852-3. There is no way of knowing the duration of trade at many of these sites, or indeed the extent to which the patents were implemented at all. Fig. 3.2., on the other hand, shows that markets patented in 1600-1650 were still going concerns by mid nineteenth century, without, it is postulated, any prolonged breaks in trading. Altogether 116 sites are shown, with a presence in all counties, except for Louth and Dublin. The preponderance of market patents date from the reign of James 1 (1603-25). Fig. 3.3. shows that fairs patented at 307 sites in 1600-1650 were still active by mid nineteenth century. All counties shared in the broadly ubiquitous pattern and the vast bulk were again awarded in the reign of James 1. The cumulative evidence points to a period of buoyant prospects and expanding economic growth.

The rapid and widespread adoption of patents for fairs and markets also related to pragmatic considerations. These were taken out by landlords for existing or proposed settlements in order to safeguard their interests and property and to ensure that no rival could lay claim to such franchises. Thus with a basis in English law, markets and fairs still carried the stamp of Irish practice. As in the medieval period, markets were regular affairs, usually weekly, and required a local surplus in production to sustain their development. Locally produced commodities were sold for cash, thereby promoting the commercialisation of agriculture. Markets also facilitated local landowners and their tenants in the purchase of goods ranging from salt to domestic utensils and agricultural implements. Enough business needed to be done to ensure a profitable turnover. Otherwise, it would not be worth the landlord's while investing in the infrastructure required for a regular market.[15] Still akin to extravagant markets, fairs were annual or seasonal events which required little outlay. At best these invested towns with custom and prestige or at base took place in the open countryside, as gathering places for the sale of livestock and the pursuit of fun and frivolity.

The proprietors of markets and fairs, to whom accrued customs or tolls on the days and at the place specified in the patent, fell into three major categories. Landed proprietors or landlords were the pre-eminent category, accounting for ownership of 81 per cent of the markets and 87 per cent of the fairs that were to prove enduring (figs. 3.2. and 3.3.). At a

34

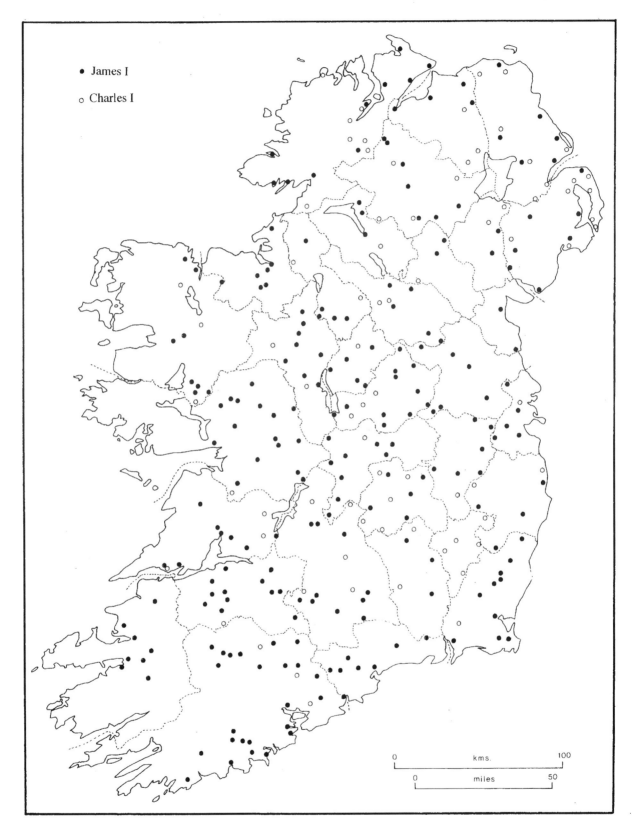

Fig. 3.3. shows fairs patented at 307 sites in the period 1600-1650, which were still active by mid nineteenth century. All counties shared in the broadly ubiquitous pattern, and the vast bulk were awarded in the reign of James I (1603-25)

time of deep transition in the history of Irish landownership they fell into three broadly recognised ethnic classes: New English, Old English and Gaelic. Next in significance, towns incorporated by charter in 1600-1650, or earlier, frequently had the ownership of fairs and markets vested in their corporations. Such towns accounted for ownership of 13 per cent of markets of an enduring nature and 9 per cent of the fairs. Thirdly, the episcopal hold on markets and fairs – a feature of the medieval period – continued into the modern. Following on from the Reformation, however, Protestant bishops increasingly succeeded to old diocesan centres, and to proprietorship of their fairs and markets. Bishops accounted for ownership of 6 and 4 per cent respectively of enduring markets and fairs.

The New English impress was striking, especially in areas that had seen land transfer and plantation in favour of intrusive landowners and colonists. In Munster plantation country names such as Herbert, Browne and Roper in Co. Kerry; Barkeley, Courtenay and Trenchard in Co. Limerick; Beecher, Boyle and Jephson in Co. Cork; and Boyle again in Co. Waterford, all accumulated extensive estates and promoted their settlement foci. Killorglin's famous 'Puck' Fair in Co. Kerry, falls within the same proprietorial remit and dates back at least to 1613, when Jenkin Conway was granted a Thursday market and a fair 'every Lammas day and two days after' at the centre of his estate.[16] The market and fairs thus granted proved their viability and longevity at the gateway to the Iveragh peninsula. Other Munster plantation towns to maintain durable markets and fairs best abounded in Cos. Limerick and Cork. In Co. Limerick the settlements of Askeaton, Rathkeale, Newcastle and Bruff all stood in long-term testament to the early endeavours of Barkeley, Dowdall, Courtenay and Fullerton respectively, while in Co. Cork the long arm of Sir Richard Boyle, earl of Cork, extended a proprietorial range from Clonakilty to Fermoy.

It was in Ulster, however, following on from 1609, that new landowners were most assiduous in their pursuit of fair and market patents at central places within their estates. Markets were potentially very profitable for a landlord through tolls and the profits of market courts, but in order to capitalise fully on them it was necessary to secure the legal right of a patent. This eager pursuit, along with the need to keep rivals at bay, may explain why 41 per cent of all market patents were taken out within the first ten years of the plantation of Ulster, together with 32 per cent of fair patents.[17] Towns, markets and fairs were the catalysts too in the promotion of a cash economy. In order to pay the cash rents increasingly under demand, tenants had to market whatever surplus they had. The Clandeboy estate in north Co. Down provides an early illustration, when in May 1621 the tenants asked for time so that they could sell some produce at nearby fairs.[18] Towns thus became rapidly integrated into the rural economy and a study of Co. Tyrone indicates that new settler families lived within walking distance of them, while the less market-focused Irish lived further away.[19]

At a time when ideas of civility were much in vogue in fleshing out plantation policy,[20] the central administration found further application in the marketplace. Accordingly, a market patented in favour of Sir George Blundell in Dundrum, Co. Down, in 1629, carried the following aspiration:[21]

> For the public good of the inhabitants residing in or near Dundrum and with the intention that they may have free trade and commerce among themselves and with other liege subjects --- by which

the rude and country people of that region may be led to a more humane and civil mode of life and the more easily procure a provision of all necessaries.

In the event, it was the fairs and not the market of Dundrum that proved longevity, but the case is illustrative of the concern of central government to exercise control over towns and their spheres of influence.

As to the facilitation of control, there was a complement of new proprietors with influence in every Ulster county, and a network of enduring markets and fairs to prove it in the period 1603-40, but especially from 1609 onwards. In the plantation county of Donegal, the last cartographic outpost of Elizabethan Ireland and one of the most Gaelic, the market towns of Buncrana (Sir Arthur Chichester), Donegal (Basil Brooke), Ramelton (Sir Richard Hansard), Ballybofey (Sir Ralph Bingley), Raphoe (Andrew, bishop of Raphoe) and Letterkenny (Sir William Simple) took off in rapid order 1609-40, along with at least eighteen other centres that ultimately proved less enduring as settings for markets, or fairs, or both.[22] The neighbouring county of Derry or Londonderry (according to its official designation) furnishes the following suite of early and enduring market towns in 1605-35: Coleraine (Thomas Phillips), Derry (Sir Henry Dockwrays), Maghera (George, bishop of Derry), Magherafelt (Randol Whistler), Draperstown (Sir John Clotsworthy), and Garvagh (George Canning), along with an indeterminable network of other centres in which markets, or fairs, or both, may have been established. All over Ulster a suite of new family names went together with a network a new market towns in the interests of fostering economic development and 'civility'.[23] Counting among these, Hamilton at Belfast, Antrim and at Killeshandra, Co. Cavan; Adair at Ballymena, Co. Antrim; and Stewart at Gortin and Newtownstewart, Co. Tyrone, betoken Scottish origins, while many others carried impeccable New English credentials.

A New English impress in the patenting of successful markets and fairs also followed on from the lesser known plantation of Cos. Leitrim and Longford *circa* 1618-20. In 1621, Henry Crofton sued for a patent for a Thursday market and an October fair at Mohill, Co. Leitrim, and long-term fairs were patented at Leitrim town (Sir F. Blundell in 1621) and at Lurganboy (James Creighton in 1622). Close synchronicity between plantation, patenting and the likely germination of village settlements is observable in Co. Leitrim, while Longford presents a more diverse profile. The old O'Farrell town of Granard fell within the patented hold of Sir Francis and Lady Margaret Aungier in 1620, and its markets and fairs enjoyed long-term viability. Longford town fell within the same proprietorial hands, with similar long-term results. Elsewhere older layers of landowner continued to prevail at Lanesborough and at Taghshinny near Ballymahon. In Co. Longford as a whole, of the nine fairs patented before 1640, only the last at Taghshinny failed by 1685.[24] In the unstable conditions of Ulster on the other hand, over 75 per cent of the fairs established by 1641 had failed by 1685.[25]

Within other strongly Gaelic areas too, plantation made a difference by introducing a New English element into the pattern of land ownership and the patenting of markets and fairs. In King's Co. (Offaly) and part of Queen's Co. (Laois) sixteenth-century land transfers and plantation were reinforced and elaborated upon *circa* 1618-20. Parsonstown (Birr) in the hands of Sir Lawrence Parsons was awarded a patent for a Thursday market and annual fair in 1618. In optimistic mode, this was added to with a patent for a Saturday market to the same proprietor in 1628. The fairs of Birr and the Saturday market

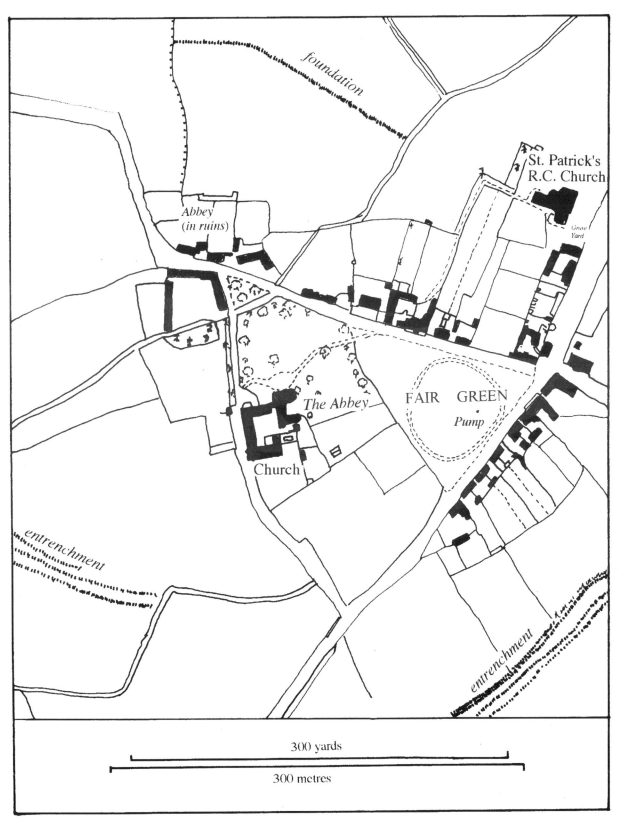

Fig. 3.4. The triangular motif at centre, a characteristic feature of pre-1641 village settlement, is well exemplified in the case of Killeigh, Co. Offaly, which was granted a patent for two annual fairs in 1620

enjoyed a successful future. So did the place itself as a landlord-designed town. Success also attended the fairs of Killeigh patented to Lady Ossaly in 1620 (see, fig. 3.4.), and the fairs of Ballycowan patented to Sir Jasper Herbert in 1622. In Queen's Co. alongside, the duke of Buckingham patented a successful fair at Borris-in-Ossory in 1624. Elsewhere, Sir Henry Wallop set the scene for an ambitious plantation scheme of north Wexford between 1611 and 1620.[26] Under Wallop's aegis, Enniscorthy was granted Thursday and Saturday markets and two annual fairs in 1611. The town attracted many newcomers. As the Franciscan, Donat Mooney, observed in 1617: 'Anglici haeretici totum oppidum inhabitant'.[27] Richard Masterson was another New English proprietor to make a mark on north Wexford, where a mixed pattern of land ownership still prevailed. Successful fairs stemmed from his 1616 patents at Clogh and Ferns respectively. Indeed the latter is testament to a changed order of patron, having served as a diocesan centre in which the medieval bishops held the powers of markets and fairs.[28]

New English proprietors therefore made a large-scale impact in the patenting of markets and fairs in recently planted regions during the period 1603-41, while exercising an appreciable influence elsewhere.[29] The ownership of the land of Ireland – the most persistent theme in modern agrarian history – was already in deep transition, as older elements compounded with new. Of these older elements, an Old English stratum persisted, although subject to varying degrees of Gaelicisation, especially in areas beyond the Pale. In the prime lands of north Leinster, starting in and about Dublin the names of Plunkett and Talbot are linked to successful long-term fairs patented at St. Margaret's and Garristown respectively. In Co. Meath, Plunkett is again linked to the successful fairs and market of Oldcastle (1619) and with the fair of Longwood (1612), while Sir F. Fitzgerald was confirmed in the patent of Ballyboggan fair in 1607. The name Nugent waxes strong in Westmeath in association with the successful fairs of Multifarnham, Finea and Fore, while Dillon commanded the fairs and markets of Moate and Kilkenny West in Westmeath, and of Abbeyshrule in Longford.[30] Elsewhere in Leinster, the Ormond Butlers took charge of the patented markets at Tullow and Hacketstown, Co. Carlow, which over the long run proved successful; William Eustace secured an enduring fair patent at Kilcullen, Co. Kildare; and the names Esmonde and Butler were linked respectively to the earliest fair patents of the little-known Limerick and Moneyheer, Co. Wexford.

Munster yields quite a diffuse pattern, with Geraldine families best in evidence in Cos. Kerry, Cork and Waterford, and yielding a crop of successful fairs and/or markets at Listowel and Ardfert in Co. Kerry; Dangan and Kildorrery, Co. Cork; and Drumana and Whitechurch, Co. Waterford. The Ormond Butlers held sway in Co. Tipperary, with their proprietorship of the fairs and markets of Cahir and Roscrea. In Co. Limerick, the power of the Geraldines had been broken, and only Lacy at Ballingarry (market and fairs), Fitzharris at Kilfinane (market), Cantwell at Galbally (fair) and Bourke at Lismullane (fair) were confirmed in patents that proved successful in the long run. One other successful upholder of Old English interests was John Power of Kilmacthomas, Co. Waterford, who received patent confirmation for a weekly market and two annual fair in 1605, and the fairs survived in the long-term.

In their Connacht hearthland, the Clanrickard Bourkes struck by far the strongest proprietorial interest in fairs and markets. Successful fairs in the longer term were confirmed to them at Ardnaree, Ballyhean, Neale, and Shrule, Co. Mayo; Athleague, Co. Roscommon; and Castlehackett, Kilconnell, Kilcorban, Loughrea, Meelick, Moylough and Portumna, Co. Galway. The market at Portumna also proved its staying power, and for extra measure, the Earl of Clanrickard owned the fair of Rathwire, Co. Westmeath, which was patented in 1617, and stood the test of long-time viability. Families of the famous 'tribes' of Galway took a hand too in the proprietorship of the fair and marketplace. Nicholas Darcy secured a patent for what proved an enduring fair at the eponymous 'Fair Hill' of Galway town in 1614. Oliver Martin was confirmed in a patent and a market with legs at Kinvara in 1619.

Gaelic proprietors – the oldest stratum of landowner in 1600-1650 – felt obliged too to adapt to the new common law order and apply to the central administration for patents for their markets and fairs. While the pattern of application is unknown, that of successful licencing shows a marked unevenness throughout the country. Clare – often taken to be the archetypal Gaelic county – yields the best results. Led by Donagh, earl of Thomond, the O'Briens, McMahons and McNamaras took impressive patented hold of the fairs and/or markets of the county between 1607 and 1627. The O'Brien earls of Thomond were inured to trading with both Galway and Limerick merchants, and probably had a fixed market at Ennis since the fifteenth century.[31] Doubtless to protect his interests and to continue drawing income under English law, the earl of Thomond was licenced in 1610 to hold a weekly market and two annual fairs at Ennis. He further amplified his trading interests at Clare town (Clarecastle) and Sixmilebridge with patents in 1607 and 1619 respectively, while Daniel O'Brien took out a patent at Ballykett in 1623. Issuing his proprietorial stamp on place, T. R. McMahon took out a patent at Kilmurry McMahon, and the McNamaras were confirmed as patentees at Quin and Broadford. Rounding off the patenting process in Gaelic hands, Luke Brady secured a patent at Tuamgraney in 1632. The market and fairs at Ennis proved their long-term mettle, and so did the fairs at all other locations.

Elsewhere Gaelic proprietors achieved best rates of the patenting of successful fairs (and of markets to a much lesser extent) at locations in counties Offaly (6), Cork (5), Roscommon (4), Galway (3), Sligo (3), Tipperary (3), Westmeath (2), Fermanagh (2) and Down (2). Included among these were some of the most famous fairs in Ireland, which were given a basis in English law at an early date, but had lost none of their Irish practice by the eighteenth and nineteenth centuries. Knockcroghery, Co. Roscommon, second only to Ballinasloe as a sheep fair,[32] was first licenced to Collo O'Kelly in 1613, and remained in O'Kelly hands when a second patent was issued in 1675. Attracting its share of lustre too at a later date, the fair of Banagher, Co. Offaly, was first licenced to John McCoghlan in 1613. Others to claim fame, and sometimes notoriety, were Drimoleague, Co. Cork (O'Donovan), Kanturk, Co. Cork (McCarthy), Clabby, Co. Fermanagh (O'Neill), Maguiresbridge, Co. Fermanagh (Maguire) and Ballinamore, Co Galway (O'Kelly). In Co. Westmeath, the name Geoghegan, which according to one source means rich in cattle,[33] was appropriately linked by early patent to the fairs of Castletown-Geoghegan and Donore. The one-off fairs of Cos. Antrim and Wexford, to be patented at an early date in Gaelic hands, also laid enduring claims to fame. The place-names are redolent: Craigbilly, Co. Antrim (O'Hara), and Scarawalsh, Co. Wexford (McBrian Kavanagh).

In the case of many leading towns the privileges of fairs and markets were vested in their corporations. Medieval towns incorporated by Jacobin charter, and patented with markets viable in the long-term, included Navan (1605), Athlone (1606), Kilkenny (1608), Clonmel (1609), Dungarvan (1609), Youghal (1609), Carrickfergus (1612), Athboy (1612), Tuam (1613) and Tralee (1613). Cashel's market, confirmed in 1638, also proved its long-term viability. All kept their fairs going, along with additions, to mid nineteenth century. There were other medieval towns where market failure ensued in the longer term, but fairs patented 1600-1650, endured. Such towns often failed to find an expansive *raison d'etre* in the modernising Ireland, and counting among them were Fethard, Co. Tipperary; Callan and Gowran, Co. Kilkenny; and Kells, Co. Meath. Also at this time there was a veneer of new town foundations, in which the privileges of markets and fairs were vested in corporations. Those to prove their mettle with markets were Belturbet, Co. Cavan; the appositely named Jamestown, Co. Leitrim; and Strabane, Co. Tyrone. Proving their mettle with fairs were Killybegs, Co. Donegal; Newtown-Limavady, Co. Derry; and St. Johnstown, Co. Longford.

The composition of many of these corporations was unambiguously New English. Even in the case of Ennis, Co. Clare, where the earl of Thomond was confirmed in fair and market privileges in 1610, the town charter of 1613 established a corporation drawn from the New English elite, with rights to hold a Saturday market.[34] In this kind of situation the rival interests of manor court and corporation remained a fertile source of conflict. A *tabula rasa* situation offered only one prospect. Such a case arose at Belturbet, the intended urban centre of the barony of Loughtee, Co. Cavan, under the terms worked out for the Ulster plantation.[35] The town was officially established in 1610, when the leading proprietor, Sir Stephen Butler, was given the projected town's land and granted a Saturday market and two annual fairs, while other proprietors in the neighbourhood were charged with procuring settlers for the new town. Fruitful productivity appears to have accompanied the enterprise, as a survey of 1618 detailed:

> Houses built of cage work, all inhabited with British tenants, and most of them tradesmen, each of these having a house and garden plot, with four acres of land, and commons for certain numbers of cows and garrons.

The commissioners for the plantation expressed pleasure with 'that well begune corporacion which is fitt to be cherished', and alluded to the 'great store' of Protestants in and about the town. As a new and vigorous market town, Belturbet came in for further warm commendation before 1641. Ruled by a Protestant oligarchy from the outset, it was the quintessential plantation town.

The old county town of Cavan on the other hand represented a very different order of urbanity. Rooted in a Gaelic culture hearth, it had at most evolved into a hybrid Anglo-Irish town by 1600. Its first charter was granted in 1610, which specified *inter alia* that the corporation be granted a weekly market and two annual fairs. The charter was issued on the direct instructions of the lord deputy, Sir Arthur Chichester, but the corporation bucked the New English trend by having Walter Brady as sovereign, and ten of its twelve burgesses as Irishmen. Moreover, an older of territoriality still prevailed in that the borough was to be defined within a radius of one mile of Walter Brady's house. Nor did the fair of Cavan lose one whit of its Gaelic practice. Writing in 1646, a Roman emissary on his way through Co. Cavan, commented on:[36]

> The great fair held in a field near Cavan. It is attended by crowds and great quantities of merchandise are brought thither by the people of the surrounding districts. I was amazed at the

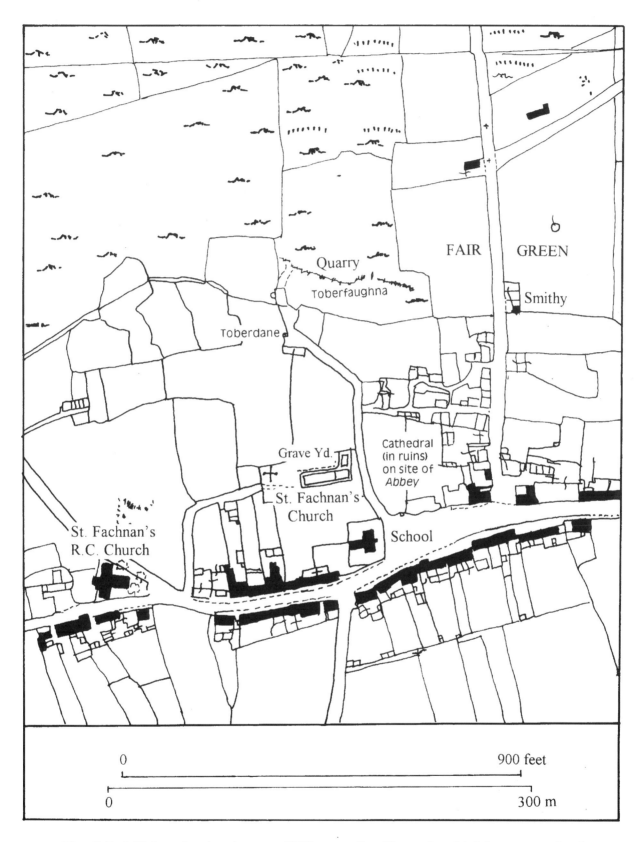

Fig. 3.5. Still keeping its shape at Kilfenora, Co. Clare, the old fair green maintains close proximity to the partly-roofed medieval cathedral, and features the 'paying stand' where accounts of the fair were settled

abundant supply especially of animals, and of all kinds of eatables, which were sold at an absurdly low price. A fat ox costs three crowns, a fine wether three guilii [6d.] or a pair of fat chickens six *baiocci* and so on, for the supplies were as plentiful as money was scarce in the country.

Neither did the inhabitants of Co. Cavan lose a whit of their long-distance droving instinct, being prepared to walk their cattle to Dublin, if they believed they would get a better price there.[37]

In general, however, the power of New English proprietorship prevailed in the patenting of fairs and markets. It is seen once again in the new episcopal order, which appropriated, or expanded upon, the medieval network of trading places under the patronage of bishops. As the religious differences arising out of the Reformation became fixed, the Anglican bishops who had acquired the temporalities of the Irish sees continued in their right to hold fairs and markets. To protect or enhance their right, patent confirmation was eagerly sought. Starting atop the hierarchy, the archbishop of Armagh, Christopher Hamilton, was confirmed in a Tuesday market at Armagh, 'where a market has been held time out of mind', and two annual fairs there.[38] Later, in 1634, another feastday fair was confirmed at Armagh. Meanwhile he further consolidated his trading and tolling interests with two annual fairs at Carnteel, Co. Tyrone, and with weekly markets at Inniskeen, Co. Monaghan, Termonfeckin, Co. Louth, Nobber, Co. Meath, and Tymon, Co Armagh. The Armagh city and Carnteel interests remained intact, while the market interests elsewhere on the property of the archbishopric had lapsed by mid nineteenth century.

In 1609, Thomas Jones, archbishop of Dublin, was confirmed in the revived weekly market of Ballymore Eustace, Co. Kildare, and in an annual fair there. These proved their durability to mid nineteenth century, as did the fairs of the old manorial centre of Swords, Co. Dublin. No more than their medieval predecessors, however, the new proprietorial order of bishops scarcely ever injected either vitality or the infrastructure of trade into the heart of their diocesan sees. At the old centre of Dromore, Co. Down, John Dodd, bishop of Down, Conor and Dromore, was granted a patent to hold a Saturday market near the cathedral, where the market cross stood. Two annual fairs were to be held in the same place. Thus locational conservatism was upheld, but the market wilted in an episcopal backwater.

Both markets and fairs did manage to survive long-term in Killala, Co. Mayo; Clogher, Co. Tyrone; and Elphin, Co. Roscommon, but again the measure of episcopal insouciance at the last named is conveyed as late as *c.* 1837, when the bishop of the time had still not got round to erecting a market house.[39] Fairs alone kept continuity to mid nineteenth century at Raphoe, Co. Donegal, and Killaloe, Co. Clare. In the modernising Ireland the old episcopal towns took on at best the look of genteel obsolescence, consistently outstripped by the secular landlords' gleaming market towns. Still charm could repose in old backwaters, as in the centre of the tiny diocese of Kilfenora, Co. Clare. Here the bishop was confirmed in a patent for a weekly market and two annual fairs in 1619. Both market and fairs are credited with survival to mid nineteenth century, but by then the trade of the landlord-inspired town of Ennistymon had decisively eclipsed it. The old fair field keeps its shape at Kilfenora, close to the partly roofed pre-Reformation cathedral (fig. 3.5.). In the middle of that stony field there is a circular stone structure about twelve feet in diameter, with battlements on top. It resembles a very large pulpit. This was the 'paying stand',[40] where accounts of the fair were settled immemorially, and where rich ecclesiastical imagery abides.

II

Figs. 3.6. and 3.7. suggest that in contrast to 1600-1650, there was a considerable contraction and reorientation in first-time patenting of markets and fairs of an enduring nature from 1651-1700. Countrywide, the tally adds up to a modest 31 freshly patented markets, successful in the longer term, and 94 (or just over three times as many) fairs. The duality of newly patented fairs and markets (with the capacity for long-term survival) related only to 25 settlement centres. From Antrim to Wexford, the eastern half of Ireland was strongly favoured in the first-time patenting of fairs, a tendency also supported in the patenting of markets. Leinster proved the outstanding province, with 13 of the markets and 43 of the fairs. A similar bias is evident in Bourk's *Almanack* of 1684, which lists some 503 fairs for the country as a whole. Of these, 43 per cent were in Leinster.[41]

It all bespeaks a difficult economic climate in a period punctuated by the Confederate and Williamite wars and the Cromwellian and Williamite plantations. The impact of the Confederate wars (1641-52) on the cattle trade and cattle numbers – the essential lubricant of the fair – was deep and negative. Later the Cattle Acts of 1665 forced a reorientation of trade away from England in favour of fresh markets on the continent of Europe and in the colonies. Inter-regional trade in Ireland was of little significance; agricultural specialisation was very limited. Given all the constraints, whatever growth there was took place in short bursts in the 1660s, 1670s and 1690s. It was all so different to Scotland, then undergoing a phase of sustained economic growth. In Scotland patent confirmation increased four-fold during the second half of the seventeenth century.[42] Relative to what had gone before from 1603-41, Ireland contracted to a quarter of new patent confirmations for enduring markets and to less than a third of those for like fairs.

From 1651-1700 once or twice weekly markets continued to serve the routine needs of a community (see, fig. 3.6.), generally within a three or four-mile radius of a market town.[43] Fairs, increasingly quarterly, or twice or thrice yearly were, as ever, the main conduit for cattle exchanges and the occasion for the purchase of non-local commodities. Dual patents for markets and fairs of a lasting nature succeeded far and away best in Co. Wicklow, which had been under-represented 1600-1650. Now the parade of Bray, Blessington, Dunlavin, Rathdrum and the hill-top village of Donard flesh out the trading network of the county impressively with once a week markets and twice or thrice yearly fairs. Elsewhere, Tyrone weighs in with Caledon, Castlederg and Moy, the last of which became known for its concourse of horses at fair, the famous 'Dancers at the Moy';[44] Down contributes Ballynahinch and Hillsborough; Galway yields the east county villages of Eyrecourt and Woodford; Mayo cedes the duo of Balla and Foxford; Offaly presents Cloghan and Edenderry. One-offs come by way of Ballyconnell (Co. Cavan); Dunmanway (Co. Cork); Ballymahon (Co. Longford); Ballybay, Co. Monaghan; Portarlington (Co. Laois); Castlerea (Co. Roscommon) Sligo town; Clogheen (Co. Tipperary); and Castlepollard (Co. Westmeath).

Once again it is tempting to seek synchronicity between settlement germination or growth and the neat symmetry of place, proprietor, and patent. Ready examples come by way of Hillsborough (Arthur Hill, proprietor), Portarlington (Lord Arlington, to whom an extensive land grant in the area was made upon the restoration of Charles II), Eyrecourt

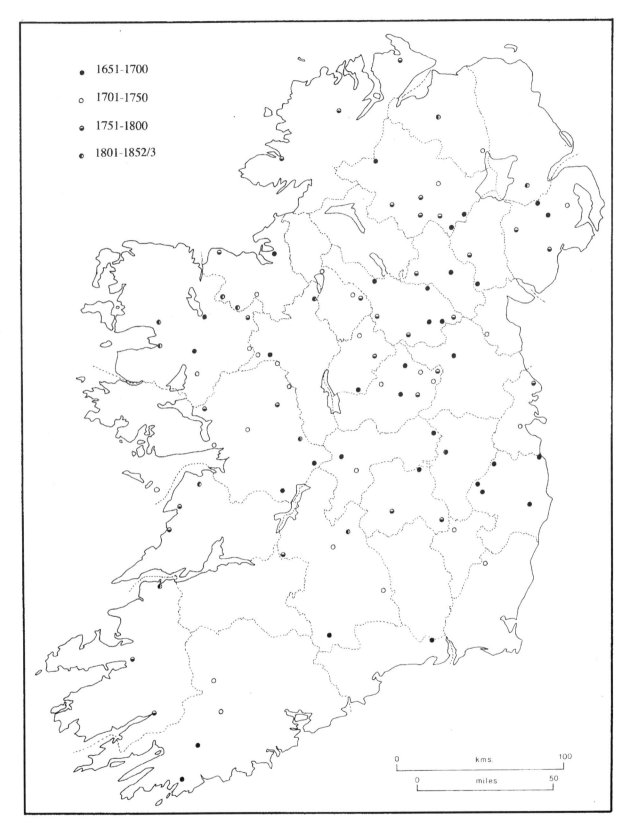

Fig. 3.6. shows the cumulative grant of market patents over the period 1651-1852/3, differentiated into separate fifty-year spans. The markets, thus confirmed, continued to faithfully serve the tributary areas of their towns

(John Eyre, whose patent also contains the Gaelic *alias* for his settlement focus) and Castlepollard (Walter Pollard, proprietor). The Restoration certainly saw the creation what was, in effect, the first generation of estate towns. Several of the dual patented settlements fall within ready ambit, including Ballinahinch (Sir George Rawdon, proprietor) Hillsborough, Blessington (archbishop of Dublin, patentee), and Castlerea (Matthew Simpson, patentee). In the case of the first of these, the detail is quite specific. Granted the manor of Kinelarty by patent of Charles II, Sir George Rawdon built the town of Ballinahinch with two mills, and appropriated a large space for the holding of markets and fairs.[45] The relationship and the timing were not, however, always as clear-cut. Moy on the Tyrone-Armagh border (patentee, John Leighley, in 1677), had to wait until 1763-4 for 'a treasure' of a small estate town to be generated by the earl of Charlemont.[46] It has as centrepiece an elongated piazza, said to have been modelled on Marengo in Lombardy - a superb setting for Muldoon's equine dancers at fair, and equally suited to marketplace (see, plate 3.1).

As distinct from fairs and markets together, fairs first patented 1651-1700 (or effectively 1661-1700) to survive *in situ* to mid nineteenth century, found clearest attestation in the province of Leinster (fig. 3.7.). County aggregates reflect the most anglicised and advanced region in Ireland, led by Kildare (7), Meath (6), Louth (4) and Dublin (4), while Kilkenny, Laois and Wexford mustered three sites each. Clearly over a period of much instability, retrenchment entered the bureaucratic mind, and deemed that the infrastructure of trade and the forward linkages from agriculture required attention within reach of metropolitan Dublin. Co. Meath featured an interesting mix of old medieval sites (Rathmoylan, Skreen, Slane) and novel settings in cattle country (Ardmaghbreague, Belgree, Culmullin). Co. Louth alongside marked a more radical departure, with Ardee as vested in the corporation representing the old order, while Castlebellingham (Henry Bellingham, patentee), Dunleer (George Legge) and Mullaghcrew (Chief Justice Keating) represented a new proprietorial order. The last went well beyond legal and legalistic etiquette in a hill-top setting renowned for its wool trade and faction fights at fair. As a gathering place patronised from the expansive plains and the pinched drumlin edge, it held the seeds of conflict.[47] Its sphere reached deep into Co. Monaghan, giving tonality to a ballad:[48]

> The Castleblaney besoms, the best that ever grew
> Were sold for two a penny on the Hill of Mullacrew.

Patented with an October fair in 1684, the tiny hill-top village had expanded its staging to twelve fairs in the year by mid nineteenth century.

Elsewhere, fairs first patented 1661-1700 to last *in situ* to mid nineteenth century, were most prolific in Co. Cork. Here Patrick Levallen proved something of a fairs entrepreneur in 1686 with Jacobin patents for twice yearly fairs at Ballinhassig, Ballinphelic and Six-mile-Water. The redoubtable earl of Orrery was confirmed in a patent for Castlemartyr in 1674, just as the place acquired the trappings of an estate town complete with a mansion, which held a household complement of sixty-six persons in 1679.[49] The Anglican bishop of Cork also made his proprietorial mark with patents for what proved lasting fairs at Aghadown and at the old diocesan centre of Ross. Thomas Mitchell at Mitchellsfort in 1686 affirmed again the pattern of place, proprietor and patent. All these preceded Cox's Dunmanway in 1693, where the market as well as the fairs survived in the long-term, and were bolstered by output from the linen industry in the eighteenth century.

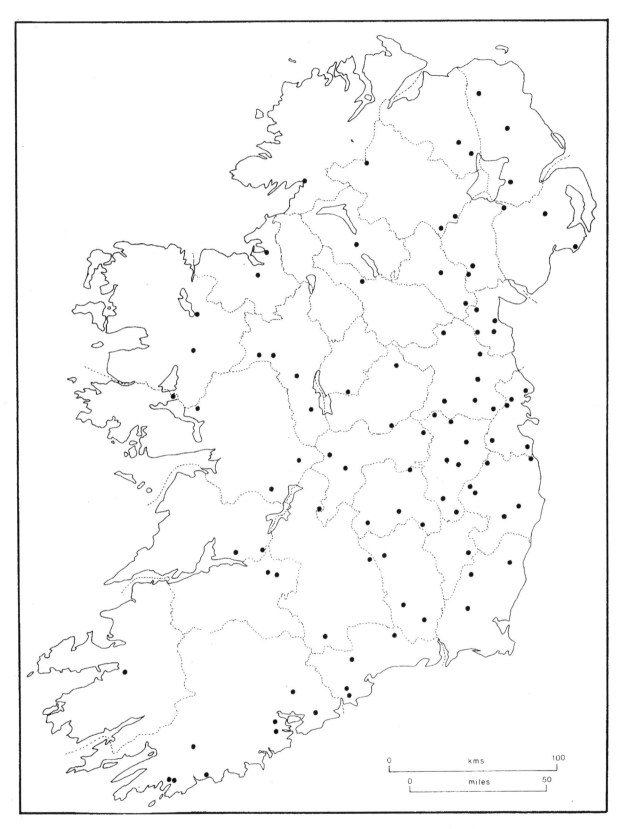

Fig. 3.7. Fairs, first patented 1651-1700 to survive *in situ* to mid nineteenth century, found clearest attestation in the province of Leinster, and elsewhere were most prolific in Co. Cork

At this time place, proprietor and patent went together well as trilogy in situations where New English landlords were in marked ascendance. It emerges in fairs patented in settings as diverse as Poyntzpass, Co. Armagh (Sir Toby Poyntz, proprietor); Mountievers or Jeverstown, Co. Clare (Henry Ivers, proprietor), Gilford, Co. Down (John M'Gill Esq., proprietor), and Castledawson, Co. Derry (Thomas Dawson, proprietor). Even in the case of Gaelic or Old English landlords, it appears certain that by the second half of the seventeenth century that they were moving within the forms of an Anglo-Irish world. Examples are few, however, and likely include the lasting fair locations of O'Brien's Bridge, Co. Clare (earl of Inchiquin, proprietor); Dunlavin, Co. Wicklow (Richard Buckley, proprietor); and Castlemorris, Co. Kilkenny (Harvey Morris, proprietor). The Scottish and New English struck the winning hand at a time when confiscation, plantation and restoration were working relentlessly in their favour. It all showed in the patenting of long-lived fairs in places like Ballymoney, Co. Antrim (Robert Stewart), Ballyconnell, Co. Cavan (Meredyth Gwyllyn); Ballymahon, Co. Longford (Daniel Molyneux); Woodford, Co. Galway (Sir Henry Waddington); and Caherconlish, Co. Limerick (Randolph Wilson).

III

For fairs and markets, which were patented and proved successful in the longer run, the period 1701-1750 is broadly comparable in aggregate to the preceding fifty years. There is a marked variation in regional preferences, however, especially in respect of fairs. Twenty-nine new and enduring markets were patented countrywide, but only twenty of these were dual sites where fairs also succeeded in the longer term. Compared to the preceding period therefore, some contraction may be noted, and though relative peace prevailed throughout the period, a black conjuncture of bad harvests and epidemics in the 1720s and 30s did much to inhibit economic growth.[50] The number of fairs, patented 1701-1750 and lasting to mid nineteenth century, shows only the most marginal increase of one over the preceding fifty-year period.

The pattern of patented markets is simply diffuse, set in a thin spread over nineteen counties. Co. Galway fares best with four patented sites, including the city, where the temporal range of the market was extended to every Monday as well as to Christmas, from 24th to 27th December inclusive. The small east Galway villages of Creggs (1720), Ballymoe (1745) and Monivea (1745) duly amplified upon the power of the marketplace. Of these Monivea was, without doubt, the most significant. Moreover, it neatly falls within the synchronised pattern of place, proprietor and patent, as Robert French, born in 1716, inherited the 6,110 acre Monivea estate in 1744.[51] The following year, he issued an early signal of entrepreneurial intent by securing a patent for a Saturday market at Monivea. Then his assertive management led to the attraction of bleacher and weavers, the establishment of the linen trade and, in time, the creation of a model village. Elsewhere in Connacht successful long-term fairs and markets were patented in Drumshanbo and Drumkeeran, Co. Leitrim; Hollymount, Co Mayo, and Ballinlough, Co. Roscommon; while long-term markets alone were perpetuated in Ballyhaunis, Co. Mayo and Tubbercurry, Co. Sligo. New English proprietors were in charge everywhere, with

Plate 3.1. shows an end-of-nineteenth century fair day at the elongated piazza of Moy, Co. Tyrone, in which cattle - and not 'equine dancers'- claim clear ascendancy. For the same period, plate 3.2. shows a horse fair on the Main Sreet of Saintfield, Co. Down

the likely exception of Creggs, Co Galway (Burke) and Ballinlough, Co. Roscommon (Mitchell).

During this period Ulster's distinctive proto-industrial economy was emerging, yet the region as a whole proved strangely deficient in the generation of patented markets of an enduring nature. Castledawson, Co. Derry, kept its Dawson lineage and developed weekly markets to supplement its quarterly fairs. Pomeroy, Co. Tyrone, could boast of a lasting market first patented in 1750. Ballybought, on the Armagh outskirts of Newry, Co. Down kept a patented market and fairs going long-term. Most success in the province, however, attended the Cavan towns of Ballyjamesduff, Bailieborough and Cootehill where dual patented markets and fairs, destined to enjoy long-term success, were first awarded in the 1720s. Proprietorship entailed a mix of Scot and New English, and serve as index of the transformation of the landownership of Co. Cavan in the hands of a new entrepreneurial class.

This emerges forcefully in the case of Cootehill, a name neatly compounded out of the families Coote (Cootehill, Co. Cavan) and Hill (Hillsborough, Co. Down), and a strategic seventeenth-century marriage, which proved heirless. Consequently it was left to a nephew, Thomas Coote, to devise a successful and profitable estate out of some 17,000 plantation acres in the barony of Tullygarvey in northeast Cavan, and in the absence of a pre-existing town, Coote commenced a new one on a site close to his residence at Magheranure.[52] Furnishing an early and telling marker of intent, Coote obtained a patent for a Friday market and quarterly fairs in 1725. Coote's interest in communications and commerce helped to make a significant nodal centre of his town, and he attracted new tenants to promote the linen industry. All this was calculated to make fairs and markets burgeon. It further promoted a state of well-being consistent with a description of the new town in the 1740s:[53]

> There are a great number of weavers and bleachers in this town and neighbourhood, and no less than ten bleach yards, the least of which bleaches a thousand pieces of cloth every year. All which was brought about by means of a colony of Protestant linen-manufacturers, who settled here on the encouragement given them by the Honourable Mr Justice Coote, who with a great deal of good management and care to have this new town so tenderly nursed and cherished in its infancy, that many of its inhabitants soon grew rich and brought it to the perfection which it is now at.

Thomas Coote's grandson, Charles, who inherited the estate in 1750, also assiduously promoted the town. From then until his death in 1800 Cootehill's markets and fairs attained their climax phase.[54]

Elsewhere in Ulster, only Saintfield, Co. Down, could claim a significant dual and enduring mandate, first patented to James Hamilton in 1701. The place was subsequently made into a town by General Price in the first half of the eighteenth century, with the settlement of linen manufacturers and other tradesmen, and improved communications to Belfast and Downpatrick. Its fortunes burgeoned in association with an expansive market and fairs. The market house dates from 1803, when the town was still under the patronage of the Price family. Premiums were given for the support of the market and fairs, so that by c. 1840 these ranked among the best in Ulster.[55] Saintfield horse fair was still going strong at the turn of the nineteenth century (plate 3.2.), while with a rare turn of enterprise its fowl market opened at 2 a.m. in the market house, in summer, to facilitate sale by poachers of pheasants thieved from an adjacent demesne.[56]

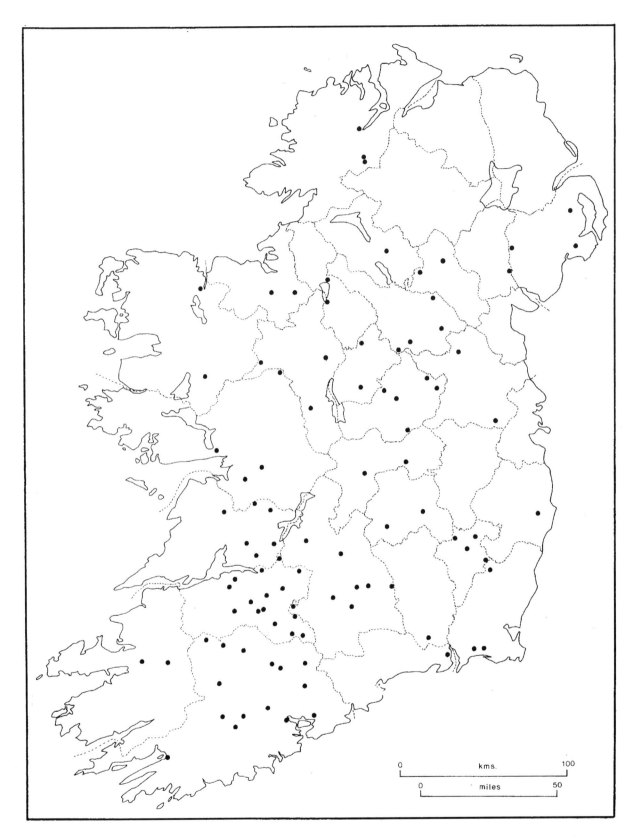

Fig. 3.8. For fair patents of an enduring nature in the period 1701-50, Munster strikes a note of unrivalled ascendancy, with the rest dispersed sparingly across the face of Ireland

In Leinster the markets of metropolitan Dublin and Carlow town were enhanced, with patents for two additional markets for buying and selling corn in the case of the former, and an additional Monday market for Carlow. Elsewhere in the province the best long-term clustering effect was achieved in Co. Westmeath with dual mandates for weekly markets and twice, thrice and quarterly fairs at the villages of Ballynacargy, Castletown Delvin, and Collinstown, respectively. To complete the Leinster network, the corporation of Ardee Co. Louth, secured a patent for market in 1712, while patents for lasting markets and fairs were secured by Drumlish, Co. Longford; Frankford, Co. Offaly; and Newtownbarry, Co. Wexford. Once more place, proprietor (James Frank) and patent go temptingly together at Frankford (later Kilcormac), and at the Maxwell settlement of Newtownbarry, planned as an estate village between 1720 and 1740, the fairs and market patented in 1728 appear wonderfully apposite.

Munster fared worst in the period 1701-50 for the first-time dual patenting of markets and fairs of a lasting nature. The meagre tally yields only Borrisoleigh, Co. Tipperary, and Millstreet and Macroom, Co. Cork. A weekly market and thrice-yearly fairs were patented at Borrisoleigh in 1731 in the hands of John or Joseph Damer. The incipient towns of Co. Cork were earlier on the move. In 1710 Donogh McCarthy secured a patent for a Friday market and three annual fairs at Millstreet, which in time became a way station on the great 'butter road' from Cork to the county of Kerry.[57] The beginnings of entrepreneurship may have been bestirred at Macroom in 1712, when Francis Bernard was granted a Wednesday and Saturday market, and quarterly fairs. Later the Bernards drew skilled cloth workers to the town and other local landowners such as Hedges-Eyre and Massy helped the vibrancy of its markets and fairs.[58]

Coming to patents for enduring fairs on their own, Munster strikes the ascendant note in the period 1701-1750, by accounting for almost one-half of the total. Moreover, the distribution pattern is refined to the extent that a distinctive fairs hearth emerges, and fans out as a broad zone commanded by the cities of Cork and Limerick. It undoubtedly relates to the rise of commercial dairying, the production of surplus calves – the key to exchange and the onward movement of cattle – and the engendering effect of the Atlantic provisions trade serviced especially from the great port city of Cork. An early source of verification of country where the cow had begun to rule is to be found in an estate album produced for the area about Newcastle, Co. Limerick, in 1709,[59] and corroboration from north Co. Cork in 1744 shows the almost complete dominance of dairying.[60]

The effects were manifold and, for one, transmitted to trading places for calves and cattle. The sale of calves and yearlings out of the dairying areas, and of heifers into them, was part and parcel of the business of newly patented fairs. Such fairs were by far the most prolific in counties Cork and Limerick in the period 1701-1750. The places at which these were held constituted a compound of old and new. Medieval parish centres still stood to the good as fair centres in Kilcummer, Kilworth and Liscarroll, Co. Cork, and in Nantinan, Dromin and Glenogra, Co. Limerick. Coming towns were represented by such as Bantry, Blarney and Midleton, Co. Cork, and by Croom and Bruree, Co. Limerick. Incipient villages also made their mark, as represented by Knockaderry, Co. Limerick, which features first on an estate map of 1710,[61] only to be awarded a patent for quarterly fairs in 1711, and also by the small Shannon village of Montpelier in the extreme north of the county, where from the start the main street and the fair green were one and the same feature. The new order of landlord left their mark on fair patent and place at Crookstown (Thomas Crook) and at Rugsborough (Henry Rugge), Co. Cork. Little known places such as Drumdear, Co. Cork, and Ballinvreena, Co. Limerick, which may never have generated any settlement, were also part of the network. Then to add a sense of completeness, lasting fairs were patented on the doorstep of the city at Singland in Limerick and at the Lough of Cork.

Outside of the Munster hearthland 1701-1750, fairs patented on their own account and successful well into the future, were dispersed sparingly throughout the rest of the island (fig. 3.8.). No county laid claim to more than a handful, and of those to strike a strong note of proprietorial resonance, we may number Brookborough, Co. Fermanagh (Henry Brooke); Scotstown and Smithsborough, Co. Monaghan (George Scott and Henry Smith respectively); and Mount Talbot, Co. Roscommon (Henry Talbot). Little known places figure well among the scattering, including Ballon, Co. Carlow; Kilgolagh, Co. Cavan; Graney, Co. Kilkenny; Carlanstown-bridge, Co. Meath, and Bunfinglass, Co. Mayo. Livestock fairs to be successful and enduring only had to keep their drawing power for all and sundry at a nondescript hamlet, a road interstice, or out in the open countryside. They were confirmed too in small central places such as Geashill, Co. Offaly, focused upon a triangular fair green, or in the wide street of a landlord-inspired town in grazier country, such as Strokestown, Co. Roscommon. The episcopal hand also remained in play, as the case of Oldtown, Co. Donegal, attests upon being patented to the bishop of Raphoe in 1725.

IV

The period 1751-1800 saw the decisive expansion of trade. Inland, the continuing and cumulative development of an elaborate network of markets and fairs carried trade to even the remotest corners of the countryside. The livestock economy was dominated by the great fairs, among which may be numbered Ballinasloe (the largest in Britain and Ireland, and one of the three largest in Europe),[62] Banagher, Mullingar and Knockcroghery. These acted as commercial hinges in the livestock trade by linking up the rearing and the fattening dairy areas. In addition, Ballinasloe, Mullingar and Knockcroghery were centres of important wool fairs, which attracted buyers from as far afield as Cork. In the south dairying peaked between 1750 and 1770, as butter buyers paying cash in advance reached into the most backward of districts. Calves and yearlings at fair amplified upon the currency of exchange, while bought-in heifers at fair replenished or expanded the dairy herd. In Ulster the growth of the linen industry was such that it counted among the world's leading half-dozen industries by 1800.[63] The success of the industry promoted intense commercialisation. A 1792 pamphleteer extolling the bounty of Co. Armagh commented:[64]

> Add to this your great weekly markets for the sale of your cloth and yarn, and we may justly say, that the county of Armagh, is a hot-bed for cash for the industrious farmer and weaver.

Within the broad Belfast hinterland, which extended into north Leinster and north Connacht, the linen industry guaranteed the vitality of towns. The brown linen markets made a pivotal contribution to transactional activity, indeed to the whole geography of exchange.

Beef, butter and linen were the great Irish exports of the second half of the eighteenth century, and in articulating a nationwide economy fairs and markets played a crucial role. These furnished the beads for commercial exchanges, which linked onward to the leading ports and outward for export. Moreover, as a pioneering geographer has shown, improved and planned roads were opening up the country in unprecedented fashion by the 1760s and 70s,[65] as traffic in linen, wool and provisions, gathered in divers marketplaces, made its way to port. Looking to fairs patented in the period 1751-1800 and lasting at least to mid-nineteenth century, we may note almost a doubling in the number of locations over the previous fifty-year period. No doubt the ban on live cattle exports, lifted in 1758, provided a major fillip to livestock fairs, which found ready venues in estate villages and were keenly supported by 'improving' landlords. By the 1770s nearly 3,000 fairs were being advertised around the country.[66]

The number of like patented markets on the other hand, remained strangely static. It may be explained in part by the cumulative number of extant locations from 1600 or before, but perhaps also by large numbers of locations, for which no patents exist, and which were certainly operative in the period 1751-1800. Take the case of Ballina, Co. Mayo, apparently devoid of a patent, but with its market in full spate in the closing decades of the eighteenth century:[67]

> In a street which shot straight as an arrow from the cross, the meat market was held. Each side of the street was lined with a row of tables and stalls from end to end. There was a large quantity of animal food for sale and from the thronged state of the market I concluded that Ballina was a place of unusual prosperity ----- We returned to the cross and saw a long line of tables running westward with piles of felt hats for sale. Opposite in another long line, the brogue markets had their standings arranged. Hatters and brogue makers were changing their value for money fast.

Thus in a poor county in agricultural terms, a leading town could still bustle with trans-actional activity and jingle with cash on a market day, with or without a market patent.

Nevertheless, in the absence of substantive evidence, market patenting provides the best available index of expansion in the range of operative markets. Thirty new locations were added countrywide in the period 1751-1800, and furnished with markets, which were still operative in 1852-3. Indeed to accord with the novelty of their standing, several of the places patented came to bear the prefix *new*, as in Newbliss, Co. Monaghan; Newtowndillon (later Bellaghy), Co. Mayo; Newtowngore, Co Leitrim; and Newport, Co. Tipperary. Luke Dillon and John Gore added their proprietorial stamp. Others to do so were Richard Edgeworth at Edgeworthstown, Co. Longford, and Michael Bellew at Mountbellewbridge, Co. Galway.

Overall, the pattern is one of dispersion, but consonant with the proto-industrial strivings of Ulster, fourteen of the thirty patented-settlements were located in the province. Twelve of these also furnished the settings for long-term fairs. They included Castlewellan, Co. Down, patented in 1754, and coincided perfectly with the high ambitions of its proprietor, Lord Annesley, who undertook the conversion of an old irregular green into a half-octagon with a market house in the centre, and added a new octagonal square for optimal measure.[68] In the same county, the 'new' Downshire town of Banbridge received a patent for a Monday market and five annual fairs in 1767. It then rose 'with uncommon rapidity as the head of the principal district of the linen manufacture'.[69] Another patented marker of landlord intentionality comes by way of Kingscourt, Co. Cavan, to where five annual

54

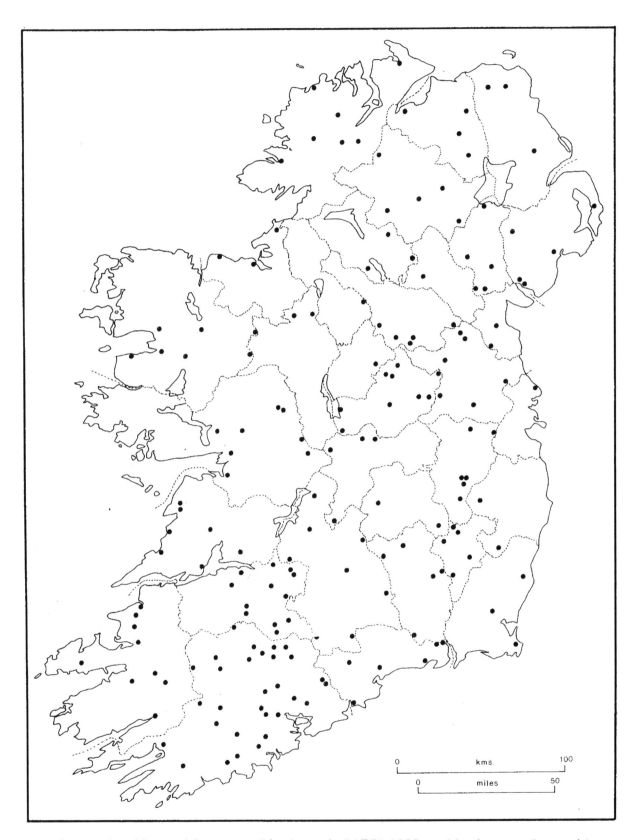

Fig. 3.9. Looking to fairs patented in the period 1751-1800, and lasting to at least mid nineteenth century, almost a doubling in the numbers may be noted over the previous fifty-year period

fairs were transferred from Cabra village in 1767, one additional fair was added, and a suite of markets duly licenced.

During this phase too inland amplifications in the patenting of lasting markets, mostly in association with fairs, occurred best in counties Tyrone (Aughnacloy, Beragh, Ballygawley and Dromore), Cavan (Arva and Kilnaleck, in addition to Kingscourt) Westmeath (Clonmellon and Killucan) and Laois (Abbeyleix and Ballickmoyler). Marketing outposts in the far west also came to connote the fleshing out of a nationwide economy. In Donegal there was Ardara, Carndonagh and Church Hill; in Clare, Ennistymon and Milltown Malbay; and in Kerry, Kenmare and Milltown. Most held attractions for the 'improving' landlord. At Ennistymon and Milltown Malbay, patents for markets and fairs were granted in 1766 and 1781 respectively. Their respective proprietors, Edward O'Brien and Thomas Moroney, developed them both as estate villages equipped with the duality of market house and fair green, and primed to tap the nascent tourist industry. At Kenmare, the second earl of Shelbourne, William Petty-Fitzmaurice, secured a patent for two weekly markets and quarterly fairs in 1764. Thus was heralded a landlord-inspired town (see, fig. 3.12.). In 1775, the proprietor found the place 'wonderfully calculated for trade', and gave instructions for building his showpiece by adapting the form of an X.[70] Significantly in this motif, the top portion of the X served as a triangular fair green and a market house and butter market helped to complete this visionary town set in superlative splendour by the Kenmare River.

Locations of patented fairs expanded rapidly in the second half of the eighteenth century, with a presence in all thirty-two counties (fig. 3.9.). Those to maintain viability to at least mid nineteenth century were carried on in 180 places countrywide, and so powerfully reinforced pre-existing patented fairs, to say nothing of a host of locations, for which no patents could ever be validated. Best rates of occurrence are to be found in the dairying hearthland of Munster, focussed upon counties Cork and Limerick. Together, these accounted for nearly one-quarter of all newly patented fairs, and elaborated minutely upon the pre-existing network. Add in outlying Kerry and the other counties to a lesser extent, to find that Munster's aggregate rises to 41 per cent of all newly patented fairs. Elsewhere the best accretions occurred in a broad zone in Meath-Westmeath-Cavan and alongside an axis running through Carlow-south Kildare. Thin dispersion marked Ulster, while in the west the culture of fair day took hold in the outermost reaches, extending all the way from Donegal to west Cork.

Above all, that culture was embedded wherever the cow was queen. We may note it well about Newcastle in west Limerick, where a land surveyor's eye ranged with acuity over the geography of getting and spending in the early 1750s. Such links cohered best on fair days and the surveyor, Joshua Wight, is on hand to tune into the rhythms of the fair, distil its magic, and portray its familiar bustle. A diary entry of 22 April 1752 says it all:[71]

> This day a great faire in Newcastle ----- a great shew of black cattel but generally small and comes from the mountains chiefly.

The town itself was rooted in land rich in grass and cream, and it drew its clientele to fair from the complementary region of the western hills. Other fair venues in cow country drew their clientele from far and wide, including those set resolutely in hill country. Such a case is Knocknagree on the Cork-Kerry borderland, which was patented for quarterly fairs in 1794, and which looks for all the world a village made for fairs (fig. 3.10.). It is

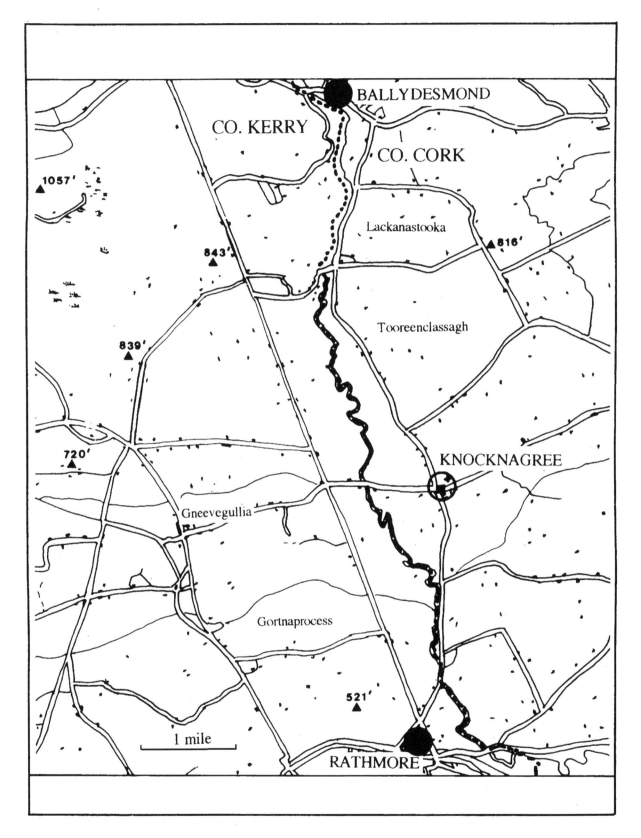

Fig. 3.10. Knocknagree, Co. Cork, which was patented with quarterly fairs in 1794, looks for all the world a place made for fairs. It is gathered upon a 'green fit/ for a fabled stud of horses/'

gathered upon a 'green fit/ for a fabled stud of horses:/ the hearth of Knocknagree,/ where the houses melt back/ from the *gleo* of the dancing tangler,/ the *caimiléireacht* of the slithery chancer.'[72]

In the dairying country *par excellence* the same bone-building facility of lime-rich soils for calves, yearlings and heifers also applied to the rearing of horses. Consequently some famous horse fairs evolved, including one patented to William Hull in 1771. This was the fair of Cahirmee, near Buttevant in north Cork, which certainly enjoyed a prior history, as 'part of Cahirmee with the fair and tolls thereof' was let to Henry Wrixon in 1750.[73] Ultimately, its origins are obscure. One source places it in immemorial remit; others assign it a medieval or early modern start. Either way, it took a hold in the popular imagination, without much direct involvement by the head landlords. The fairground came to measure 24 statute acres and the open countryside fair on 12th and 13th July each year (after eleven days had been added to the calendar in 1752) outstripped those of nearby towns and had made an indelible name for itself as a horse fair before the end of the eighteenth century.

From 1751-1800 expansiveness was the keynote of the fair. It shows in the stepping up in number of fairs held annually, and in additional fairs being added by patent. For example, in Co. Cork, three additions were made by patent to Sir John Freke's fairs at Newmill, and two each were made to the Countess of Barrymore's fairs at Castlelyons, and to Viscount Midleton's at Glanworth. At Kilfinane in Co. Limerick, Silver Oliver was granted an additional fair and a change of fair date to coincide with a fresh colonising influx, settlement genesis and further improvements to his estate.[74] Altogether, in Co. Cork, 103 additional fairs were patented annually at thirty-one locations, while Co. Limerick accrued 39 additional fairs in twelve, and Co. Kerry added 31 more fairs in ten. It all bespeaks the temper of the times in country set fair for growth in transactions around commercial dairying. Specialist fairs also received impetus, as in the case of Newport, Co. Tipperary, an exchange point for the transmission of store cattle which grew appreciably in the 1760s,[75] and got a fresh supplement of two additional fairs by patent in 1775.

In the west, the pace of transactional activity and economic pulse of the countryside was linked to the great Ballinasloe fairs.[76] These gathered the Connacht stock for the Cork victualling trade, the great supply source for the navies and the North American colonies of England and France. At the October fair, fat cattle were sold for slaughter in Limerick or Cork, or for transport to the Dublin market. Later the same fair met the demand from the north and east of Ireland for horses. In May, lean cattle were purchased by graziers for fattening in Meath or Tipperary, before slaughter in Dublin, or live shipment, to the English market. In July, Ballinasloe furnished the central fair for the wool trade. It supplied spinners from as far away as Co. Cork, and increased demand in the 1770s boosted this trade as well as that to Dublin. During this time too, 'improving' landlords in the west found scope to sue for patents and schedule fairs in times of slack not met by Ballinasloe. Their newly-created estate villages provided the venues, and in east Galway alone, the network of fairs was added to by Monivea (1752), Newtownbellew (1768), Mountbellew Bridge (1777), and Laurencetown (1789).

Known from an early date for its fairs for black cattle, the street fair of Glenties at the turn of the nineteenth century was favoured for sheep (plate 3.3.), while cattle kept monopoly at the harvest fair on the village edge (plate 3.4.)

Indeed estate villages counted among the most fertile sources of fair venue in the second half of the eighteenth century. The point is well made alongside an axis running through Carlow-south Kildare, where Ballitore, Co. Kildare (1776), joins with Palatine Town (1761) and Staplestown, Co. Carlow (1769). The last had already established itself as a seventeenth-century estate village, with its triangular green furnishing a ready-made setting for fairs; while Palatine Town named after German immigrants in their colonising phase, kept its name and its Burton proprietorship, long after the Germans had departed.[77] Stratford-on-Slaney, Co. Wicklow, a textile village founded by Edward Strafford, also belongs in this company, and its patented fair of 1776 may be taken at least as a signal of intended genesis. Elsewhere in the zone of high patenting in the north midlands, estate cores gathered the fair as key mechanism of trade in villages such as Mount Nugent, Co. Cavan (1762); Clommellon, Co. Westmeath (1776); and Summerhill, Co. Meath (1780).

The only other salient characteristic to emerge from the distribution of fair patents from 1751-1800 is that in reaching host venues in the far west, fairs may be truly said to have been critical in articulating a nationwide economy. In Co. Donegal, we may point to Ardara (1760), Ballyness (1769) and Carndonagh (1766); in Co. Sligo, to Bunnanadden (1759), Cliffony (1781) and Easkey (1782); in Co. Mayo to Louisburgh (1796), Newport (1788) and Westport (1781); in Co. Clare to Ennistymon (1766), Milltown Malbay (1781) and Doonbeg (1794); and in Co. Kerry to Benmore or Ballyduff (1764), Ballinclare (1758) and Kenmare (1764). Clearly, from the 1750s to the 1790s small farm surpluses in the 'new' west were transferring to new nodal points at periodic fairs, and engendering the fresh pulses of trade.

Also, proprietors knew that if they took out patents for markets and fairs, they could request the grand jury (in effect, the forerunner of the local authority) to link their new settlements to neighbouring market towns.[78] Thus in the 1760s a 'great road' was laid out from long patented Killybegs to the newly patented town of Ardara. A road from Ardara to Glenties was built at the same time, and no doubt prompted the establishment of markets and fairs at the latter, without legitimation by patent (plates 3.3. and 3.4.). The local entrepreneurial spirit proved undaunted, however. By the 1780s Glenties had gained a reputation as 'one of the most considerable fairs ---- for black cattle in the north of Ireland'.[79] In the far southwest too, the success of Kenmare's fairs and markets and its overall well being as a town depended on the building of two new roads, first to Bantry in 1785, and later to Killarney. Paved roads offered wonderful facilitation to fair and marketplace, besides the hazards of rough mountain tracks.

V

To complete the series of fifty-year spans to mid nineteenth century, an emphatic downturn may be noted in the numbers of first-time patented markets and fairs of a viable nature. Thus there was little to enhance the pre-existing network, as fig. 3.11. clearly shows. Innovation by way of generating the mechanisms of trade – towns/villages, fairs, markets – tailed away altogether over large swathes of Ireland. Relative to any other fifty-year period since 1600, the lowest crop of patent confirmations was registered from 1801-1850. Many contributory factors may be cited including, rising population and

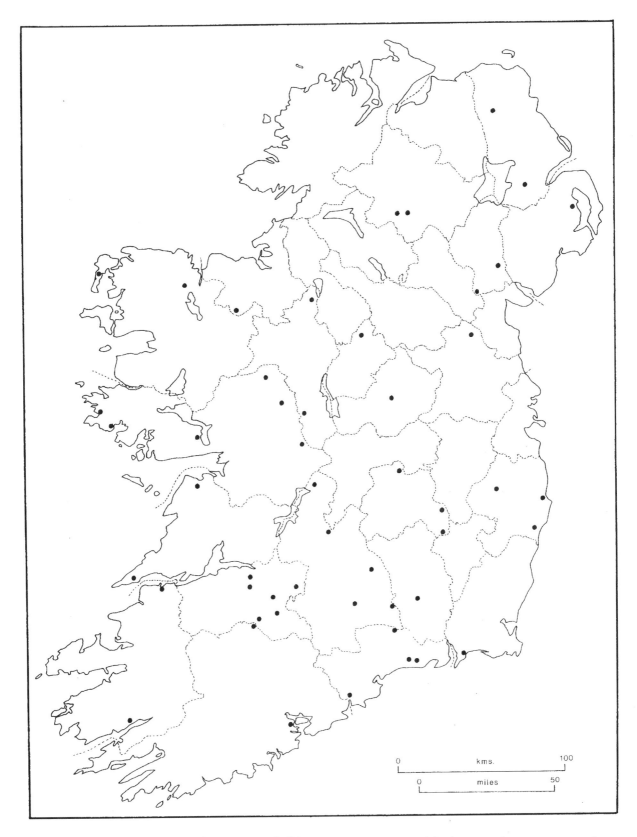

Fig 3.11. completes the series of fifty-year spans to mid-nineteenth century, and shows that there was relatively little to enhance the pre-existing network of fairs in the period 1801-1852/3

increasing marginalisation, a weakening in the landlord's economic position and a decline in his creative impulses, years of falling prices following on from 1815 and cyclical oscillations thereafter, a gathering rural crisis and, outside the north, the wholesale stagnation of towns and villages.[80] Ultimately, everything culminated in the Great Famine 1845-51, when the population fell by about two million. In a mammoth conjunction of pestilence with insouciance, Ireland's population was most cruelly adjusted to its narrowing economic prospects.

Evidence of such narrowing is well attested in the nine markets and fifty fairs freshly patented in the period 1801-1850. Dual patents for markets and fairs at the same location were confirmed in only four cases: Crumlin, Co. Antrim; Ballyvaughan, Co. Clare; Keadue, Co. Roscommon; and Bellaghy on the Sligo-Mayo border. Well within the urban sphere of Belfast, Crumlin traces its genesis to flour and corn mills erected in 1765, and the development of a street village across the Crumlin River.[81] On Mondays from 1804 pedlar's goods, yarn and crockery were sold at market, to be amplified by cattle, sheep and pigs at the monthly fair. Ballyvaughan continued the recent motif of western road head development as a McNamara village, germinated in the 1830s, and endowed with market and fair days from 1834. The Tennison village of Keadue in north Roscommon was confirmed in a patent in 1814, and a market house was duly erected. Bellaghy on the Sligo borderland with Mayo enjoyed the benefit of a weighing scales and recognised markets and fairs, having been patented in 1819, but it was subsequently eclipsed by Charlestown, located cheek-by-jowl across the border, and established in a fit of pique by a rival landlord's agent.[82] Elsewhere, patented markets were latecomers to towns such as Ballinasloe, Westport and Templemore, which must have enjoyed a prior existence as marketplaces. Latest of all was Ballylongford, Co. Kerry, patented in the name of the head landlord, Trinity College Dublin, just in time to be recorded by the fairs and market commissioners of 1852-3.

Also in relation to fairs, many of the patents awarded from 1801-1850 went to towns and villages, in which fairs had long been held. This was certainly true of Kilmallock, Adare and Old Pallasgreen in Co. Limerick, while in the same county Herbertstown (1802), Patrickswell (1806), and the open countryside venue of Knocktoran (1819) may have marked new additions to the network. Such additions were scarce. The prefix *new* is apt and allusive for Newbirmingham (1802) and New Inn (1810), both in Co. Tipperary, and for Newbridge (1839) *alias* Newtowngerrard, Co. Galway. Of these, Newbirmingham is best known, mainly because of the obvious, grandiose ambitions of its proprietor, Sir Vere Hunt of Currah Chase, Co. Limerick. Here, patent confirmation for twelve annual fairs may be taken as an early signal of intent, and *c.* 1813 Vere Hunt was actively lobbying government officers and people of influence on behalf of his new town near the coal deposits of the Slieveardagh Hills. Sore disappointment was to be his sorry lot. Symptomatic of this, his diary entry of 14th April 1815, is instructive:[83]

> Fine day and New Birmingham Fair. Many pigs and few stock of any other kind at it. No pig buyers and pigs in no demand. Bought five small ones at £4. 1s. for the purpose of having, on a reasonable rate, twenty hams and gams for Currah and the rest for New Birmingham. A cheap bargain if a computation was made. No masons at work and all the other tradesmen and labourers idle, and merry-making at the Fair.

It all made for poor prospects for a new town, and Vere Hunt's perfunctory entries on other fair days suggest that things remained that way.

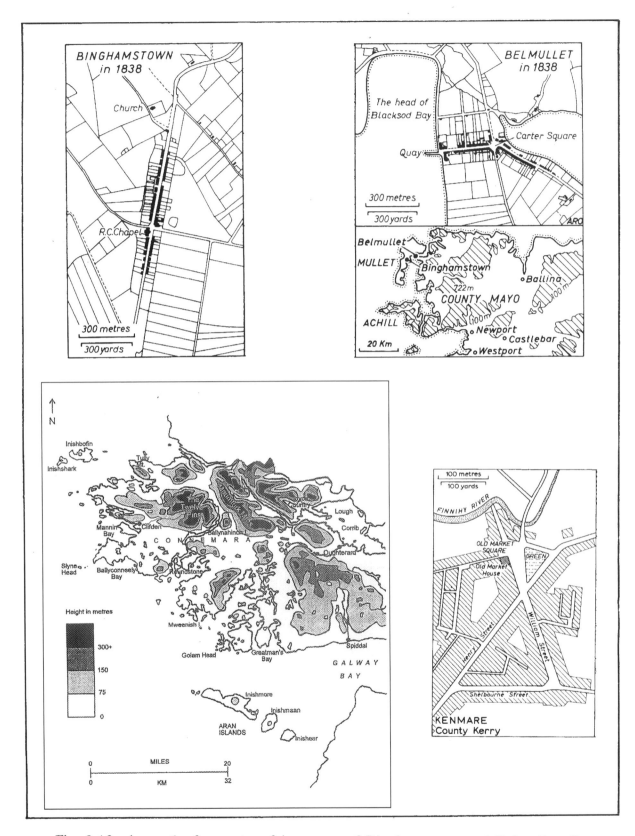

Fig. 3.12. shows the far western fair venues of Binghamstown and Belmullet, Co. Mayo; Clifden and Roundstone, Co. Galway; and Kenmare, Co. Kerry, a town 'wonderfully calculated for trade'

Elsewhere, new village settlements attracting patent confirmation for fairs are best represented in the outer west near end of road situations. Clifden, Co. Galway, declared in 1809, to be followed by Binghamstown on the Mullet peninsula of Co. Mayo (1820), and Roundstone (1830), further on from Clifden in the distant recesses of *Iar Chonnacht*. Trade like the English language followed the roads west, and the first road to Clifden led to the establishment of a town there by John Darcy *c.* 1812. Darcy was the patentee of four annual fairs, and subsequent Darcy patronage saw the establishment of a Wednesday and Saturday market in a neat market house. Characteristically, Binghamstown in Erris took its name from its proprietor, Major Bingham, who founded it in the 1790s, and the twelve annual fairs patented to him, gave it subsequent impetus. However, it ultimately failed owing to the growth of rival Belmullet, strategically located by William Carter on the neck of peninsula in 1825.[84] No such fate attended the small growth point of Roundstone laid out in the 1820s by Scots engineer, Alexander Nimmo, after he had built the first road to Clifden. Thomas Martyn subsequently secured a patent for four annual fairs in its favour, Thus, having reached the *Ultima Thule* of Irish fair venues in the remote west, a nationwide economy drawn together by the proprietorial classes, had become fully articulated.

CHAPTER FOUR

Climax Phase of Fairs and Markets

In demarcating a context to mark the fullest expression of fairs and markets in Irish culture, we are drawn to a largely rural, pre-industrial society at a time approaching peak population numbers. It was a time to coincide with the decline of creative impulses within the estate or landlord system, when the network of small towns and villages had run out of much further infill or extension. It was also a time when village and small town had claimed their place at the heart of the rhythms of the countryside. Such rhythms were modulated by menial and mundane needs on a weekly, seasonal or annual basis, and were consonant with a population distribution, which according to the first accurate census of Ireland in 1841, was four-fifths rural.[1] That represented 6,519,900 persons out of a total aggregate of 8,175,000. The qualifying criterion for the 1,655,000 persons living in towns and villages was a nucleated settlement containing twenty or more inhabited houses, and from among the immense array of these settlements came a clear majority of the host venues for fairs and markets, as well as the vast majority of events, duly held. Moreover, the census of 1841 marks Irish population numbers at their recorded peak. Given that and the accompanying cast of culture and society, and a persuasive case may be made for locating the climax phase of Irish fairs and markets on either side of this temporal benchmark.

Such a time frame happily manages to coincide with the period of optimum document-ation on the fairs and markets of Ireland. It also furnishes the best approaches to standard source materials, thereby facilitating an all-Ireland perspective. It was at this time *c.* 1840 that central government had entered forthrightly into the lives of the vast majority of the people of Ireland by providing rudimentary social services, establishing numerous commissions, making reports and sometimes acting on them, mapping the entire country at a scale of 1:10,560 (making Ireland the first country in the world to be mapped on so small a scale),[2] and using the survey as the basis for rateable valuation and taxation of all the land and tenements. The last task was undertaken by the Ordnance Survey, which apart from the maps as indispensable sources on the absolute and relative location of features such as market streets and market squares, market houses and fair greens, also furnished a whole range of ancillary materials. Of these, the *Name Books* provide nationwide, if uneven, data on fairs and markets, while the *Ordnance Survey Memoirs* often issue exquisitely detailed data on the fairs and markets in the northern part of Ireland.[3]

The great mainstay source is, of course, the *Fair and Markets Commission Report* of 1852-3. This source purportedly gives a complete listing of all the extant fairs and markets in Ireland by place and county, their proprietors, dates (if any) of first and subsequent patents, days mentioned in patents, and the days or dates on which fairs and markets were currently being held in 1852-3. Its major defects have been alluded to in

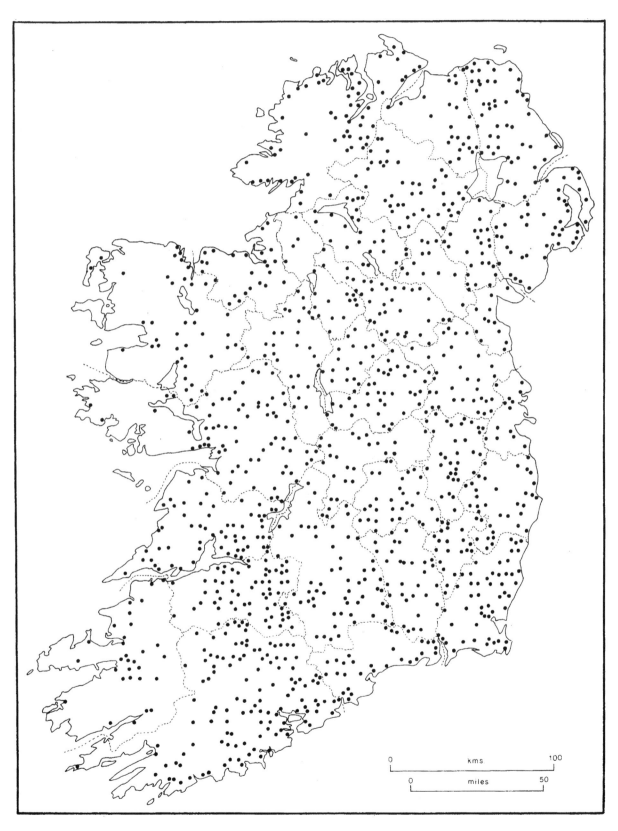

Fig. 4.1. The drumlin belt establishes its primacy in the distribution of fairs in 1852-3. Elsewhere, general ubiquity is the keynote of the fair, except where it is thwarted by large stretches of unproductive land

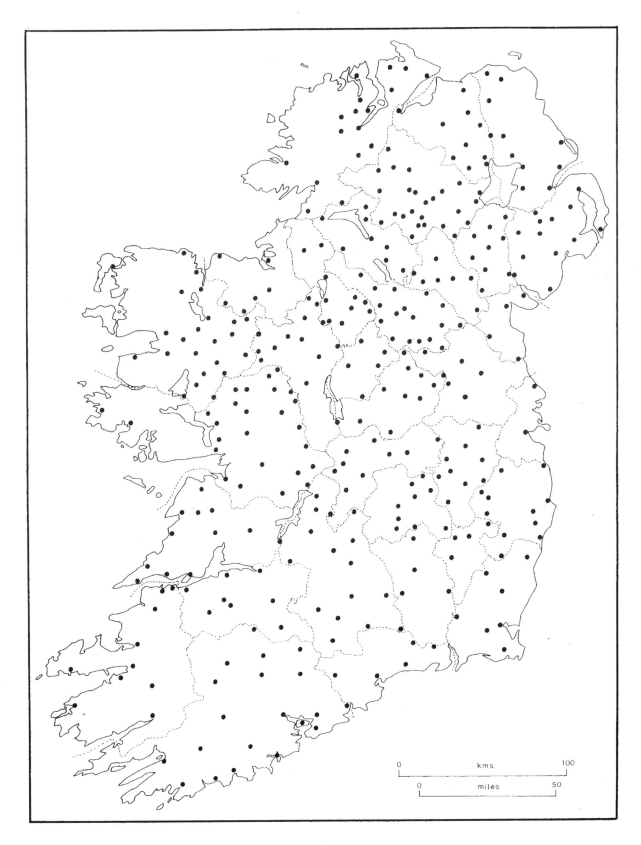

Fig. 4.2. In 1852-3, there is no doubting the area of highest market incidence, as it tracks the drumlin belt from Mayo to Down and epitomises Irish small farm country, close settlement, high demand, a cash economy, and a leavening of the linen industry

chapter three, and while not completely accurate, it remains nevertheless the best approach to a standard inventory. That its availability should coincide with the climax phase of Irish fairs and markets also provides the optimal timing for such a source. It is supplemented by other source materials, including all-Ireland topographies through which threads of consistency run, parliamentary and state papers, and the accounts of travellers. Taken together, all the foregoing sources furnish the basis for an exploration of the cultural geography of fair and market day at a time of maximum spread and import to the lives of the people of Ireland.

I

According to the data of 1852-3, markets were being conducted at 349 locations throughout Ireland and fairs were going concerns at 1,297 different locations.[4] In 125 instances (36 per cent) no patents could be discovered to authorize the holding of markets, while in the case of 103 locations for which patents existed, the markets were held on different days from those specified in the grants. The proportion of fairs without patent is almost identical: 485 or 37 per cent. Once again there is significant divergence (324 out of 812) between the days mentioned in patents and the days on which the fairs were actually held. It all led to two important legal considerations: 1) Whether it was necessary to obtain a grant from the Crown to establish a fair or market, and whether markets and fairs held without any such authority were illegal, even if no toll was levied? and 2) Whether fairs or markets held on other days than those mentioned in the letters patent were illegal? These were issues, which the commissioners ducked. It appears that the ecology of fairs and markets was predicated at best upon the prospering of the fittest or at worst upon their survival as functioning trading days. Competition and/or insufficient patronage could be left, it appears, to ruthlessly weed out the weakest nodes in the network.

Figs. 4.1. and 4.2. show the respective nationwide distributions of markets and fairs in 1852-3. In the case of market distribution, pronounced regional contrasts may be noted within individual counties and throughout the country as a whole. For example, the zone of market town activity heavily favours the kinder east in the Atlantic seaboard counties of Donegal, Mayo and Galway, while Clare and Kerry present a more equitable spread. Equability is broadly observable across the south of Ireland and the commanding status of Dublin's markets may account for their absence in its nearby tributary area. There is no doubting the area of highest incidence countrywide, as it tracks the drumlin belt transversely from Mayo to Down and epitomises Irish small farm country, close settlement, high demand, a cash economy, and the leavening of the linen industry. That belt of country also establishes its primacy in the distribution of fairs, although visually it is less striking than the broad zone in the south across the heart of dairying country from Cork harbour to the Shannon estuary and beyond. Elsewhere, ubiquity is the keynote of the fair, except where it is thwarted by large stretches of unproductive land.

Fig. 4.3. shows the density index of markets on a county basis in 1852-3. The archetypal drumlin county of Cavan yields best results with a ratio of 1: 44 sq. miles. Tyrone, Armagh and Leitrim follow in rank order, to keep fidelity with Ulster and the drumlin

68

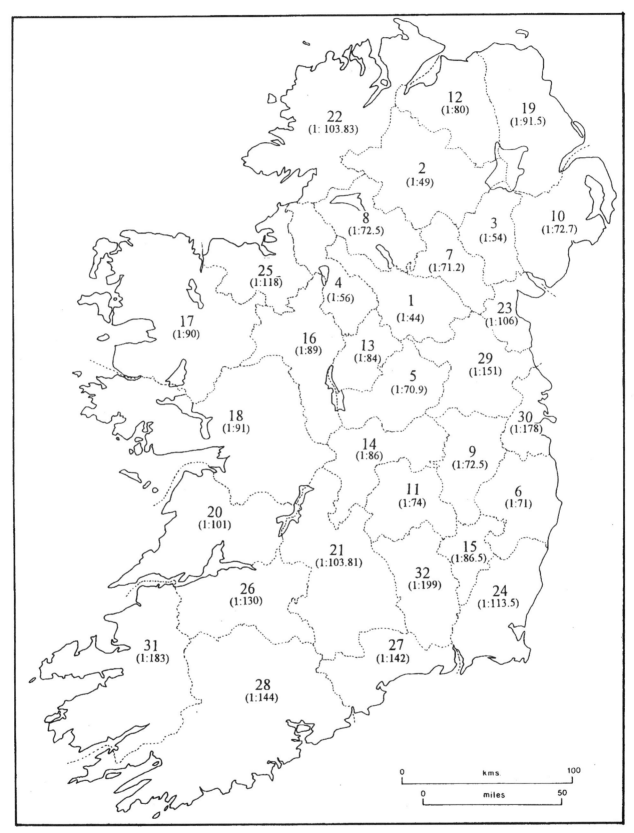

Fig. 4.3. shows the density index of markets on a county basis in 1852-3. The archetypal drumlin county of Cavan ranks first with a ratio of 1:44 sq. miles, while Kilkenny fares worst with a ratio of 1:199 sq. miles

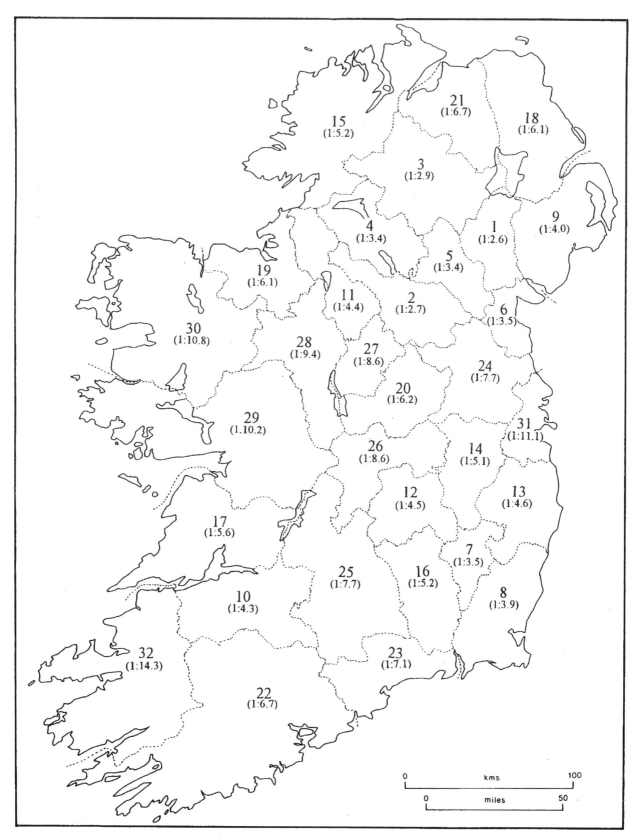

Fig. 4.4. The frequency/ density index of fairs shows reasonable congruence with the rank order for markets. However, a broad, compact and contiguous zone much more effectively defines the premier network of fairs, led by Co. Armagh (1:2.6 sq. miles)

belt as the region of optimal dispersion of small market towns. Westmeath and Wicklow then lend their diversity to the order of density, before Monaghan and Fermanagh again resume the northern ascendancy in market town preferment. At the other end of the spectrum Dublin ranks thirtieth due to metropolitan monopoly. Kerry ranks thirty-first for its very porous network, and Kilkenny ranks worst of all for its paucity of market centres, the centrality and strength of its county town, and the easy re-direction of produce and products for export through the ports of New Ross and Waterford. The frequency/ density index of fairs shows reasonable congruence with the rank order for markets (fig. 4. 4.). However, a broad, compact and contiguous zone embracing counties Armagh, Cavan, Tyrone, Fermanagh, Monaghan, and Louth much more effectively defines the premier network of fairs in 1852-3. It is made all the more striking by the generally far lower order of frequency/ density in the adjoining counties. At the other extreme, Dublin joins with the western counties of Galway, Mayo and Kerry for the greatest porosity in the pattern of fairs.

The sum total for fairs held throughout the country in 1852 was 5650, which bears no comparison with any earlier data set, but represents for certain a massive increase over the numbers that were being advertised in the 1770s.[5] Counties of the drumlin belt and the north offer the most concentrated patterns with, for example, Fermanagh hosting four or more fairs annually at 22 of its 25 venues, while the comparable figures show Monaghan with 14 out of 14, Leitrim with 16 out of 19, Cavan with 31 out of 38, and Tyrone with 41 out of 48. These were also among the counties with towns and villages, which had graduated best to the holding of monthly or near monthly fairs by the mid nineteenth century. Tyrone furnished 28 such venues, while Cavan provided 16, Monaghan 11, Fermanagh 9, and Leitrim 7. It is clear therefore that in these counties with poor urban traditions, towns and villages when germinated in the seventeenth and eighteenth centuries evolved rapidly into central places to serve their surrounding rural hinterlands.

The point is well made in relation to Co. Fermanagh, which came to boast a significant cattle trade and the dedicated provision of space in its towns and villages to host its frequent fairs.[6] By·the 1830s the Ordnance Survey was on hand to map the fair greens of Co. Fermanagh, including the expansive 7 acre setting opposite the jail in the county town of Enniskillen, at which 13 fairs were held annually. Others declared on the edges of the smaller towns such as at Ballinamallard, which hosted fairs on the 6th of every month, at Lowtherstown (later known as Irvinestown) with fairs on the 8th of every month, and at Belleek and Kesh with their bi-monthly fairs, while at Tempo the epony-mous Fairhill characteristically had a pound for abutment (fig. 4. 5.). Elsewhere, monthly fairs found ready venues on the main streets of such small towns as Garrison, Derrygonnelly, Monea, Lisnaskea and Maguiresbridge. It all made for a great frequency of concourses for buying and selling, bartering and bargaining, getting and spending. At Tempo fair alone, the estimated average of livestock and merchandise sold in the years 1832-3 may convey some idea of the business done: cattle, 5,060; horses, 20; pigs, 2,640; sheep, 360; fowl, 360; eggs, 120,000; oats, 30 tons; potatoes 15 tons; meal 3 tons; flour, 6 tons; butter, 264 casks; whiskey, 26 puncheons; beer, 70 barrels; yarn, 28,800 hanks; turf, 120 gauges; linen 31, 200 yards.[7]

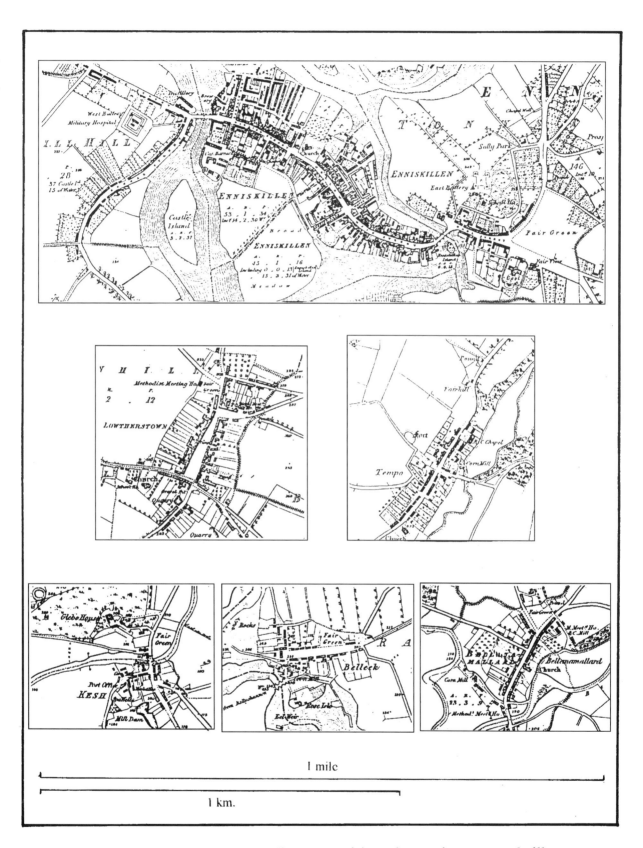

Fig. 4.5. In Co. Fermanagh, the dedicated provision of space in towns and villages to host its frequent fairs is striking. *Circa* 1840, fair greens were a feature of Enniskillen, Irvinestown, Kesh, Belleek, and Ballinamallard, while Tempo boasted a 'Fairhill'

However, it was the frequency of Fermanagh fairs and all the ancillary activities focused upon them, which really caught the eye and fired the imagination of another compiler of memoirs for the Ordnance Survey.[8]

> Monthly fairs, the bane and demoralisation of nine-tenths of the Irish population, are held in Derrygonnelly on the 24th of each month, in Garrison on the 18th, in Belleek on the 10th and in Monea on the 13th, for the sale of horses, cows, sheep and pigs. Annual or half-yearly assemblies would be quite sufficient for the wants and necessities of the country, and would lead to habits of sobriety, industry and accumulation. Immense crowds attend, having no direct agricultural object whatever, and however valuable the time or favourable the season, it is prostituted at the shrine of these perpetual fairs and gatherings of the people.

The outsider/ insider perspectives explored to such powerful effect in the Friel play *Translations*[9] find similar constructions here. The unsympathetic outsider sees only a cold world of utility and infrequent transactional activity. The insider on the other hand, sees a whole culture world drawn together at nodal centre where fun, frivolity, fertility and fighting are vented around the fair. Even as polemic, the observations of the Ordnance Survey memoir-writer serve to highlight the fair as a cultural phenomenon, around which a whole concatenation of events dance and dive, and out of which a whole cultural geography may be distilled. It also unambiguously signals the climax phase of the fair, drawing in 'nine-tenths of the Irish population' at its peak.

Such was the populist drawing power of the fair, its frequency and its ubiquity that it is worth testing the correlation at county level between the fairs data of 1852-3 and the census of population of population, 1851.[10] In correlating the annual aggregate of fairs in a county with its overall aggregate population in 1851, the findings indicate a ratio of 1 fair to less than every 1,000 persons in as many as thirteen counties. This makes it easier to understand the exasperation of the Ordnance Survey memoir-writer at an earlier date. Indeed it is rendered all the more comprehensible when Fermanagh is seen to emerge with a ratio of 1 fair for every 601 persons in 1851. That puts it second overall, behind Wicklow (1:586). Next come the archetypal fair counties of Tyrone (1:604) and Cavan (1:640), which also score high in the frequency/ density index. In contrast, the most populous counties of all – Armagh and Monaghan – figure well down the rank order. Monaghan (1:971) comes twelfth, while Armagh, which boasted the highest population density in the country in 1841, ranks fifteenth. In these small counties with highly concentrated rural populations, the frequency/ density index ranks them at first and fifth respectively. There is no mistaking the backmarkers, although for entirely different reasons. Kerry ranks last but one, having its scattered rural population served by a paucity of fair venues and a paucity of fairs at them to enliven the yearly cycle. Last of all, Dublin's metropolitan needs were still being met by Smithfield Market,[11] and a network of small fair venues around the county satisfied the needs of the scarcer Dublin countryman.

II

At the heart of every fair and market transactional activity occurred, which to a greater or lesser extent, determined the long-term viability of the gathering. Whether at livestock fairs in general, or cattle fairs, horse fairs, hiring fairs or pleasure fairs, proceedings were lubricated by transactions. The buying, the selling and the bargaining gave a leavening and an aura to a cultural phenomenon where wit and ingenuity were tested and the skills of brokerage abounded. In the marketplaces butter and fowl, meat and fish, flax and linen, clothes and pedlary may all have been assembled at market house, stall or bothie of a weekly market day, to await the grist of dealing.

Let the dealing at market then commence, as in Dunmanway, Co. Cork, in 1842, where the English writer, Thackeray, is on hand to offer his distillation:[12]

> Here it was market day too, and as usual no lack of attendants: swarms of peasants in their blue cloaks squatting by their stalls here and there. There is a little miserable old market house where a few women were selling buttermilk; another bullocks' hearts, liver, and such like scraps of meat; another had dried mackerel on a board, and plenty of people huckstering of course.

The same writer had resort to Killarney, Co. Kerry, by then much frequented by tourists, looked out his hotel window, and saw the market house:[13]

> A dismal rickety building with a slated face that looks like an ex-townhall ------ A sort of market is held here and the place is swarming with blue cloaks and groups of men talking: here and there is a stall with coarse linens, crockery, a cheese and crowds of egg and milk women are squatted on the pavement with their ragged customers or gossips.

To get away from unprepossessing scenes at market, Thackeray was obliged to go north to Coleraine, Co. Derry, where the bell was rung at 8 a.m. to tell the butchers to bring their meat into the market. It was rung again at 9 a.m., and after that no more meat was admitted. The traveller was on standby to observe that:[14]

> The scene as we entered the Diamond was rather a lively one. A score of little stalls were brilliant with lights; the people were thronging in the place making their Saturday bargains: the town clock began to toll nine.

Customers could inspect the meat before buying it, and haggle over the price of it. The Shambles or meat market was situated on the street leading south from the west end of the Diamond, where live sheep were also sold.

Coleraine market at its peak of a Saturday offered for sale linens, linen yarn, butter, pork, oats, barley, wheat, potatoes and rye.[15] Consistent with market provision everywhere, these commodities were brought in from the surrounding countryside, and their supply was regular according to season. Butter, pork and grain was bought by merchants for exportation. Linen on the other hand was purchased by bleachers in an unfinished brown state, who then bleached it for English or foreign markets. In the 1830s, increase in the supply of grain and agricultural produce in general more than offset a slippage in linen, so much so that it was found necessary to open a new market place on the south side of town, comprising 1.75 statute acres. Alongside a cattle market was held in open space, while still habituating the Diamond at centre, travelling haberdashers and fruit and vegetable sellers set out their stalls. There too, to lend an exotic touch, roach lime was sold by the barrel. Then to copperfasten all from an early date, it was enacted 'that no market be hereafter granted to any within seven miles compass of the town'.[16]

For market day at its superlative best, however, the traveller might repair to the town of Lisburn, Co. Antrim, at the apex of the famous linen triangle,[17] and within seven miles of Belfast. Take one day, Tuesday 7th March 1837, when items and commodities were priced, and a splurge of transactional activity occurred.[18] To be bought and sold amid a highly sensate ambience, there was oats, oatmeal, potatoes, fresh butter; beef, mutton, bacon, pork, fed veal, slink veal; cheese; salt herrings; duck eggs, hen eggs; turkeys, geese, ducks, hens; onions; salt; calf skins, cow hides; woollen hats; men's and women's shoes, woollen socks, woollen stockings from Co. Donegal; cambric or fine linen, sack cloth; shovel, spade and pitchfork handles; straw baskets, saddlery old and new; deal bedsteads, kitchen tables, kitchen stools; clothes baskets, hand baskets, potato baskets; rods, hampers, stable brooms; farm riddles, spades, hatchets; old and new hemp ropes; pig troughs; and forest trees.

Delph and china, in great supply, came partly from England and partly Belfast. Glazed earthenware carried the 22 mile fetch from Coalisland and red earthenware made the shorter trip from the Maze. Tinware was supplied partly from Belfast, and from Lisburn and the surrounding countryside. The same applied to old and new, black and whitesmith work, for farm and house use. Old and new ready-made clothes, and all of men's and women's wearables as well as bedding, were supplied from England, Scotland, Belfast, Lisburn and other neighbouring towns. The last took up 49 stands in the market. Old and new books, and ballads, had the same sourcing as clothes, and suggest the rising impetus of education and of literacy.

There was more. Quicks for thatching sold by the thousand, and were accrued from the forests within seven miles of Lisburn. Dairy churns, wash tubs, buckets and watering cans were all priced and sold. Other dairy utensils duly branded came in good supply from Dromore, seven miles distant. Beans and peas sold by the gallon. For the populace there was coarse grey linen, home-made drugget, dressed flax and woolen yarn and flannels. For the affluent there were silks, cottons, muslins and hosiery. For everyone with the means there was fruit, bread, gingerbread, vegetables and toys. Moreover, all of the foregoing ensured that the market of Lisburn handsomely surpassed in volume any other market that the Ordnance Survey memoir-writer had inventoried.

Take one day (7th March 1837) with another, 14th March 1837. Further amplification occurs to an already impressive inventory. Livestock are enumerated and priced: 147 black cattle in stalls; springers £7 - £12; strippers £4 - £5; heifers £3 - £4;[20] calves £1 - £2; 159 pigs in stalls (various prices); sucking pigs 9s. - 12s.-6d.; 5 goats in stalls 2s.-6s each. Fat cattle and pigs were supplied mainly from counties Antrim, Down, Derry and Tyrone for home consumption and for the English and Scottish markets. All black cattle at market bore a characteristic signature – a tether made of a hemp or straw rope, fastened round their head or horns, and held by their anxious owners. Fresh herrings from Ardglass, Co. Down, and along the coast for 20 miles or upwards, sold at 6d. per dozen. From the town's hinterland, there were turkey eggs and goose eggs; from more exotic climes, oranges and lemons. Primed for planting time were cup potatoes, seed potatoes, and potato baskets made of hazel. Bent bottomed chairs came from Castlewellan, Co. Down. Band boxes, hat boxes and horse whips were supplied from Belfast, and straw mattresses from Lurgan.

To frequent Lisburn's markets, carters had been coming for some 60 years from such remote districts as Glenties and Dungloe, Co. Donegal, laden with cargoes of woollen stockings. More generally on the supply side, however, the market exercised a magnetising power over hinterland that had all the force of a gravity model. Cheeses, for example, were brought from Magheragall, Glenavy, Ballinderry, Saintfield, Ballinahinch and other districts of counties Antrim and Down within a range of 5 to 18 miles. The supply of wickerwork came from within similar parameters. Furniture at market was partly made in Lisburn, Lambeg, Magheragall, Hillsborough and other districts within a 10-mile radius. The proximity of Belfast was of major significance for supply and demand. Thus relative location counted supremely, and so did the absolute location of Lisburn at the apex of the linen triangle. To uphold keen demand, leading cloth merchants were in regular attendance at Lisburn markets for the purchase of linen cloth. They came from as far afield as Suffolk in England, nearer home from Belfast, from Finaghy and Dunmurry, Co. Antrim, and from Comber, Co. Down. On the supply side of cattle at market, the tributary area extended into neighbouring counties. On the side of demand from April till June, large numbers of one and two-year old black cattle (preferably *moileys*)[20] were bought by Scotch and Down jobbers for export to Scotland.

For buying and selling at market the ascendancy of the linen trade was a recurrent feature of the towns of Ulster. It was particularly conspicuous in Co. Armagh, which at 511 persons per sq. mile, boasted easily the highest rural population density of any Irish county in 1841. In Lurgan, for example, superior damasks and cambrics were made in large quantities, and sales in the weekly market were worth in the order of £2,500 - £3,000 *c.* 1837. There was scarcely a family in its tributary area not connected with the linen trade.[21] At Tanderagee, the Wednesday market was largely supplied with flax, with its weekly sale amounting to £7,000 *c.* 1837, while sales of butter and pork averaged only some £3,000 weekly.[22] In addition, an extensive linen trade was being conducted at such markets as Charlemount, Keady, Killeleagh, Moy and Portadown. It also appears likely that all these linen markets were operating near their optimal performance, given still the labour-intensive nature of the industry in Co. Armagh at a time of transition from dispersed handicraft industry to one centred increasingly upon mechanisation in linen mills.[23]

Sometimes, marketplace provision and the trading it engendered came under impressive patronage, as in the strong market towns of Co. Cork.[24] In Bandon, for instance, weekly markets on Wednesdays and Saturdays were generously supplied with all kinds of provisions, dispersed over two major marketplaces, built at the expense of the Duke of Devonshire: 1) meat and fish markets on the north side of the River Bandon set in an capacious building in the form of a polygon, surrounded by stalls, and forming a piazza for the market clientele, 2) potato, corn and eggs market on the south side of the river set in an oblong building in which *c.* 1837 more than 20,000 eggs were sold every week for conveyance to Cork, and thence to the English market. Mallow's marketplace, built at the expense of the Jephson landlord family came to occupy an area of 75 x 50 yards, in which on Tuesdays and Fridays large quantities of corn were bought by agents for the Cork merchants, and everyday butter, celebrated for its sweetness, was sold to eager customers. Butchers' meat, eggs, pigs, sheep, potatoes and general provisions amplified upon the range of transactional activity. Clear signals of intent were evident too in Macroom, with its newly erected market house forming one side of the market square, and the sale on account of corn brought daily to town by farmers amounted to more than 39,000 barrels to Cork merchants in 1835. The market on Saturday drew an abundant supply of butcher's meat, vegetables and provisions, and a weekly market for pigs was held from January till May.

Aside from the ruthless application of central place theory and the tenets of competition,[25] a range of variables made market towns viable. At Kenmare, Co. Kerry, a stunning location, together with patronage and road-making, combined to lift the market profile of the town. As the local informant for Lewis' *Topographical dictionary* reported *c.* 1837:[26]

> Under the hotel is a sort of market house for potatoes, and it is expected that a regular market for provisions will be established, in consequence of the probable influx of visitors on the opening of the new road to Bantry.

In contrast, market towns with old roots and a measure of resilience could still draw upon an extensive tributary area for getting and spending. Callan, Co. Kilkenny, presents such a case. *Circa* 1837 the market was held in a small market-house on Tuesdays and Saturdays, and a large market for pigs was held every Monday from January to May, attended by buyers from Waterford, Kilkenny, Clonmel and Carrick-on-Suir. Sales of pigs were very extensive, a point amplified upon in the contemporary diary of a local merchant.[27] Span new villages were also able to exploit gaps in market provision, as in Kiltyclogher, Co. Leitrim. Lying under the north-eastern range of the Glenfarne Mountains, the village was only a recent landlord creation *c.* 1837. Still, it contained a 'good' market house, had a well-attended market every Friday, and was able to exploit purposefully the lack of market provision, 'there being no other within seven miles'.[28]

Elsewhere, presenting opportunities were also taken up, as in Mullinahone, Co. Tipperary. This village generated considerable traffic by virtue of its situation on a through-route, making it a convenient way-station for carters plying their journey from Carrick-on-Suir to the colliery district in the Slieve Ardagh hill country about Ballingarry. It became famous, not least for a market held on Thursdays, at which the merchants of Carrick-on-Suir, Kilkenny, and Clonmel purchased great quantities of the sweetest butter. Lying in the shadow of Mount Leinster in north Co. Wexford, the patrons and people of Bunclody saw to it that their well established market remained unchallenged within a 10-mile radius *c.* 1840. This helps to understand how its Saturday market for provisions enjoyed the vaunted reputation as one of the best attended in the south of Ireland. At the heart of Ireland too, the proprietors of Lanesborough, Co. Longford, proved adept at exploiting its location on the River Shannon, and later an easy land connection to the head of the Royal Canal gave it access to the Dublin markets. Its marketplace pulsated on Wednesdays; corn, pigs and eggs in 'vast quantities' went the onward way of barges on the Shannon and the Royal Canal to distant destinations.[29]

Indeed, as evidence from the markets of Co. Roscommon shows *c.* 1840, the network of trade inter-connections forged from the Irish interior, was impressive.[30] At Strokestown, the market held weekly was well frequented, and gave the place a bustling appearance. From the hinterland, the country people came with provisions, also linen, linen yarn and tow, woollen stockings, webs of flannel, wollen yarn and worsted. The textiles were bought by dyers and dressed in the town. There was an abundance of eels and river fish, salt-water fish, and laver – a preparation of seaweed – from Sligo. Some 7,000 barrels of wheat, produce of the locality, were sold in the year. It was purchased mainly for the flour mills of Sligo. Much grain was also sent to the head of the Royal Canal, some 7 miles distant, for the Dublin market, or for exportation. At Boyle market, corn and butter were the staple items, procured mainly for Sligo, or for exportation. Additionally, yarn was sold in large quantities, attracting buyers from the north on Saturday market days, while fish from river, lake and sea were well supplied and well procured. Roscommon market, also on a Saturday, scored high for supply and for attendance. Corn and provisions constituted the staple fare. In addition, frieze, coarse woollens, flannels and a little linen diversified the supply profile, while coarse brown pottery made in the neighbourhood and sourced from clay from the borders of the River Shannon, gave a distinctive potters' stamp to marketplace.

Turning from the general to the specific, it may confidently be asserted that of the specialist markets in nineteenth century Ireland, none come more famously than the Cork butter market. The Butter Exchange located in the city of Cork was the linchpin in a great trading and marketing network. It therefore played a highly significant role in both the Irish agricultural economy and the international butter trade.[31] Shipments of butter from Cork were virtually all inspected and branded at its celebrated market, the largest in the world. These same exports dominated the Irish export trade in accounting for nearly one-third of the total volume of some 527,000 cwt. dispatched from Irish ports in 1835. By 1850, Cork's ascendancy in the butter trade had remained undiminished. Its monopolistic status as supply source to the foreign trade still brooked no challenge, and despite the establishment of some 25 small firkin-butter markets throughout Munster in the period 1850-1880, the quantity of product passing through the Cork weigh-house registered a steady increase. From 269,190 firkins in 1827 to 342,260 firkins worth over £800,000 in 1850, to an average of 407,000 firkins per year in 1875-80, is the measure of the significance of the Cork butter market at best.[32]

From an early date a sophisticated and regulated market structure reinforced the power of Cork's location to draw dairy-owners and dairymen overwhelmingly to the city.[33] Beginning in 1769, a committee of distinguished Cork merchants sought to eliminate fraud by insisting that its members 'ship no butter which shall not be publicly inspected, marked and branded'.[34] Such codes of practice found speedy legislative backing from the opening of the Butter Exchange in 1770, when the internal organisation of the market was regulated, in minute detail, by acts of parliament. Then with the lapse of legislative controls in 1829, Cork merchants dealing in butter adopted a series of regulations whereby they not only monopolised market facilities, but also assumed the authority to enforce their regulations by way of fines or expulsions from the trade. These rigid controls were lacking for the most part in other firkin-butter markets after 1829. Cork merchants held steadfastly on to them, thereby perpetuating a commercial organisation that regulated quality, manipulated prices, and influenced the volume of production through credit controls. The exercise of such powers was seen to serve the market well at least until period 1875-80, when it could count upon a producing clientele of 70,000 to 80,000 dairy farmers. In the broad sweep of Cork's hinterland, the cow ruled as undisputed queen.

Almost all the butter brought to the Cork Butter Exchange came by land, making for many an arduous journey.[35] Carts were scarce until the end of the eighteenth century, and in their absence the usual practice was to sling the firkins across the horse's back. Round trips to the Exchange at Shandon could take up to a week. Small dairymen, starved of cash, often had no option but to face the road. It is all neatly encapsulated in evidence given to a select committee on employment of the poor in 1823, when the small tenant farmer from the remote barony of Iveragh, Co Kerry:[36]

> Had to travel a distance of about seventy miles from his house and his load was generally two firkins of butter, that was one hundredweight; they travel without lodging , with merely buying a piece of bread or a sup of milk upon the road, and so they make their journey and return again -----

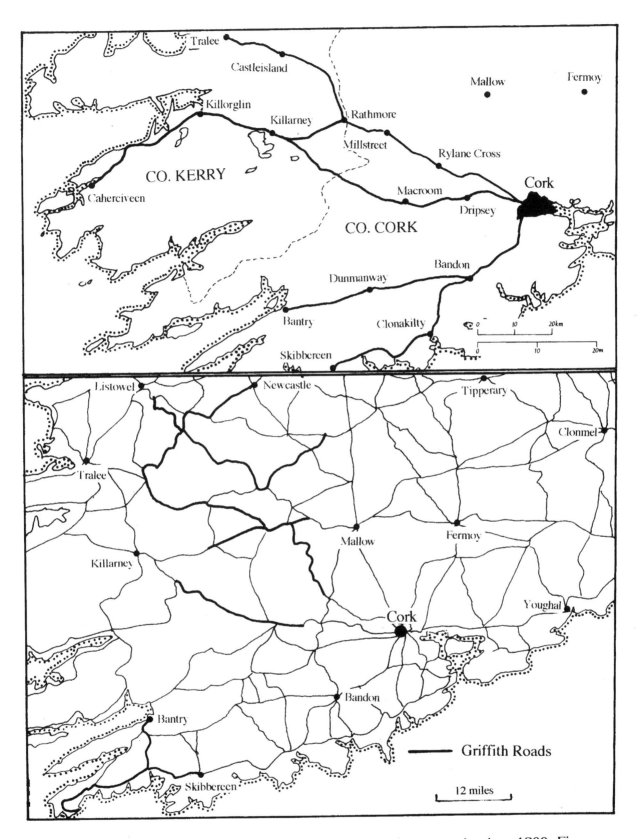

Fig. 4.6. shows the principal routes of the Cork-Kerry butter roads *circa* 1800. Fig. 4.7. shows the roads built by Richard Griffith in the 1820s and 30s, which greatly facilitated access to the Cork butter market

As the witness stated, these poor men in their quest of a meagre existence, felt obliged to travel 'night and day' without respite. In 1822, road-maker, Richard Griffith was on hand on the borderlands of counties Limerick, Cork and Kerry to provide corroboration:[37]

> At present, a farmer going with his produce to Cork, is absent from home six days, at great expense as well as loss of time.

Griffith was charged for the first time by government to construct new roads in the region as a stratagem to help quell agrarian disturbances, offer employment, and make the butter routes to Cork as direct as possible.

A shrewd and stringent observer, Griffith quickly ascertained that every year some 50,000 firkins of butter were brought to Cork from north Kerry and west Limerick. He commented on the *modus operandi* in vogue for fetching the butter to the great Exchange at Shandon:[38]

> In order to save the great length of road by Tralee and Killarney, the small farmers are in the habit, during the summer season, of sending their butter on the backs of horses by the present mountain path, as far as Newmarket, where a few join together and place the butter in carts, from whence it is drawn to Cork. The distance between Newmarket and Listowel, the nearest part from whence the butter is sent, is 25 Irish and nearly 32 miles British, and for this distance, from eight to twelve horses, and as many men, are employed to convey twenty-four firkins of butter, the common load for a single horse cart!

Griffith's new road reduced the distance between Listowel and Cork, via Newmarket, from 102 to 66 statute miles. He similarly worked a wonder in south Kerry, from which upwards of 10,000 firkins of butter were conveyed to Cork each year. His new carriage road between Glenflesk and Macroom succeeded in reducing the mileage from Cork to Kenmare by 31 statute miles. Thenceforth one man and a horse could with facility do the same work as had required twelve men and as many horses. Altogether, between 1822 and 1836 Griffith was responsible for the construction of some 234 miles of road in counties Cork, Kerry, Limerick and Tipperary. In the process, he made the butter roads to Cork Exchange smoother and straighter, and the journey sweeter.

New and improved roads transformed the geography of getting and spending, as predicated upon the Cork butter market. The journey time from Killarney to Cork or Castleisland to Cork, for example, was reduced from two days to a manageable seven hours, allowing men such as William Costello (d. 1882) of Kilscanlon, Currow, Castleisland, to regularly drive a butter cart to Cork, and reputedly bring the first cartload of Indian meal back to Castleisland.[39] From the 1820s too, carmen from south west Cork carried both butter firkins and bolts of linen cloth from weavers in the Bandon and Dunmanway areas. The cloth was deposited at the finishing yards in Hammond's Marsh, before making the steep rise to the Butter Exchange at Shandon.[40] In the broad hinterland of Cork, new and better roads facilitated the procurement and the spread of lime for land reclamation and improvement, thus enabling higher crop and milk yields. It all translated into more remunerative and regular cash returns for the dairymen and dairy farmers who supplied butter to the great Cork market.

The cow's head on the portico of the new Exchange, completed by Sir John Benson in 1849, is talismanic of the Cork Butter Market at its apogee. It may well connote symbolic continuity from the original Exchange building. The 'sign of the cow' (*sign na bó nár duireadh*) also features in the lament *Caoine Dhiarmaid' 'ic Eóghan*, which mourns the loss of a Millstreet merchant, Diarmaid Mac Eóghan na Tuinne Mac Carthaigh, who died at the Cork Butter Exchange, and whose mother travelled from

Millstreet to Cork to retrieve her son's body.[41] She bitterly resents the atmospheric coldness of the Exchange and the indifference of its patrons to her grief. Thus the lament may serve as an evocation of the hold of the Cork Butter Exchange over its trading clientele, and reminds us that great institutions, like great processes, in the nineteenth century could make for painful experiences for those caught up in their grip.

III

For transactional activity at the height of its power, livestock fairs still tended to be bumper versions of weekly markets. The point is well made in relation to some Co. Derry fairs, for which detailed data are available from the 1830s. The great monthly fair in Moneymore (said to be one of the oldest established in Ulster) occurred on the 21st of every month. As a cattle and horse fair, Moneymore was renowned and resorted to by buyers and sellers from a wide tributary area that included Derry and its neighbouring counties. Take the August fair of 1836.[42] At 697 head, there were black cattle in abundance at prices from £3 - £11. Presenting horses numbered 523, and fetched prices from £3 - £25. For the 374 sheep on offer, prices varied from 10s. - 50s.. Asses and goats were much scarcer at prices of from 15s. to 25s. and 6s. to 10s. respectively. There was an indeterminate number of suckling pigs and an estimable 371 store pigs at varying prices.

At Moneymore fair, a whole range of goods and commodities were offered for sale at specific prices or fell within a range of prices. These included the requisites of dairying – dairy churns, milk pails, stable buckets, butter firkins – and the requisites of farm – wash tubs, water cans, stable brooms, potato baskets, hop rakes, farm gates. Some of these saw service indoors, as did quart noggins, piece crocks, kitchen chairs, bed ropes and bedsteads. Cowhides sold by the hundredweight; fine linen yarn and coarse yarn by the spangle; web linen and flannel by the yard; cotton and woollen stockings and socks by the pair; wool by the pound; coarse flax, dressed flax and tow by the stone. Footwear and hats were priced and offered for sale. There was beef, bacon, mutton and cheese priced by the pound (lb.) to tempt aspiring customers; salt herrings, fresh herrings and pullins were priced by the dozen.

Other commodities were in abundant supply: Old and new ready made clothes; old and new books and ballads; silks, calicoes, cottons, linen, sacken; hardware; hosiery; delph, china, earthenware, tinware; smith work and turner's work for house and farm; glass windows; and bread, gingerbread, fruit, vegetables, and garden seeds. Thus the range and volume of supply was extraordinarily generous at a small village fair in harvest time. What of demand? Although perfunctory, the answer is nevertheless indicative. The demand for middle and lower quality horses was brisk, while slow for those of top quality valued at £25 - £35. Black cattle and pigs were in fair demand, with the latter registering an advance in prices.

The November fair of Dungiven in 1834 was equally well provisioned, and on this occasion the hinterland of supply and demand was set by local informants within clear spatial parameters.[43] Cattle and other livestock and all the usual provisions clearly came from the immediate neighbourhood of the little south Derry town. Herrings were brought from Derry and Coleraine, and oysters in carts came from Magilligan. Hazel, ash and sally rods used in different types of farming basket work were brought from the nearby extensive woods of Walworth and Faughan. The crockery sold at fair was brought from the neighbouring town of Castledawson, Co. Derry, and from Castle Island, Co. Down. China and delph came from Belfast and Derry. Flannel and hosiery were sourced through importation, with some also supplied from the neighbouring parishes of Dungiven and Banagher.

Pedlars at Dungiven fair were a peripatetic lot, given to wandering with their backpacks or laden carts from one fair to another throughout the province of Ulster. They were in attendance with clothes, jewellery and many types of utensil. Licenced owners who did the rounds of the fairs of Ulster, offering facilitation, provided two auction stands for them. The pedlars themselves put up to auction muslins, cottons, hosiery and trimmings. These all met with local demand, and in addition items and commodities at the fair found avid buyers from Derry, Coleraine, Limavady, Ballymena, Ballymoney, Belfast, Strabane and Cookstown.

All over Ireland, fair-day locations attracted distinctiveness and allure *c.* 1840.[44] For example, the cattle, sheep and pig fairs of Clonakilty, Co. Cork, were greatly enhanced in the months of October and November by a large supply of turkeys and other fowl. Similarly, the October fair of Aughrim, Co. Galway, was renowned for the sale of turkeys, of which some 20,000 were usually sold. The January fair of Mallow, Co. Cork, was mostly for pigs, of which some 2,000 were sold in 1836; the St. Stephen's Day fair at the little triangular village of Geashill, Co. Offaly, staked its bold claim as one of the largest pig fairs in Ireland; and the February fair at Kilgobnet in the parish of Knockane in south Kerry could be regularly depended upon to sell pigs to the value of £4,000. At the way-station venue of Mullinahone, Co. Tipperary, fairs for all types of livestock drew remarkable attendances and pigs, in particular, sold in great numbers. Knockcroghery, Co. Roscommmon, still kept its sheen as a great October sheep fair, while the September fair of the small village of Ruan, Co. Clare, also earned kudos for its sheep sales. The November fair of Fethard, Co. Tipperary, re-vivified the old walled town, being the largest in the county for the sale of fat cattle. In Co. Meath, the village of Carlanstown took the same title, its November fair being the largest and best in the county. Ballymahon, Co. Longford, did even better with a variant, as its May fair was much resorted to by graziers. It was thus accorded a leading status in the province of Leinster for the sale of store cattle.

Other fairs too struck a redolent chord in reportage. The September fair of Banagher, Co. Offaly, for example, was so famous for its livestock sales that it was ranked second only to the great fairs of Ballinasloe. At Belnagare, Co. Roscommon, the January fair was noted for pigs and young horses, and at Ballybay, Co. Monaghan, the fair held on the third Saturday of every month achieved remarkable success in its sales of horses, horned cattle and pigs. In Co. Louth, the tiny hill-top village of Mullacrew had long been famed for its great fairs for sheep, cattle and pigs,[45] and it held its status *c.* 1840 as one of the most extensive wool marts in Ireland, with its June fair, in particular, primed for the shearing season. Another small village, Hilltown, Co. Down, hosted large fairs monthly for cattle and linen yarn. Clearly custom, practice and patronage gelled at small, and sometimes unprepossessing venues, made for great fairs *c.* 1840 before the thrust of modernisation had caused a largely rural, pre-industrial society to focus upon a sparer network.

In the extensive network that prevailed *c*. 1840 premiums were sometimes offered in support of fairs. The practice was especially common in Ulster, and was often availed to kick-start new fairs. One such case is Manorcunningham, a street village on the banks of Lough Swilly in Co. Donegal, where lapsed fairs had recently re-commenced and local landlords gave small premiums to the buyers and sellers of the best farming stock, yarn and flax exhibited for sale. At Saintfield, Co. Down, the proprietor, Nicholas Price, gave premiums for the encouragement of fairs and markets which helped to make them rank among the best in the north of Ireland. Similar support was forthcoming at Brookborough, Co. Fermanagh, where monthly fairs were held for the sale of cattle, sheep, pigs, butter, cloth and yarn, and premiums given every fair day to the largest purchasers and sellers. There was also a decisive increase in the frequency of fairs at the climax phase. In Borris, Co. Wexford, 4 more were added to the 7 already in existence. Here the July fair bulked large for wool, in addition to the more staple fare of cattle, sheep and pigs. In the same county, the village of Taghmon hosted no less than 23 annual fairs, a feature integrally tied in with the well being of the place.

Above all others, the celebrated fair of Ballinasloe kept its place as the greatest cattle mart in Ireland during the heyday of the fairs. It was held on the Galway side of the River Suck from the 5th to the 9th of October. Black and horned cattle were exhibited in an extensive area set aside for the fair outside the town, while a plot of ground in Garbally Park was appropriated for the show and sale of sheep. Unsold sheep were subsequently driven to the fair green for further exposure. By the 1830s the wool mart had diminished due to direct competition from Dublin merchants and those in other major towns. The quantity and range of goods on offer, however, still attracted every type of dealer. At the October fair of 1835, 61,632 sheep were exhibited and 54,974 sold. Of 7,443 cattle, 6,827 were sold.[46] Ballinasloe as fair setting continued to burnish in the popular mind, it being described *c*. 1845 as 'the cynosure of much the larger part of the western province of Ireland'.[47] Situated on one of the sinuous gravel ridges or eskers that wind cross-country, Ballinasloe was the great node of the drove roads, for which the eskers provided dry footing, and along which drovers, cattle and sheep headed for the fattening pastures and markets of eastern Ireland. The fair of Ballinasloe served the west of Ireland in much the same way as the great trysts of Crieff and Falkirk served the Scottish Highlands.[48] Moreover, it was timed to allow for the optimal movement of livestock on to the fattening grounds before winter or to the English fairs by All-Hallows or Martinmas.

IV

As well as general livestock fairs, more specialist horse fairs were also a feature of the climax phase. Among those to claim renown were the fairs at Cahirmee, near Buttevant, Co. Cork, and at Oldstone, near Antrim town. Both were esteemed to be the greatest horse fairs in their respective provinces. Horse dealing was by no means the only business conducted at either venue, but each was certainly synonymous with the equine world in the nineteenth century. Local tradition upholds the belief that both 'Marengo' and 'Copenhagen', the respective mounts of Napoleon and the duke of Wellington at Waterloo, were purchased at Cahirmee.[49] The great fair, held on the 12th of July each year, won fame and renown. In 1846, for instance, a newspaper report stated that:[50]

> Celebrated as it has been for the large number of horses usually offered for sale, there was not within the last thirty years so large a fair at that of Monday [12th of July]. Horses for general use that is, for harness and saddle were in brisk demand and fetched large prices, several of them having changed owners at £120 each.

Civilian horse dealers from England and Scotland were in regular attendance and military purchasers could also be counted on to attend Cahirmee fair. This was an attribute shared with Oldstone fair in Co. Antrim where buyers for the artillery and cavalry were in regular attendance, along with a civilian clientele from England, Scotland and distant parts of Ireland.

Like Cahirmee, Oldstone suggests that an unprepossessing location might in no way inhibit the draw of a famous fair. It attests to the cult of fairs in high places, and the name of the place is instinct with allure. An Ordnance Survey memoir-writer, however, renders it in straightforwardly prosaic terms:[51]

> The hamlet of Oldstone is situated on the summit of a hill, the highest and most conspicuous point in the Grange [of Muckamore], in the townland of Oldstone and near the centre of the grange. The hamlet straggles for some 250 yards along a by-road near the point where it intersects the old road from Antrim to Lisburn. The appearance of the hamlet is uninteresting in the extreme, consisting as it does merely of 47 cabins of an inferior description straggling along the highway. There is a trifling craggy knoll on the summit of Oldstone hill, on which are some very large unshapely stones said to have formed part of a druidical circle or altar, which is remembered only by the very old people in the neighbourhood. From this the hamlet probably derived its name.

Everything about the place was transmuted on the day of the 12th of June, the date of the annual fair. There was no early morning start. On the contrary, it was preceded by a curtain-raiser in the town of Antrim:[52]

> The fair of Oldstone does not commence there until between 12 and 1 o'clock on the day appointed. By that hour Antrim, which had previously been crowded with horses and buyers, is then deserted by all who have not effected their business, and the fair at Oldstone only then commences. The horses are shown along the highway, a hard, rough and hilly road. Cows, sheep and pigs are exposed in an open space at an opposite end of the hamlet. Tents, stalls and standings are ranged along this space and along the side of the highway.

Thus the territoriality of the fair is striking as between horses and other livestock, with the interconnection between these micro-worlds being forged by whiskey sellers, hucksters and pedlars in tents, stalls and standings.

At the June fair of 1838, 600 horses were exposed for sale.[53] Of these, 400 were sold. Prices ranged from £20 to 100 guineas, and working animals suited to farming and domestic purposes constituted the majority. English and Scottish dealers bought about 150. Several were also purchased for the cavalry and artillery. Other livestock were traded on the strength of the horse fair. Some 300 cows were exposed, of which about 200 sold. About one-half of the 400 pigs on offer were sold. The same applied to presenting sheep numbers. It was adjudged to have been the smallest fair for horned cattle for many years, but a good fair for horses, despite some misgivings about quality.

However, in the rounded sense of Irish fair days, Oldstone was a fair for pleasure as well as for business. Its broad appeal whetted other forms of transactional activity. Chief among these was the sale of whiskey for which 38 covered tents were provided by vendors, together with 9 outlets in private houses, which were mostly licenced. Thus the capacity to slake thirsts was immense, and so was the capacity to stave off hunger. Four covered stands were provided for the sale of victuals, while a grand total of 36 plied the lines of gingerbread, cheese and an edible seaweed known as dulse. Sales of soft goods and hardware were accommodated at 17 stands; wooden vessels at 4; delph at 2; tinware at 2; beehives at 2; hats, prints and small pictures at 2; old clothes at 1; and books at 1.

For those intent on pleasure or a combination of business and pleasure there was showtime, as represented by three shows or exhibitions. Admission to each cost 1d. Gambling commanded the clear ascendancy, pitching halfpence, thimble rigging,[54] and other games of a trifling nature. Indeed, the Ordnance Survey memoir-writer adjudged that the number of attendees for amusement was the equal of that who came for business only. Furthermore one-half of the total was female, among them domestic servants, who looked forward to Oldstone fair as one of their few days of amusement and relaxation from work. The fair was accounted remarkable too for the number of well-dressed women in attendance, and it must have been a place where love stories or matches began.

Other locations too established the primacy of their horse fairs during the climax phase of the fairs. Such was the case, for instance, at Rathkeale, Co. Limerick, where verifiably from c. 1840 Traveller families, like the Sheridans, who won fame as judges of horses, were wont to sojourn in the town around the time of the June horse fair. The fair provided the mid summer marker for the itinerant horse traders, so that it became common for the Travellers to arrive some weeks before the fair and stay for some time after it.[55] Then as children were born a growing identification with the place developed. Another horse fair in the month of September served to further the causes of trade and sojourn, and in the larger context it is worth recalling that the total number of fairs at Rathkeale increased from 5 in 1787, to 7 in 1824, to 12 in 1852-3. Rathkeale became a growing fixing point on the Travellers' circuit, a sustaining place between elsewheres. It was all predicated initially on the draw of horse dealer to fair.

V

The draw to fair served multifold purposes. Hiring labour was one such purpose and c. 1840 the hiring fair had clearly entered the parlance of the day. The Ordnance Survey memoir-writer for Antrim town, however, displayed no easy familiarity with the practice, when writing under the heading of 'hiring fairs':[56]

> Attending the summer fairs is a source of amusement, particularly to the females. A curious custom exists in the manner in which they engage their servants. There are two annual fairs at Antrim, one on the 12th of May, the other on the 12th of November. These are the seasons at which the period of servants' engagements throughout the county terminate. On these days all the servants in the neighbourhood for several miles around, whether they are to continue with their former master or not, come to this fair and are there re-engaged by him or enter into the service of another. Each male servant who comes in quest of service carries a rod, and on being hired receives a shilling as earnest. The women attend the fairs for a similar purpose.

These counted among the few days in the year when servants were at liberty and free from the restraint of their masters and mistresses. They often made the most of their day out, their excesses being described as 'saturnalia and disgusting scenes of the most brutish brawling'.

Stereotypes are presented of hirer and hired. On the one side, the farmers who did the hiring are depicted as 'above the middle stature', as usually prevailed in country where the people were well-nourished. They were the possessors of good countenances, high foreheads and strongly marked features. On the other, the labouring classes were rather stunted and by no means vigorous or well formed, due to the early age at which they were put to labour. In general, the labourers were well-fed; they were sinewy and capable of enduring much fatigue. The real stars of the fair, however, were the young women of the parish, the 'Killead girls' who were proverbial for their beauty, which they also betook to the neighbouring fairs. They were striking not only for their good looks, but also for their neat style of dressing and pretty figures. Fair of complexion, with light blue or hazel eyes, their well-formed features riveted the interest of the men at hiring fair.

Antrim furnishes the best early example of the hiring fair as a going concern, and although the practice was widespread by *c.* 1840, there is a dearth of documentary evidence.[57] The best early reference to the practice comes by way of the eighteenth-century poem, *An spailpín fánach*, in which a Kerryman describes the contempt with which he was treated in the hiring fairs of Tipperary and other counties:[58]

Go deo deo arís ní raghad go Caiseal	I'll never again go to Cashel
Ag díol ná ag reic mo shláinte,	selling or bartering my health,
Ná ar mhargadh na saoire im shuí cois balla	nor hang about the street
Im scaoinse ar leataoibh sráide	at the hiring fair seated by a wall,
Bodairí na tire ag tíocht ar a gcapall	the boors of the district on their horses
Dá fhiafrai an bhfuilim híráita.	asking if I'm hired.
Ó! téanam chun siúil, tá an cúrsa fada;	Let's start, the journey's long;
Seo ar siúl an spailpín fánach.	It's off with the wandering labourer.

He then imagines himself in a later verse not with a reaping hook, flail or spade in his hand, but carrying a pike under the French flag.

In Ulster, one of the first known references to the hiring fair proper dates back only to 1814 and a small town setting in Co. Tyrone:[59]

> They usually hire themselves to a farmer, but never for a longer term than six months at a time. There are two stated days in the year, when they assemble at Newtown Stewart for this purpose.

From the start there was little variation in the dates of the hiring fairs or the nature of the hiring agreement. Nearly always, as in Antrim and Newtown Stewart, they were held twice a year, with early summer and early winter as markers of the yearly cycle. The most important hiring fairs therefore coincided with the large annual May and November fairs, and the usual business of the day pertained to the selling of livestock and the hiring of farm servants.

Rampant population growth and increasing marginalisation after 1815 certainly fuelled the numbers of landless labourers and popularised the hiring fair. Still the documentation remains restrained in the 1830s, when the Ordnance Survey memoir-writers were recording the fruits of their fieldwork. To add to the detailing of Antrim hiring fair, there were others at Newtownhamilton, Co. Armagh; Wheathill, Co. Fermanagh; Newtown-limavady, Co. Derry; and Clady on the Donegal-Derry borderland. True to form, at Newtownhamilton, the largest fairs were held on the last Saturdays in November and May, when the hiring of farm servants swelled the attendance:[60]

> The town on those days is crowded to excess and for some market days after it, for the servants who are hired on fair days, when on going to their place they find it not so agreeable as they expected, they then come the following market day to look out for another master.

At Wheathill, Co. Fermanagh, at the May and November fairs young stock from the neighbouring farms jostled with the farm servants who were hired at wages, which varied according to term, from 6s to £5. At Limavady, hiring day was advanced to the Monday before Christmas, and was known as 'Galloping Monday'. On that day servants came from all parts of the neighbouring baronies to be hired. The name 'Galloping Monday' was said to derive from the hurry and uncertainty that attended the occasion. At Clady, a small village on the Finn River, two of its fairs had been ceded to nearby Strabane. It retained two others on the 16th of May and the 16th of November. These were called 'rabble fairs',[61] to which no cattle were brought, but servants were hired, coarse stockings and socks were sold, and whiskey was drunk.

Most of the documentation and memory of the hiring fairs comes much later. However, it is scarcely conceivable that at a time of peak population numbers, marginalisation and landlessness that the hiring fair as mechanism had anything other than a pronounced profile. In Ireland as a whole, the ratio of farm workers to farmers was 2.71:1 and 2.29:1 in 1841 and 1851 respectively.[62] By 1861 and 1871, these figures had declined to 1.8:1 and 1.6:1 respectively. The diminution continued steadily. In these circumstances the important hiring fairs still operating at the beginning of the twentieth century must have enjoyed their heyday at the climax phase of the fairs from the 1830s to the 1850s. In Ulster alone the venues may have included Antrim, Armagh, Aughnacloy, Ballymena, Ballymoney, Bailieborough, Banbridge, Ballinahinch, Cavan, Cookstown, Coleraine, Cootehill, Comber, Dungannon, Derrygonnelly, Enniskilllen, Irvinestown, Killyleagh, Lisbellaw, Letterkenny, Monaghan, Magherafelt, Newry, Newtownards, Newtown-hamilton and Strabane.[63] Elsewhere ready venues declared in the hinge-towns that filtered labour movement from the west to the east such as Bandon, Co. Cork; Newcastle West, Co. Limerick; and Athenry, Co. Galway. Venues like Tullow, Co. Carlow, and New Ross, Co. Wexford commanded the flow of labour to tillage fields, and close to the city of Dublin the outlying village of Tallaght re-directed agricultural labour by way of its hiring fair.

VI

Above all, fair day was a day out, a day away, and an occasion to be celebrated. 'A fair for pleasure as well as for business' was a frequent refrain adopted by the O.S. memoir-writers, with as one of their number put it 'nine-tenths of the Irish population' acting as a captive clientele.[64] All over the country the major outlet of pleasure and amusement consisted of attending the spring and summer fairs. In north-east Ulster, for example, fairs, explicitly for pleasure, put the spring in many a step. Right on the doorstep of Belfast:[65]

> On Easter Monday and Tuesday numbers from this parish [Carnmoney] flock to the Cave Hill in the adjoining parish of Shankhill, at which hundreds from the surrounding districts congregate on those days. Tents for the sale of spirits and refreshments are pitched on it, and the days are spent in rolling coloured eggs and in a variety of other amusements.

At the bridge of Toome, later to be celebrated in song, the annual fair on Easter Monday drew a concourse from the Antrim-Derry borderland strictly for amusement, as no livestock were proferred for sale.[66] Still, as in Cavehill and elsewhere transactional activity occurred, with crockery and pedlar's goods being exposed and whiskey and cakes offered for sale.

At the Giant's Causeway in north Antrim a fair, exclusively for amusement, was held on the 12th of August. As the O.S. memoir-writer relates:[67]

> It is anxiously looked forward to by the inhabitants of the surrounding country, who flock to it from even distant parts, and there is no part of Ireland where so great an assemblage of well-dressed country people may be seen. Dancing, strolling about the rocks and cliffs, and eating and drinking in the tents form the amusements of the day and if the weather be fine, there is no time when the Causeway is seen to the same advantage.

At nearby Portstewart, Co. Derry, a pleasure fair took place annually on Lammas day in August. Their amusements during the day consisted of short boating excursions, dancing and drinking. Conduct was good and most retired at nightfall without any fighting. Another pleasure fair to be tenaciously upheld occurred at Boveedy village in the parish of Tamlaght O'Crilly in south east Derry. This was held of a Christmas time, with the day and the greater part of the night devoted to amusements such as shooting for bets, common playing, cock-fighting, dancing, singing and drinking.

Ballykelly in Tamlaght Finlagan parish in the same county furnishes the interesting case of a livestock fair, which lapsed in 1807 but continued as a pleasure fair. On the appointed day, the 12th of August, dealers in cakes, fruit, spirits and dulse swelled the attendance, and dancing, drinking and gambling held monopoly over amusements. Another Lammas fair with old roots was held at Greencastle, Co. Down. It was known as the 'Ram fair', and maintaining the same motif as the famous 'Puck fair' of Killorglin, a ram was enthroned high on the walls of the ruined castle during the time of the fair.[68] In this scenic setting tents were spread in the fields about the castle. Very large numbers attended, drink was dispensed and consumed, and music was put under the feet of dancers.

The last was an art well practiced in the Glens of Antrim, where the fairs of Cushendall were as much resorted to for pleasure as for business, and:[69]

> Until very lately, each public house regularly employed two fiddlers or pipers on fair days and two rooms in each of these houses were set apart for dancing -------------- Dancing, until very lately, was their favourite amusement and they frequently indulged in it both in their own houses and at the fairs at Cushendall, to which many came for no other purpose. But their priest, within the last year [c.1833], put a total stop to it; and since it has ceased, there has been much drunken rioting at the fairs of this parish.

The spoil-sport priest of a spoil-sport Church had taken to the implementation of official ordinance,[70] and in the process of curbing fun had unwittingly led to the exacerbation of violence.

Sometimes, the clergy targeted pattern/ pleasure fairs for outright elimination. These were occasions of festivity to mark a saint's day in the calendar, which mostly focused upon a holy well dedicated to the saint. It often happened that devotional rituals of a morning gave way later to fun and frivolity, as sanctity ceded to profanity. Clerical opposition certainly had an effect on Brideswell, Co. Roscommon, a village that derived

88

its name from a holy well dedicated to St. Brighid. Weld, writing in 1832, describes how attendance at the pattern fair had been prohibited by the Catholic clergy:[71]

> Their mandates had been implicitly obeyed during the two years which preceded my visit. Nothing can more decidedly show the great influence of the priesthood than the ready compliance of the people with their orders to abandon festivities which, during a long series of years, had been hailed both by young and old as a source of annual delight and enjoyment.

In the short term the *raison d'etre* of the little village built around a level green on which the pattern fair was celebrated had been dealt a cruel blow. However, tenacity of tradition saw to it that the fair was later revived.

Sometimes pattern fairs displayed extraordinary resilience in the face of official Church strictures. Try as they might, metropolitan and episcopal authorities could not suppress the assembly at St. John's well, in Warrenstown, Co. Meath, which according to an early nineteenth century report bore 'a greater resemblance to a fair than an assembly for the purpose of devotion'.[72] Nor had archbishops of Dublin any greater success in seeking to suppress gatherings at another St. John's well, at Kilmainham, on the outskirts of the city. On St. John's Eve *c.* 1840, it continued to be much patronised by the working classes of Dublin, for whom tents were pitched and the usual entertainments of pattern day provided. Western counties proved a fertile source of pattern fair venues, which filled out nodes of assembly and entertainment in countrysides where towns, villages and ordinary livestock fairs were scarce. Such was conspicuously the case in Co. Kerry, where fairs and markets were thin on the ground, and where Ballinageragh, a village in Kilcaragh parish near Lixnaw, offered concourse as one of the largest pattern fairs in the county on the 29th of September, the feastday of St. Michael.

Indeed, there were many long-time pattern fairs, which despite clerical opposition continued to thrive and to throng from the 1830s to the 1850s and beyond. Take Croagh Patrick, near Westport, Co. Mayo, the holiest mountain in Ireland and setting for the greatest pilgrimage, where Thackeray was on hand at the foot of the mountain on a wet day in 1842, to distill the senses of the pattern fair:[73]

> The pleasures of the poor people – for after the business on the mountain came the dancing and love-making at its foot – was woefully spoiled by the rain, which rendered dancing on the grass impossible, nor were the tents big enough for that exercise. Indeed, the whole sight was as dismal and half-savage a one as I have seen. There may have been fifty of these tents squatted round a plain of the most brilliant green grass, behind which the mist-curtains seemed to rise immediately; for you could not even see the mountain-side beyond them. Here was a great crowd of men and women, all ugly, as the fortune of the day would have it (for the sagacious reader has, no doubt, remarked that there are ugly and pretty days in life). Stalls were spread about, whereof the owners were shrieking out the praises of their wares – great, coarse, damp-looking bannocks of bread for the most part, or mayhap, a dirty collection of pigs'-feet, and such refreshments. Several of the booths professed to belong to 'confectioners' from Westport or Castlebar, the confectionery consisting of huge biscuits and doubtful looking-looking ginger-beer – ginger-ale, or gingeretta, it is called in this country, by a fanciful people, who love the finest titles. Add to these, cauldrons containing water for tay, at the door of the booths, other pots full of masses of pale legs of mutton (the owner 'prodding' every now and then, for a bit, and holding it up and asking the passenger to buy). In these booths, it was impossible to stand upright, or to see much, on account of smoke. Men and women were crowded in these rude tents, huddled together, and disappearing in the darkness. Owners came bustling out to replenish the empty water-jugs, and landladies stood outside in the rain calling strenuously upon all passers-by to enter.

On the most miserable of days, when everyone was wet through, business and pleasure co-mingled to enliven the play of the pattern fair. Everyone was happy.

Plate 4.1. shows scenes from *The Festival of St. Kevin at the Seven Churches*, Glendalough, by Joseph Peacock, 1813 (Ulster Museum), which appear perfectly congruent with Sir William Wilde's written portraiture of the pattern fair *circa* 1850

Some thirty years later, Sir William Wilde, was able to wax expansive about the pattern fair of Glendalough, Co. Wicklow, enraptured setting of a monastic proto-town, dedicated to St. Kevin. Long-practiced in his visitations, he was well equipped to report on pattern eve and pattern day, as he encountered it *c.* 1850:[74]

> The scene was remarkable, and I and my friends often spent a large portion of the night walking among the ruins where an immense crowd usually had bivouacked or were putting up tents and booths, or cooking their evening meal, gypsy-wise, throughout the space of the sacred enclosure -- ----------[Next day] dancing, drinking, thimble-rigging, prick-o-the-loop, and other amusements, even while the bareheaded venerable pilgrims and bare kneed voteens were going their prescribed rounds, continued. Towards evening the fun became became fast and furious, the pilgrimages ceased, the dancing was arrested, the pipers and fiddlers escaped to places of security, the keepers of tents and booths looked to their gear, the crowd thickened, the brandishing of sticks, the 'hoshings' and 'wheelings and 'hieings' for their respective parties showed that the faction fight was about to commence among the tombstones and monuments and that all religious observances and even refreshments were at an end. Police and magistrates were often required.

Clerical intervention helped to assuage some of the worst excesses, but by the time of Wilde's reflections the pattern fair of Glendalough, depicted so tellingly in Peacock's painting of 1813 (plate 4.1.), was no longer celebrated.

Another great concourse to come a cropper during the heyday of the fairs was the infamous fair of Donnybrook, Co. Dublin, which came to lend its name as synonym for 'riotous behaviour' all over the English-speaking world. This fifteen-day fair under an old patent was often a matter of contention in the late eighteenth and early nineteenth century, as its carnivalesque element eclipsed that of business. Still a great deal of business was carried on, and being so near a large city the constant demand for draught horses made it the rival of Ballinasloe. In 1841, for instance, 2,500 horses were presented for sale.[75] Most were adapted for the saddle or light draught. Cattle and sheep were also sold. There was no gainsaying, however, the fair's principal function: it was for pleasure, amusement and diversion. One calculation places 74,792 people in attendance on a single day in 1841. Eating and drinking were cardinal activities, for which leading hoteliers and vintners of the city often made sumptuous provision. For the ordinary run of attendee, side-stalls of gingerbread, fruit, cheese and sweets were dispersed all over the green. Frolicsome games and races held the interest of the day. Showtime summoned up the circus, travelling show or penny theatre. Commencing on the 26th of August, Donnybrook fair was a moral holiday for the great numbers in attendance.[76] It was predicated upon the sway of popular culture; its role was cathartic, with a lingering fertility magic underlying its excitement.

The popular conception of the fair as a battleground for faction fights was well earned in the eighteenth century, when two opposing factions focussed in on the great concourse to maximize impact and publicity. The factions had an occupational, as well as a territorial and sectarian basis, and thus made for incendiary possibilities, whenever assembled *en masse*. By the early nineteenth century large-scale engagements had abated, at which time in certain circles the fair was upheld as a microcosm of the Irish national character.[77] However, a great deal of violence still took place, as witnessed, for instance, in the sequel to Donnybrook reported from a metropolitan police station in 1822:[78]

> College St. – Donnybrook, being in this division, there were made of the occasion of the fair the customary number of complaints for broken heads, black eyes, bloody noses, squeezed hats, singed, cut and torn inexpressibles, jocks, and upper benjamins, loodies, frocks, tippets, reels and damaged leghorns, together with sundry assaults, fibbings, cross buttocks, chancey lodgements, and ground floorings, too numerous to mention.

Plate 4.2. shows William Sadler's drawing of Donnybrook Fair, 1830 (National Library of Ireland). Plate 4.3. shows Donnybrook Fair in full swing in 1845-9 from a painting by Erskine Nichol (Tate Gallery, London)

Then in 1834 gangs of ruffians looking for money and armed with crowbars and bludgeons, broke into tents in the early hours of a fair morning, attacking employees and proprietors alike. More generally, drunkards and coteries of thieves and hooligans ensured that Donnybrook fair kept its reputation for violence up to the time of its suppression.

Notwithstanding this, one of the last images of the fair conveys the sense of a vast throng assembled, regulated and peaceable.[79] It comes by way of a large painting by Erskine Nichol, which hangs in the Tate Gallery in London (plate 4.3.). Nicol was a Scotsman who visited Ireland between 1845 and 1849. His painting purports to depict the great commercial gathering in all its glory. In the foreground well-dressed figures are conversing, playing or engaging in transactions. The background features an assemblage of show booths and showmen's caravans arranged in order, with Bell's fantastic American Circus taking the part of prominence. On the far side, swinging boats and other amusements hold fast a youthful and captive clientele. All is the essence of ease and conviviality.

The end to legal fairs came soon afterwards. A new curate arriving in the combined Irishtown, Ringsend, Sandymount and Donnybrook parish in 1853 determined that the annual blot on the good name of parishioners entrusted to his care should be erased forthwith. The fair of 1854 was targeted to be the last. He enlisted the support of the patentee and of the lord mayor of Dublin. The timing was also optimal as the Catholic Church began to move magisterially in post-Famine Ireland and could count on the mores of an urban bourgeoisie for solid support. Donnybrook's fair green hosted its last legal fair in 1854, an event which coincided with the advent of photography. Photographs were taken, but none survive. Thus within clear sight of a major representational innovation, had come the demise of a fair and a name forever calculated to bestir imagination.

VII

It is apparent from the experience of Donnybrook fair and many others that fighting was still apt to occur in the course of the climax phase of fairs from the 1830s to the 50s. Pre-famine Ireland was a violent society in which public order was at best problematic and at worst non-existent. Violence at fairs and at markets, to a much lesser degree, took several forms. Not surprisingly in a divided plural society, sectarian animosities were a source of recurrent fighting, for the most part in Ulster (where it was known as party fighting). Party fights and market brawls were, for instance, an endemic source of conflict in the cock-pit county of Armagh as early as 1784-6.[80] There was also the random violence of brawls and assaults, which could take place casually on any occasion but which were especially common at fairs and similar social gatherings. These same gatherings also provided a familiar battleground for local factions, often formidable alliances and capable in some cases of mustering armies several hundred strong. Common animosity towards the opposing party constituted the main animating impulse, and from the early nineteenth century onwards power conflicts between lineages tended to displace the older, territorially based, fued.[81] At times clashes between factions may have amounted to little more than a pastime, governed by ritual and convention. In other cases they developed with ferocity of intent into murderous feuds. They could also undermine or even set at naught the viability of the fair, as could party fights.

The last point is well made in relation to the well-known fair of Crebilly, near Ballymena, Co. Antrim, where an O.S. memoir-writer was on hand to assess the the scene in 1832:[82]

> These fairs used to be the scene of dreadful party riots, which were tending much to their injury, dealers being afraid to attend them -------- No outrages have lately occurred. Crebilly was, until the last three years, the scene of many a bloody party fight. Previous to the last eight years these fights were as regular as the fairs, and though lives were but seldom lost on the ground, still many never recovered [from] the beatings they received. Latterly these riots have ceased. The last that took place was a year ago and it was but trifling. Had they continued the fair must have been ruined, as respectable dealers were afraid to come to it, but the presence of the constabulary has put an end to them. Both parties are equally disposed to riot. Their fights [began] by a volley or two of stones and an immediate rush to close quarters. They have but few firearms, and even these they do not use, but they have much more dangerous weapons called 'colts' which are made of osiers or woodbine plaited to the thickness of an inch, and loaded with a heavy knob of lead at one or both ends. They are about 18 inches long and are generally concealed under the sleeve. A stick will not throw off a blow from one of these as, from its elasticity, it will bend over ----- The engagement --- continued until the rout of one party, who in their retreat never met with any mercy.

Thus the stakes were high for the two annual fairs of Crebilly on the 26th of June and the 1st of August, all the more so when its immense draw for business and pleasure is taken into account. Horses were brought from counties Derry and Antrim; black cattle from Fermanagh and the western counties of Mayo, Sligo and Roscommon; pigs from the surrounding countryside; and sheep from the Scottish Highlands (they landed at Cushendun) and the Antrim plateau. Dealers came from far afield to buy up pigs and black cattle for wholesale exportation. Up to 50 tentholders served refreshments. Broth was dispensed in quart noggins and whiskey in advisedly lesser measures.

Abatement of fights at fair sometimes had a beneficial effect on settlement that went well beyond ensuring viability of the fairs themselves. At Draperstown, Co. Derry, for example, a relocated fair was integral to village genesis, so that by 1836 the village at the foot of a sloping hill was comprised mainly of a street and fairground, a large irregular open space. It was then adjudged ripe for development on the part of the Draper's Company. Its origins, however, were humble in the extreme, having started with a quarrel of a fair day. According to an O.S. memoir-writer of 1836, Laughlin McNamee, a local publican, founded the village in 1798. The story is related as follows:[83]

> Before 1797 the cattle fair had always been held in the townland of Moneyneany. In that year, at one of the fairs, the company in McNamee's tent became quarrelsome over their liquor. Their ideas suddenly received a new turn by one of the drunkards exclaiming that if he had a house at the crossroads he would 'have a comfortable place to take his glass in', upon which, after some further altercation, another rushed out and, leaping on a cart, proclaimed to the multitudes that the next fair would be held at the crossroads of Moyheyland. They accordingly resorted thither at the time appointed and immediately Laughlin McNamee removed to it and built the first houses. He also soon established a weekly market by giving free carnage and entertainment, and to this day it, as well as the principal part of the fair, is held about his doorway.

Betokening a clear sense of progress, the place went through several name mutations.

> With the priest's aid at first, and then the gentry, he kept down quarrelling, and soon had the satisfaction of seeing the fair in a flourishing state and the number of houses increasing. Its name was first Borbury or the 'yellow road', then Moyheyland, then Ballynascreen, then Cross, then Draperstown Cross and finally Draperstown, the name given to it by the General Post Office and the Company of Drapers.

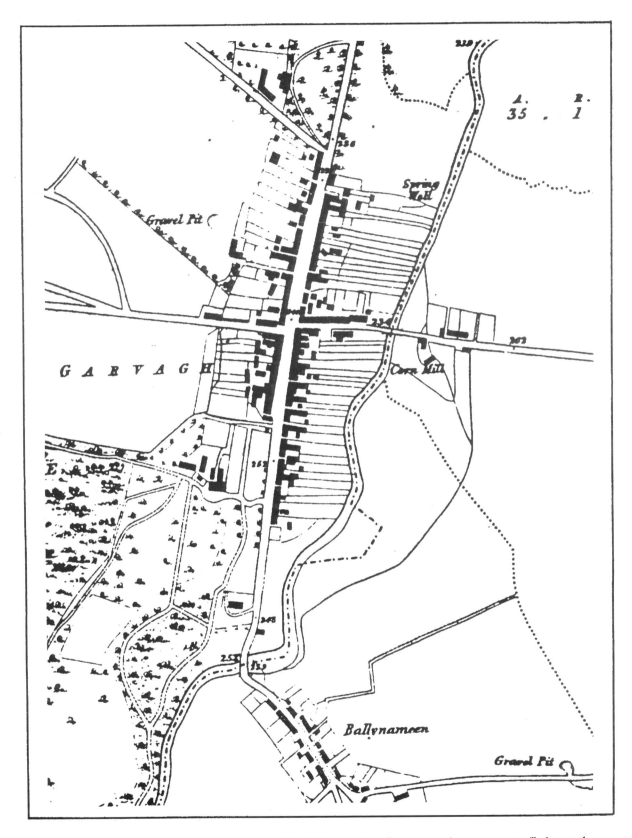

Fig. 4.8. Garvagh, Co. Derry, furnished the setting for a murderous party fight at the July fair of 1813, which became immortalised in a ballad known as 'The Battle of Garvagh'

It also acquired the markers of civility – parish church, inn, market house – and many more buildings were planned.

Having left fights and quarrelling well behind, the fairs of Draperstown thrived. The October fair of 1836 is symptomatic for the 389 horses on offer, the 1,225 black cattle, the 1,035 sheep and lambs, and the 217 pigs together with 7 stands of sucklings pigs or bonhams. There was linen yarn to be had by the spangle, and coarse linen by the yard, coarse flax and fine flax. Requisites for wear included woollen socks and woollen stockings, wollen hats, and men's and women's shoes. Flannel, sacken and wool were priced for the taking and making up. Beef, mutton, bacon, cheese, eggs, eels and salt herrings could be had at a price for home consumption. Items as diverse as slide cars, potato baskets, stable brooms, noggins and piece crocks offered the prospect of everyday utility in home and on farm. The fruits of the harvest – apples and plums – were on sale for 2s. a bushel. Furthermore supply met or bettered demand for old and new ready-made clothes, bedclothes; old and new books and ballads; silks, cottons and calicoes; hardware, delph, china and crockery; tinware, black and whitesmith work, the range of turner's work; and the staple eatables of bread and gingerbread.

Extrapolation suggests that Draperstown fair on the first Friday of every month and its market on a Wednesday waxed expansive in the climax phase from the 1830s onwards. Not all places were as fortunate. At the newly founded village of Newtown Crommelin in the Glens of Antrim, fairs had to be stopped c. 1830 since they were frequently the target of riot and bloodshed. Maguiresbridge, Co. Fermanagh, famous for its horse sales, hosted as many as 16 fairs in the year c. 1800, but then saw its role decline due to 'the curse of faction fights',[85] and in a re-cast fairs pattern nearby Lisnaskea proffered superior competition. Famously at Garvagh, Co. Derry, a party fight at the July fair of 1813 became immortalised in a ballad entitled 'The battle of Garvagh', in which the contenders took up station with murderous intent:[86]

The day before the July fair	The Protestants and Orangemen
The Ribbonmen they did prepare	Like brothers did assemble then
For three miles round to sack and tear	To keep the town they did intend
The loyal town of Garvagh.	Or die like men in Garvagh.

The effects were deep and negative, so much so that monthly fairs and a weekly market needed to be re-established at Garvagh in 1829 and the earlier unsavoury episode was air-brushed out of the O.S. memoir writing of the 1830s.

All over the country the lure of fair day proved irresistible to rival factions and the drive to maximise impact is well exemplified by the setting for one of the earliest incidents to be recorded in Co. Limerick. This was Montpelier, the tiny Shannon-side village below Killaloe, where fair green and main street formed the same feature. Here in 1814, in the absence of one of the factions, the other continued in possession of the village for the whole of a fair day, while 'committing every sort of excess, firing shots, etc.'.[87] Most of the other planned confrontations actually did take place along with a great many casual encounters. Everywhere, the bustle of the fair appears to have had the potential to transmute combative urges into battle and in Co. Limerick alone fair venues such as Ballyagran, Dromin, Shanagolden, Abbeyfeale, Newcastle, Abington, Kilteely and Knocklong yielded up some of the most notorious of the faction fights in the early decades of the nineteenth century.[88] It was potentially the same everywhere. As a local magistrate reported from Co. Cork: 'there are twenty-three fairs in my district, all of which are remarkable for faction fights'.[89] The effects on transactional activity and long-term viability can only have been deeply regressive.

Much, however, had been sorted out by the climax phase of fairs and markets, as holds inspired by state, church and middle classes firmed over society, and thoroughgoing reforms were introduced. To test a sequence of fair days (1828-33), it is worth tracking the observations of Amlaoibh Ó Súilleabháin, schoolteacher and merchant of Callan, Co. Kilkenny.[90] The town's repuation as *Callainn an Chlampair* ('Callan of the Ructions') no doubt signifies its favoured venue status for faction fighters, as rival parties of Caravats (*Carabhaití*, 'the Cravats') and Shanavests (*Sean-Bheisteanna*, 'the Old Waistcoats') were wont to assemble and fight the day of a fair. Ó Súilleabháin appears a trustworthy and phlegmatic witness with a fine command of language. His observations of St. John's fair day (10th July) in his adopted town suggest that Callan was already living down its image.

He begins with the fair of 1828 at which there was a good trade in cattle, and a clear instance of police brutality:

Do buaileadh a lán daoine neamhchiontach leis na píleirí diabhail. Bhuaileadar beirt cheannaithe ina dtithe féin. Ní féidir seasamh leo.	The devilish peelers beat up a lot of innocent people. They beat up two merchants in their own houses. They can't be tolerated.

The fair of 1830 also engendered a lively trade, but passed without rancour:

Cia go raibh mórán daoine ann ní raibh brúion ná achrann eatarthu.	Although there was a large crowd at the fair there were no arguments or fighting.

Nor was there much to report by way of disturbance at another good fair in 1832:

Ni raibh bruíon ná achrann ann ach idir beagán dailtíní i ndeireadh an lae.	No quarrelling or fighting except among a few brats at the end of the day.

There was more to report of the fair of 1833, but no indication of orchestrated violence:

Bhí coimheascar idir dailtíní. Do lámhaigh na píléirí bean sinséara sa chromán agus do loitear beirt nó triúr eile.	The rowdies were fighting. The peelers shot a woman gingerbread seller in the hip and they injured two or three others.

Altogether, Amlaoibh's evidence suggests little disturbance of transactional activity and little concerted fighting at fair.

In fact, the faction fighters appear intent on avoiding the *peelers* or police on a pre-determined fair day and arrange to strike on a different day instead. One of a number of Callan's known faction fights is carried in a newspaper report of 3rd September 1834, well away from the fair days of 21st August and 10th October:[91]

> We have just heard that the streets of Callan exhibited on Thursday last a dreadful scene of riot and disorder arising from the assemblage of two factions – the Shanavest and Caravat ..... The parties met in considerable force, we believe by previous consent, in the streets of the town, and it soon became necessary to read the riot act. It was not until the police under Major Browne, chief magistrate, had charged the combatants and driven them at the point of the bayonet out of the town that order was restored.

Police interventions had become much more effective, and the establishment of the Irish Constabulary along unmistakable modern lines in 1836 made them much more efficient. The world of faction fighting at fair became more and more a tangled world in recession, while in contradistinction fairs and markets struck their best pattern of returns and of frequency.

VIII

Except in the cities and leading towns, the infrastructure of trade, to facilitate fair and market days, was rudimentary. In relation to fairs, main street or market square – often with overspill into adjoining streets – formed the basis of accommodation and facilitation. There was little specific provision by way of dedicated fair greens on the edges of towns and villages, and it was not until the early nineteenth century that fairs attained the kind of frequency that might merit special spatial arrangements.[92] Wherever the issue arose, however, there was stiff resistance from shopkeepers and publicans to the removal of fairs from the centres of towns and villages.

In Newtownlimavady, Co. Derry, for example, the issue is given a good airing. On the one hand, the householders are recorded as finding the lack of a dedicated 'cow market' a great inconvenience.[93] In its absence, 'the cows stand promiscuously in the narrow streets and frequently become very restive'. The publicans, in contrast, were apt to vent their stern opposition, given that their chief support came from the crowds that filled the town of a fair and market day. Easy facilitation to their services was offered. No tolls or customs were levied, and in the absence of fairs and markets one-half of the total complement of public houses would suffice for the town's own needs. Business interests in general would not countenance change. Nor would the proprietor.[94]

> There is not at present, nor never had been, a fair green set apart in or about the town of Newtown-limavady for the sale of cattle, other than the streets, though many of the local inhabitants at various times solicited the sanction of Mr. Ogilby, the lord of the soil, to have a fair green set apart in the suburbs and have the cattle removed off the streets, as they not only occupy the principal streets in the town but also endanger the lives and safe access of young and old on fair and market days. The above solicitations are not only neglected by the lord of the soil, without whose consent the cattle could not be removed, but are also opposed by several persons in trade in different parts of the town, believing that if the cattle were removed from the streets, that their callings would suffer materially; therefore under all these circumstances the streets continue filthy and the access of local and foreign visitants [is] unsafe and unpleasant on fair and market days.

Thus in Limavady the rationale for fairs and markets on the main streets of the town was integrally tied to resident trading interests, despite the danger, dung and inconvenience. The same pattern prevailed in the vast majority of Irish fair venues.

Over the country as a whole there is relatively little evidence of dedicated space set aside in towns and villages for the use of monthly or less frequent fairs. Indeed, wherever the urban network was best developed as in the south and east, there is a dearth of fair green provision at the margins. This is apparent from an inspection of the Ordnance Survey 1:10,560 sheets, which provided pioneer coverage for the whole island from 1833 – 45.[95] It is clear that trading interests at centre held the preponderant sway and that, except for certain estate towns, fair green delimitation at edge was relatively rare. The motif of market house at centre and fair green on the periphery is conspicuous in such estate towns as Dunlavin, Co. Wicklow, and Milltown Malbay, Co. Clare, and much has been made of the symbolic interplay between these worlds representing coloniser and colon-ised .[96] We may certainly allow for the integrity of both as cultural phenomena, but the longevity of fair greens as active venues for trade is open to serious question. Take the case of Callan, Co. Kilkenny, which boasted both a central market house and a peripheral fair green. Writing about the latter, Amlaoibh Ó Súilleabháin in the early 1830s appears to place it on the disreputable edge of the town, the setting for wakes, hurling, cock-

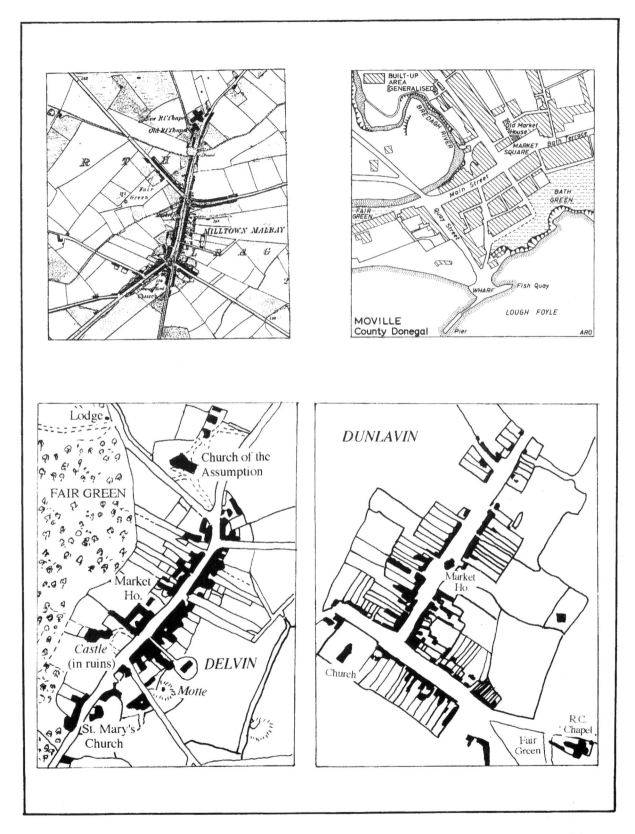

Fig. 4.9. The duality of market house/ square and fair green is well illustrated in Milltown Malbay, Co. Clare; Moville, Co. Donegal; Delvin, Co. Westmeath; and Dunlavin, Co. Wicklow. The longevity of fair greens is, however, open to question

fights, strolling etc.,[97] but nary a mention of fairs. In an old town such as Callan, the trading interests at centre would hold the commanding sway. In landlord-inspired towns and villages too, commercial interests often ensured that the fair green at edge did not long remain the place of fairs. Even in towns with weak urban traditions fair greens were apt to appear as main street appendages rather than discrete entities in their own right (fig. 4.5.). In this way the role of main street as trading artery remained undiminished.

Other than the space fairs filled, little further demand was made, except (wherever applicable), a facility for collecting customs and tolls. By the 1830s and 40s these were coming more and more into disuse, as competition between neighbouring venues sharpened. Sometimes the end was abrupt as in Raphoe, Co. Donegal, an old diocesan centre in which the tolls were let by the bishop to a tenant. Toll collectors and toll gates, however, proved no match for the clientele of the summer fair of 1833, who assembled and drove their cattle past with a sufficient degree of terror to ensure that no tolls on cattle were levied thereafter. The elaborate series of toll gates on the approaches to Lisburn, Co. Antrim, appears to have been quite singular in the 1830s, and doubtless this network was sustainable because of proximity to Belfast, large-scale supply and demand, and the presence thriving fairs and markets. Elsewhere, toll collection rarely finds such specification as at the fairs of the little village of Claudy, Co. Derry, where:[98]

> All persons passing the custom gate are required by the collector to pay the sum annexed to whatever article he has. If he has not been able to sell the article, an oath is immediately administered.

The extent to which the practice was followed at all is unclear, and the greater weight of evidence from fair venues suggests either diminution in returns or outright abolition.

At the fairs of Ballyconnell, Co. Cavan, customs and tolls had been much reduced by the 1830s, when their collection realised only £10 - £20. At Comber, Co. Down, tolls in the gift of the Marquess of Londonderry were not levied with strictness. At Randalstown, Co. Antrim, the customs of two annual fairs amounted to about £1-10-0, and at Clogh in the same county four annual fairs yielded a modest £8. At Ballymena a scale of tolls payable to the proprietor, William Adair, was posted at each end of the town, but there is silence regarding collection. By the 1830s tolls were being actively withdrawn or allowed to lapse. At Carrickmacross, Co. Monaghan, tools were withdrawn by sufferance of the proprietor, Lord Bath and Shirley, his tenant. They were allowed to lapse in Garvagh, Co. Derry, in 1829, when the fairs were put on a firm new footing. Similarly, tolls and customs were abolished in Antrim town c. 1820, at Bellaghy, Co. Derry, c. 1830, and at Moneymore, Co. Derry, in 1835. No doubt the detriment of fairs and markets gave compelling reason, as it did in Ballymoney, Co. Antrim, in 1835, when a successful petition of the townspeople overturned notice of renewal.

At a great many locations throughout Ireland tolls and customs had ceased to be levied by the climax phase of fairs and markets from the 1830s to the 50s. In coverage afforded by O.S. memoir-writers in the 1830s, 23 of the 36 locations in Ulster for which details are given, had come to enjoy toll-free status. Far from following diminishing returns and suffering the thrust of keener competition, some proprietors appeared eager to bolster fair and market prospects at their estate cores by making improved provision. In Castlederg, Co. Tyrone, Sir Richard Ferguson gave a large piece of ground free of toll for a cattle and pig market, and enclosed it with a stone wall at his own expense. On the O.S. 1:10,560 map, an impressive statement is issued with the market house centrally placed in a

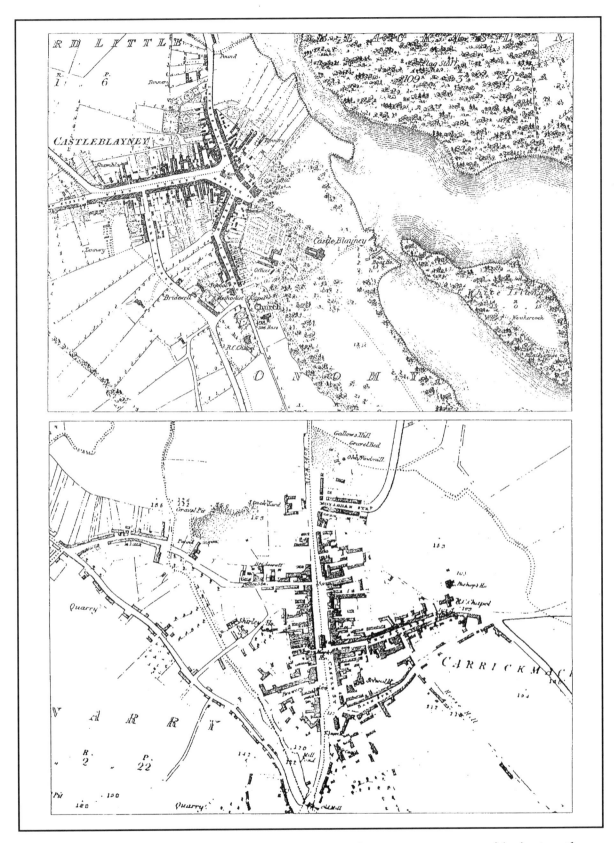

Fig 4.10. Set in a zone where the market network was strongest at mid nineteenth century, the centrality of the market house is tellingly illustrated by the Co. Monaghan towns of Castleblaney and Carrickmacross

triangular open space at the head of the village, and a place of animal impoundment mediating between it and a large enclosure known as the 'cattle market'. Similarly, at Ballycarry, Co. Antrim, the proprietor put fairs on a new and improved footing by enclosing 'a suitable and commodious space for cattle', which was to be custom free and without tolls. At Moneymore, Co. Derry, a village in which markets and fairs were thriving, the Draper's Company took the bold step in 1835 of abolishing all tolls and customs, despite these being set at a considerable yearly rent. Not only that, but they allowed their tenant £100 per annum compensation.

Infrastructural provision on the part of proprietors spanned the spectrum of non-existent to excellent. It was often meagre, as in the small village of Feeny, Co. Derry. Here in the summer of 1833 the proprietor, Richard Hunter, appointed Friday as market day and exempted dealers from all charges of carnage or customs, with the view to encouraging trade. Such was the proximity to the well-supplied markets of Dungiven, however, that those at Feeny never really took off. Still the triangular crane remained in the street for the free use of buyers and sellers, especially at the eight annual fairs there.[99] Other places, such as Bellaghy, Co. Sligo, and Ballingarry, Co. Limerick, could only boast of a public weighing scales in the open street in support of their markets, and although the former acquired a market house, the latter apparently did not. Even in Tralee, the county town of Kerry, there were no regular marketplaces.[100] Dealings were carried on in the public street, where the provost acted as clerk of the market. He examined weights and measures, corrected abuses, and decided disputes.

Still there is no gainsaying the draw of the market place and the power of the market town. Fortunately too, the Ordnance surveyors were at hand *c.* 1840 to depict the topographic make-up of towns and villages on their pioneering sheets of six-inch maps. One of the commonest prevailing motifs sees market house as centrepiece. Thus the functional role of a settlement was proclaimed, and practical as well as subliminal messages are implicit in the absolute and relative location of the market house. Take example from the belt of country where the market network was strongest at mid nineteenth century. Co. Monaghan yields exemplary cases.

Start with Castleblaney, where three streets meet in a triangular marketplace, in the centre of which is the market house. It stands on an elevated spot, commands every vista, and leads directly to the proprietor's big house. Betokening patronage, the market house is a neat and ornamental building, with a spacious room on the second storey, and a bell turret above the roof. The place hummed on Wednesdays when considerable quantities of yarn and flax were sold and also at the corn and butter markets on Thursdays and Fridays. Doubtless too, the market house served as linchpin on the first Wednesday of every month, when standings festooned its precincts and the livestock fair spilled on to adjoining streets. The only thin note sounded applied to a nearby shambles, which was well supplied with meat in winter, but not in summer.[101]

Centrality was again proclaimed in Monaghan town where market house and linen hall shared the diamond or marketplace. This was the hub of the town, to which recourse was had on Monday for the pig and linen market; on Tuesday for wheat, bere, barley and rye; on Wednesday for oats; and on Saturday for oats and potatoes. Supplying all markets flax, yarn, butter and provisions yielded appreciable sales, while monthly fairs focusing

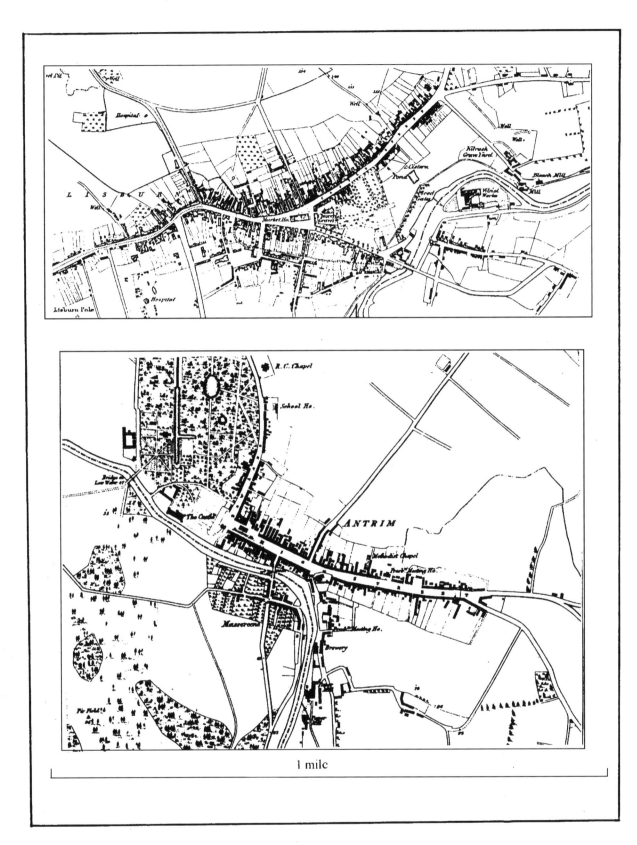

Fig. 4.11. In Lisburn, Co. Antrim, the market house was 'a great ornament to the centre of the town', while *circa* 1840 a similarly impressive statement was made at the core of Antrim town

upon the same compact zone commanded ample provisioning and drew large attendances. At Clones, a triangular open space at centre carried the stamp of a market house and hosted a weekly market and monthly fair. In Carrickmacross, the market house dominated the main street from its central vantage at the town's major junction. It facilitated corn markets on Wednesdays and Saturdays and a general market on Thursdays, to which the pig dealers of Dundalk, Newry and Belfast made eager resort. Betraying the customary influence of the proprietor, the market house was built from the ruins of his castle. Betokening the same influence elsewhere in the county, Ballybay, Newbliss and Rockcorry were all the possessors of neat market houses at centre and weekly markets that spilled into ambient space.

Set like a diadem, the market house was apt to make a statement about relative well-being and functional diversity, as well as give witness to the term 'market town'. It often formed part of a larger complex, incorporating in addition such functions as courtroom(s), assembly room(s), reading room(s) etc. Its building could incur significant expenditure, as in Edenderry, Co. Offaly, where the cost to the proprietor, the Marquess of Downshire, was £5,000, in 1826. From the outset the handsome stone building took on a diversity of functions, by affording accommodation for market at ground level and overhead a large room for assemblies and public meetings, together with several offices in which petty sessions and other courts could be held.[102] In Armagh, a centrally situated and elegant market house of hewn stone was erected by the Archbishop at a cost of £3,000, while more peripherally markets for grain, stores, weigh-house etc. were erected in 1829 by the committee with responsibility for tolls. Tasteful, apt and judicious use of space came with the market/courthouse of Mitchelstown, Co. Cork, which was erected in 1823 at a cost of £3,000 to the proprietor, the Earl of Kingston. There was also a departure from the usual leitmotiv in that the Catholic chapel and not the Protestant church, was located on an eminence overlooking the market house and market square. Good value could also be had for lesser expenditure, as at Clonakilty, Co. Cork. Here a spacious market house was built at a cost of £600 to the corporation in 1833. The site was let rent free by the proprietor, the Earl of Shannon.

The market house could be 'a great ornament to the centre of the town', as it was claimed on behalf of Lisburn, Co. Antrim.[103] Standing in a triangular open space at the junction of the three main streets, its command of ambient space is reminiscent of Castleblaney. It was erected, improved and kept in repair by the Marquis of Hertford. A rectilinear two-storey structure, its ground floor comprised a spacious hall with apartments, stores for market stalls with selling facilities, a library, a spacious, well-appointed newsroom, and the recent addition of a gymnasium. Overhead there was a beautiful ballroom, which also saw service as a dining room and courtroom. Surmounted by a steeple, cupola and clock, surrounded by a wrought metal railing, and fronted by an attractive entrance gate, the cut stone market house of Lisburn made an impressive iconographic statement at the heart of the town. A similarly impressive was made at the core of Antrim town (fig. 4.11.).

Statements of a generally lesser order were being made c. 1840 all over Ireland, sometimes picked up by the Ordnance surveyors and recorded, and sometimes not. In Cavan, the archetypal county of small market towns, the market house stamped the centres of Arva, Ballinagh, Ballyhaise, Belturbet, Cootehill, Killeshandra and Kingscourt. Capacious Cork yielded a nexus for market day in its varied urban settings: Bandon,

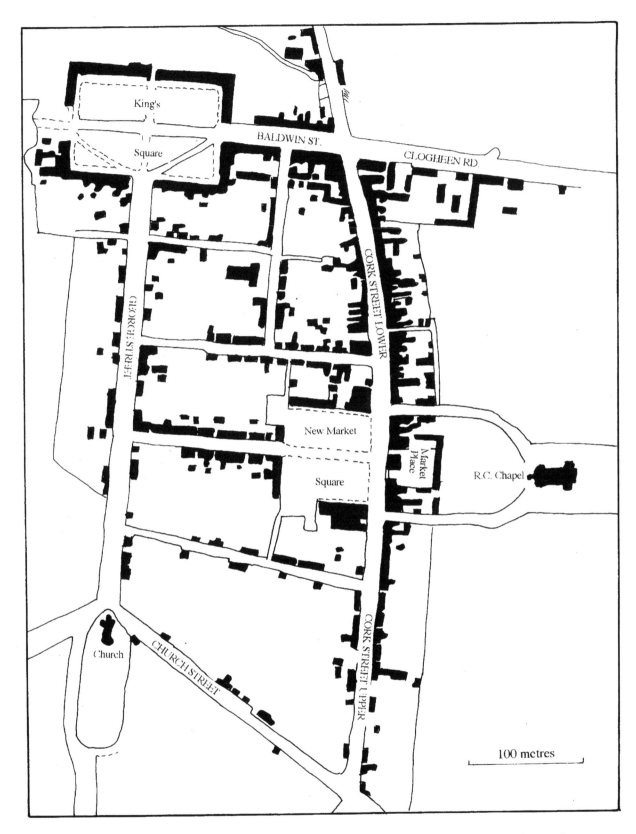

Fig. 4.12. Tasteful, apt and judicious use of space came with the market/ courthouse of Mitchelstown, Co. Cork, set in a surround of market place and new market square, and overlooked by the Catholic church

Buttevant, Castlemartyr, Clonakilty, Cobh, Doneraile, Dunmanway, Fermoy, Glanworth, Kilworth, Macroom, Mallow, Midleton, Mitchelstown, Rathcormack, Rosscarbury, Skibbereen and Youghal. The West was awake too to facilitation for a weekly market. In the small north Mayo village of Ballycastle, for example, most of what counted was new *c.* 1840, including the market house. A pattern of recent vintage was amplified elsewhere in Co. Mayo in humble small-scale settings as well as the major towns. Over much of Ireland the theme of 'historical lumpiness'[104] prevailed from the 1820s to the 50s in the provision of market houses. In this way concrete expression was given to the term 'market town' at the height of its powers.

CHAPTER FIVE

Writing Fair and Market Day

As time passes, written accounts of fairs and markets may appear more and more the accepted record of what happened. The rate at which first-hand memory has gone with its holders is now at an advanced stage, as fairs and markets underwent decline, and ultimately a near total eclipse in the 1960s. Forces of modernity, never mind post-modernity, sufficed to see off the mire and magic of the fair and dealt wholesale death to the haggling of the marketplace. Life and the memory of fair and market day is no longer compressed. Memory comprises a shifting, fading record of what happened.[1] One story is good; another is told. No one has the last word. Meanwhile, the written record remains, flawed and flavoured, diffuse and disassembled, to challenge the interpretative mind. Let us therefore gather up the senses of fair and market days.

In assembling that record we may commence with the diary of a nineteenth century merchant of Callan, Co. Kilkenny, who plied his wares and did the rounds of fairs and markets of south Leinster and east Munster in 1827-35. It proved a sufficiently remunerative way of life to lure him out of schoolteaching, while the record he kept attests to the disciplines of schooling. Other nineteenth century fairs were given forceful rendering by writers such as W.M. Thackeray and Seamus Fenton. Also a duo of Kerry novelists, the one writing in English, the other in Irish, sought to authenticate fair day in popular settings for a popular audience. In the early twentieth century the full shaft of light was turned up on the hiring fair, and the perspectives come in both English and Irish. At the same time, Sean O'Faolain gives a shape to the modalities of both fair and market day, while to amplify upon the power of market, the domain of the marketplace has been atmospherically charged by the Listowel writer, Bryan MacMahon. The Monaghan poet, Patrick Kavanagh, sweeps up a raft of memory and takes some liberty with the fairs and markets of Louth and Monaghan. Old harvest fairs that continue to be celebrated find their own dedicated writers such as E. Estyn Evans on the Lammas Fair of Ballycastle and Richard Hayward on the Puck Fair of Killorglin. The local historian too may claim a part of prominence and there is, as ever, the distilled power of vivid memory to take the fair and market beyond description.

I

The Callan schoolmaster, Amlaoibh Ó Súilleabháin, first offers insight into the local market, while he was still teaching, but perhaps also dealing in merchandise. Consonant with the mind of a merchant, his eye and ear are well attuned to prices on 7th April, 1827:[2]

| Margadh mór potátaí, coirce, móna | A large market of potatoes, oats, turf |

agus guail. Sé pingine ar chloic potátaí; ó seacht scillinge déag go punt ar bhairille coirce; deich fichead ar chruithneacht ag Muileann an Bhrianaigh; deich bpingine ar chéad guail; dá scilling ar chisín móna Pholl na Caillí; leathchoróin ar chisín móna Pholl an Chapaill; ó thoistiún is leathphingin go réal is leathphingin ar chéad plandaí cabáiste; cúig pingine ar phota mine nó fiche scilling ar chéad mine ...

and coal. Sixpence a stone for potatoes, from seventeen shillings to a pound a barrel for oats; thirty shillings for wheat at Muileann an Bhrianaigh; ten pence for a cwt. of coal; two shillings a small basket of turf from Poll na Caillí, a half-crown for the same from Poll an Chapaill; from fourpence halfpenny to sixpence half-penny a hundred for cabbage; fivepence a pot or a pound a hundredweight for meal ...

In Amhlaoibh's mind, the focus of the marketplace combined with the loving recital of the places of origin of the products offered for sale and the price differentials between them. He is more perfunctory at the 12th January market the following year, citing again a big market, for coal, culm and potatoes, and issuing the asking prices.

Most of his other references to the Callan markets relate to the sale of pigs. He cites 'a good pig market' on the 7th February, 1831, and another good one on 23rd January, 1832, at which he never saw as many suckling piglets or bonhams for sale. On 4th November, 1833, small pigs and piglets were sold at poor prices as potatoes were being dug, and the pig market of 2nd February, 1835, elicited the following poetic commentary:[3]

Muca rua rathúla,
Muca dubha dathúla,
Muca breaca líonann cró
Muca glasa níl gnó leo,
Muca ganna odhar mar a bheadh gabhair
Muc dhaingean dhroimleathan chinnéadrom
Is í sin an mhuc ba mhéin liom.

There are brown prolific pigs,
Black handsome pigs
Spotted pigs that fill the sty,
Grey unwanted pigs,
And thin dun-coloured pigs like goats,
But a sturdy wide-backed light-headed pig
Is the pig for me.

A knowledgeable man on the attributes of pigs, he took his acuity of observation to appraise another item at the market of 18th April, 1835:[4]

Chím scuaba ar an margadh déanta de
fhraoch agus scuaba déanta de dhilliúr
.i. an rasán ar a dtagann an fraochán.
Is ón duilliúr leathan air ghairtear a
ainm.

At the market I see brushes made of
heather and brushes made of the shrub
on which the whortle-berry grows. It is
called *duilliúr* from the broad leaf that
grows on it.

As in the marketplaces of the north of Ireland homemade brushes and brooms featured at Callan market. Other than Amhlaoibh Ó Súilleabháin, who else would have known the Irish and Latin names of the vegetation from which these were fashioned?

Ó Súilleabháin also betook himself to Thomastown assizes, a distance of some 12 miles, and stayed on for the market. On 23rd July, 1830, he accounts it:[5]

A small poor town. The dwelling houses are falling down. The stores are are without wheat, oats, barley or flour, without butter, bacon or beef. The storehouse doors are falling off their hinges; their windows are without glass and grass is growing in their yards and porches ------ There has been no prosperity in Thomastown since Waterford Bridge was built. Before that there used to be a good market in the town, and grain, meat and butter used to be sent down to Ross and Waterford by boat. But since the bridges were built, nothing is sold in Thomastown – *Baile an Chandáin*, *baile an chanráin* ('the town of Mac Andáin', 'the town of complaints'). The only things I saw for sale were two small churns of milk-and-water.

Thus he furnishes an insight into market decline in a county which had the fewest markets in the country at mid nineteenth century. It was all to the advantage of the port of Waterford and its enhanced nodal role. Ó Súilleabháin had seen Thomastown at its worst.[6]

108

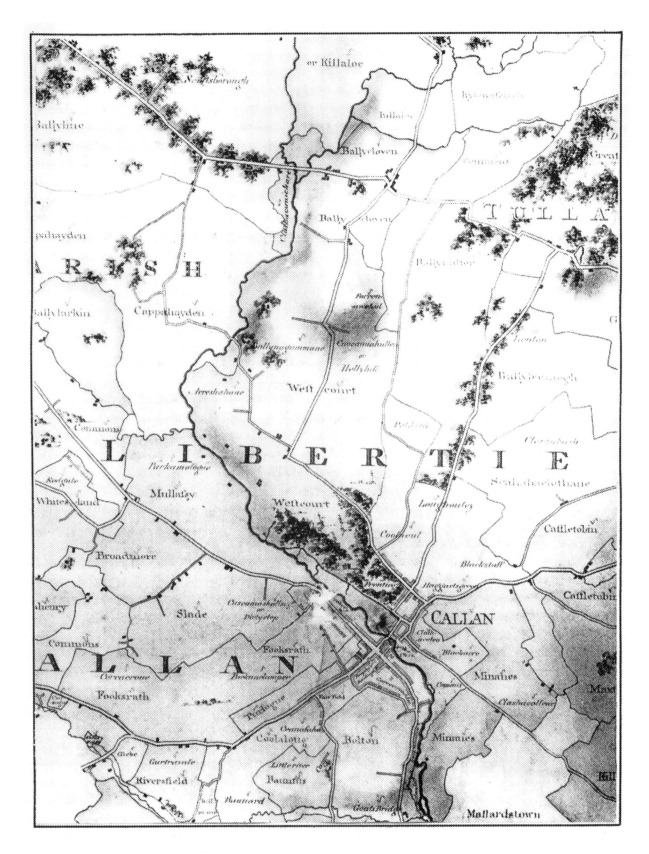

Fig. 5.1. Aher and Clements map of Callan and its neighbourhood *circa* 1817 exemplifies the intimate sphere of Amlaoibh Ó Súilleabháin's traverses to fair and market in the period 1827-35

The Callan schoolteacher and merchant was adept too at flagging fair days within his preferred sphere. Thus on 26th May 1828 he notes the Whit Monday fair of Ballingarry or *Cill Baoithín* Fair, which he accounted the most vicious in Munster or Leinster. Set in the Slieve Ardagh hill country of Co. Tipperary where societal fissures ran deep, it fed off a much-vaunted reputation for violence. That is how Ó Súilleabháin introduces the mindless mayhem:[7]

> For there's many a devilish blackguard with a stealthy stick, many a yeoman, tricky lout, a large headed rogue with a white knobbed ashplant cracking senseless skulls and brainless mindless mannerless heads.

He then proceeds by way of elaboration to cite a long narrative poem that depicts stone-throwing, invasion, cacophony, and maiming at fair. The characterisation of people and animals is vivid, if somewhat stereotyped and stylised, and the overriding sense of the fair as gather-all is powerfully conveyed.

As counter to the stylisation of Ballingarry, later that same year, the Michaelmas Fair of Callan proved altogether agreeable and peaceable. The catchphrase being proffered by everyone, *fógraim féirím ort* or *m'fhéirín ort* ('you owe me a fair-day gift') set an accordant tone. Amlaoibh noted a lot of hornless cattle at the fair.[8] The old proverb about never buying or selling a hornless cow was clearly being discountenanced, as these engendered an easy trade. Sticking to pigs, the diarist bought two castrated male slips himself for £3-7-6, and paid fourpence custom. Waxing expansive, he detailed:[9]

Is iomdha earra agus aiméis ar an aonach, mar atá capaill, ba, caiorigh, muca, turcaíthe géanna, lachain, cearca, coiligh, eiroga, sicíní, oinniúin, úlla, mionearraí, soithí adhmaid agus cria, líon, olann. Bhi luach maith ar gach ní, go háirithe ar bha is ar chaoirigh ramhra.	A great variety of articles, livestock and fowl for sale at the fair, for example, horses, cattle, sheep, pigs, turkeys, geese, ducks, hens, cocks, pullets, chicks, onions, apples, wooden and delph ware, flax, wool, and small goods. A good price was got for every thing, especially for cattle and fat sheep.

No rows took place, and not a blow was struck.

Amiability was the preponderant mood at Callan fairs. Not a blow was struck either at another Michaelmas fair on 10th October, 1831. Many people, cattle, small pigs, birds, etc. were in attendance, and to reflect the bounty of harvest, quantities of onions were offered for sale. In suitable accord, Amlaoibh and his son Donncha were kept very busy selling goods in their shop. Good July fairs too were the norm in Callan, as a number on the Feast of St. John of the Fair (10th of the month) demonstrate. Large crowds were in attendance, trade in cattle was brisk, and goods were in high demand. At St. John's Fair in 1832, for example, the Ó Súilleabháin family – Donncha, Anastás, Amhlaoibh (Jun.), Séamas and Amhlaoibh (Snr.) sold 'an amount of goods'. Amhlaoibh Ó Súilleabháin was also apt to attend the Corpus Christi Fair in Kilkenny in late May or early June to round off the energetic merchant's record of attendance at trading places from 1827-35. His legacy endures in the Callan area in the popular remembrance of 'Old Humphrey'.[10]

II

Soon after Amhlaoibh Ó Súilleabháin's record of a fairs and markets circuit in Co. Kilkenny, the English writer, W.M. Thackeray, made the wider circuit of Ireland and took in markets and fairs on his route. We have already noted his brief distillations of the sense of marketplace, and his expansive rendering of the pattern fair of Croagh Patrick (chapter 4). For the last of his 'agricultural excursions' in 1842, he went to the fair of Castledermot, Co. Kildare, which was celebrated in a lush borderland setting for its show of cattle, and attended by the farmers and gentry of the neighbouring counties:[11]

> Long before reaching the place we met troops of cattle coming from it – stock of a beautiful kind, for the most part large, sleek, white, long-backed, most of the larger animals being bound for England. There was very near as fine a show in the pastures along the road, which lies across a light green country, with plenty of trees to ornament the landscape, and some neat cottages along the roadside.

With Dublin close at hand, the finest of fat cattle from the short-grass county were following the drove road to port.

Nearer fair town the scene became more animated and thronged.[12]

> At the turnpike of Castledermot the droves of cattle met us by scores no longer, but by hundreds, and the long street of the place was thronged with oxen, sheep, and horses; and with those who wished to see, to sell, or to buy. The squires were altogether in a cluster at the police houses; the owners of the horses rode up and down, showing the best paces of their brutes; among whom you might see Paddy, in his ragged frieze coat, seated on his donkey's bare rump, and proposing him for sale. I think I saw a score of this humble, though useful breed, that were brought for sale to the fair .... Besides the donkeys, of course, there was plenty of poultry, and there were pigs without number, shrieking and struggling, and pushing hither and thither among the crowd, rebellious to the straw-rope.

Here Thackeray adverts to the well-remembered custom of driving a pig with a straw rope tied to one of its legs. Then the ceremonial attending the loading of a big, fat pig on to a cart tested both strength and ingenuity.[13]

> It was a fine thing to see one huge grunter, and the manner in which he was landed into the cart. The cart was let down on an easy inclined plane, to tempt him; two men, ascending, urged him by the fore legs, other two entreated him by the tail. At length, when more than half of his body had been coaxed upon the cart, it was suddenly whisked up, causing the animal thereby to fall forward: a parting shove sent him altogether into the cart, the two gentlemen inside jump out, and the monster is left to ride home.

With reference to the pig proprietor, Thackeray suggested that it was the pig who paid his rent, 'squeaking at the end of a straw rope'. All in all, the sights he witnessed at the fair counted among the most agreeable of his visit to Ireland.

Another difficult animal to deal with was the *bradaighe* ('thief') recalled by the Kerry writer, Seamus Fenton, on the open road to Sneem fair *c.* 1885. He accounts her:[14]

> A type of beast that was in almost every mountain herd, a survival, no doubt from the age when all the Kerry cattle roamed the mountains wild. She would walk quietly along in the herd, noticing no breaks in road-fences and no cross-roads one would think, until suddenly she plunged out of her company, wheeled right around and with the speed of a hound made for a mountain path, and on home to freedom.

Still, for an eleven-year old boy the experience was numinous, driving in the company of other boys, a herd of black mountain cattle to Sneem fair green, with the southern slopes of the Dunkerrons as backdrop at the dawning of a June morning.

Then the seasoned owner-dealers took over on the fair green, had no difficulty in striking an agreeable price, and in adjusting a *luach impidhe* ('luck penny'). Flannel and frieze were sold at the fair by dealers from the Beara peninsula, and measured by the *bannlámh* or bandle, of twenty-five inches. It was also the only fair at which the author saw bogdeal ropes (*téada giumhaise*) exposed for sale. These were fashioned from unknotted logs of bogdeal, which were seasoned, cleaved and splintered almost as fine as flax fibre. It was then twisted into strands, three of which were braided to form a strong rope that met with an eager demand from farmers and boatmen. It all bespeaks a world well recessed in terms of raw materials, time and space.

There is an insight into the cast of characters at the fair:[15]

> The Coffeys, the leading tinsmiths, whose long tribal line claimed certain fair-day privileges, were largely in evidence --- assisting in making bargains and in displaying the finer points of an ass or a pony belonging to a particularly hospitable farmer who never refused them food or fodder. A very ancient race, the tinkers appear to have no blood relation with the land-men.

Their itinerancy and endogamy had set them apart, and the occupational lines they followed were given expression in 'a great fair-day tin teapot' used to dispense strong tea in a local hostelry, as well as their brokerage and dealing at fair. With the dealing and the feasting done, the diversions of the day commenced. Dancing master, Morty O'Moriarty from Glenbeigh, adjudicated over purportedly no less than an 'inter-parish dance championship', and ballad singers, only one of whom sang in Irish, regaled the attendance. Accounts were paid, shop bills met, and matches made. All the while fair day characters had a chance to shine, including one Colonel Prince Patrick O'Sullivan who held court 'adorned with medals which he believed were bestowed upon him by his Holiness --- and by kings at war with England'.[16]

III

In his novel *The road to nowhere*, the north Kerry writer, Maurice Walsh (1879-1964) offers an authentic portrayal of fair day, Listowel, and stays true to the topography of the town. For him, as for D.H. Lawrence, the spirit of place was to be a great reality.[17] He wrote with a painter's eye of a time within clear ambit of memory, and placed indeterminately in the late nineteenth century:[18]

> It was early afternoon of the big November fair at the town of Listowel, and most of the cattle had already been sold. From earliest dawn the fine old square – with its ivied Protestant church in the middle – had been close-crowded with clumps of cattle, each guarded by two or three country lads – lean, shrill-voiced fellows, armed with ash-plants that they used mercilessly on beasts that tried to break away or trespass – but now all the best cattle had been sold and railed: the polled-Angus crosses, the Shorthorns, white-fronted Herefords, blue-and white Frisians [sic], and there were left only scattered remnants of throw-outs, long-horns, frenchies. Here and there a felt-hatted dealer still moved from group to group, and high voices decried ridiculous offers or protestingly accepted equally ridiculous ones; but for all practical purposes the sale was over.

The vividness of the scene-setting bears the stamp of first-hand knowledge, befitting a boy who grew up within easy reach of the town of Listowel.

The scene and the action shifts from open square to public house an an easy rounding up of the numbers:[19]

> The public-houses – and there are fourscore in that town – were reaping their brief harvest; for the breeders, having been paid for their cattle, were engaged in soothing long throats strained from hard bargaining, and no farmer would care to leave Listowel with, as they say, the curse of the town on him. Before each and every public-house was a row of red-painted, springless, country carts harnessed to donkeys, jennets, or short-coupled horses with remarkably clean legs; and the hum of the high-pitched Kerry voices came out from the bars like the song of bees swarming.

That last is an entrancing metaphor of the post-fair buzz that came with lubrication.

THE SQUARE, FAIR DAY, LISTOWEL, CO. KERRY. 8229. W.L.

Plate 5.1. fits in neatly with Maurice Walsh's depiction of fair day, Listowel, placed indeterminately in the late nineteenth century. Plate 5.2. evokes Bryan MacMahon's youthful ambience of carts and their owners in Market Street, Listowel

Walsh attends to the atmospherics of the day and the dialogue of the fair.[20] Heavy rain had yielded to blustering wind, which had dried out most of the mired pavements. Soon another Atlantic front would come swirling in. With the pubs crowded, the out-of-doors domain of the Square was left to a trio of tinkers, conversing of indoor sanctuary. Question was countered by question: 'Could you absorb a drink?', 'Could a duck swim?', holds authentic resonance. En route from the Square to a main street destination they reached a wide cobbled elbow on the left, where a derelict old ballad singer with a sheaf of broadsheet ballads under his oxter, marched slowly up and down, singing. People paused to listen, an odd one tossed him a copper, and passed on. No one bought a broadsheet.

The people of the road paused too as the ballad singer launched into an air that diffused to the American West as the 'Streets of Loredo', and reached main street, Listowel, as 'The Bard of Armagh', a confessional anthem of the north of Ireland:

> At a fair or a wake I could twist my shillelagh
> Or trip thro' the jig with my brogues bound with straw,
> And all the pretty colleens in village and valley
> Loved the bold Phelim Brady, the Bard of Armagh.

The singer was exhorted to 'lift it a taste!', and seeking a further rise he was commended for 'doing a roaring trade'. To which he delivered the withering reply: 'Trade is it? The hobs o' hell before Listowel town for trade!'. His voice was gone. The best of his fair days were well behind him.

The freshness of fair day is evoked by another fiction-writer, Pádraig Ó Siochfhradha (1883-1964), who took 'An Seabhac' for a pseudonym. It is illustrative too of the fascination the fair held for Kerry writers, which may well have been sparked by the relative paucity of fairs and fair venues within the county.[21] In Ó Siochfhradha's classic comic tale, *Jimín Mháire Thaidhg*, the fair day of Dingle is given the stamp of vivid description:[22]

D'éiríomar – mé féin is Daid – ar a cúig a chlog agus chuamar leis an ngealaigh 'on Daingean. Cheithre cinn de bheithígh a bhí Again. Gach aon bhearna a bhuaileadh linn ar thaobh an bhóthair, thugaidís fé dul isteach ann agus bhíodh Daid gach 'ra neomat á rá liom "Jimín, a bhuachaill, rith rompa agus sáraigh iad."	We rose, myself and Dad, at 5 o'clock and we set off with the moon to Dingle. We drove a complement of four beasts. They took to every roadside gap and Dad every second minute would cry out " Jimín, run ahead of them like a good boy and put a stop to them."

Despite his best efforts Jimín did many the circuit of a field to restore a beast to road, but before he knew it, they had hit Green Street and the fair green of Dingle. He never thought there was so much stock in Ireland between cattle and sheep, and all the frenzied bleating and bellowing and breaking away.

The fair is shot through with little vignettes of scatterings including three of their own, yelping dogs, and an old man with a solitary tethered cow, which broke away from him under the duress of other breakaways. Then the business of the day commenced:[23]

Timpeall a hocht a chlog tháinig na ceannathóirí Ar an aonach. Fir reamhra b'ea iad ar fad. Casóga móra orthu, órlach de bhonn féna mbróga acu; bróga geanncacha orthu; coisbhearta leathair go glúinibh orthu, bataí siúil ag gach fear agus rian a choda ar gach éinne acu.	About 8 o'clock the dealers arrived at the fair. They were all big, fat men. They wore big jackets, pinched boots with hob-nails and leggings to their knees, a walking stick to every man of them and a well-fed look about everyone of them.

They came to deal and for openers belittled the stock they inspected. The vendor responded by asking an extravagant price. Bargaining proved protracted and loquacious, punctuated by withdrawal on the part of dealer, ritualistic hand slapping and the splitting of differences. Eventually, the deal was struck, the cattle put on the train (of the Dingle-Tralee light railway!) and the agreed price paid over. Then the town of Dingle revealed itself to the little country boy.

IV

For a perspective on the hiring fair in the early years of the twentieth century, Donegal furnishes favoured country of the mind, given the huge supply of labour in the county and the location of all the important hiring fairs in west Ulster to tap into that market.[24] Moreover, there are the perspectives of participant observers, among them Patrick MacGill (1891-1963), whose experience mirrored that of many of his peers. Essentially the Donegal workers were first sent to the hiring fairs to gain employment and experience with Ulster farmers, before embarking on a career as migratory workers to Scotland. They served their apprenticeship in the Lagan, an indeterminate swathe of prime agricultural land with the Letterkenny-Derry axis at its core. This was to be MacGill's fate, starting at the age of twelve to push his fortune by "goin' away beyont the mountains in the mornin' ".[25]

The sadness of family parting soon yielded to the contagion of communal leavetaking:[26]
> On the road several boys and girls, all bound for the hiring market of Strabane, joined me. When we were all together there was none amongst us over fourteen years of age. The girls carried their boots in their hands. They were so used to running barefoot on the moors that they found themselves more comfortable walking along the gritty road in that manner.

The last was obviously a common practice that MacGill noted elsewhere in relation to the fair of Greenanore.[27] This time they were bound for the hiring fair of Strabane, for which they boarded a train at a desolate station. They awaited their fate:[28]
> We stood huddled together like sheep for sale in the market-place of Strabane. Over our heads the town clock rang out every passing quarter of an hour. I had never in my life before seen a clock so big ------ The boys who had been sold at the fair before said that the best masters came from near the town of Omagh, and so everyone waited eagerly until eleven o'clock, the hour at which the train was due. It was easy to know when the Omagh men came, for they overcrowded an already big market. Most of them were fat, angry-looking fellows, who kept moving up and down examining us after the manner of men who seek out the good and bad points of horses which they intend to buy.

Looked up and down, tried and tested like a farm animal, the young MacGill wrung an offer from a Lagan farmer, and the 'cub' was his for six months.

It was the practice at many fairs for the hiring workers to carry or wear an emblem such as a straw or a stick. The stick was often a peeled sally or willow rod; the straw might have been held in the hand or sown on to a coat or jacket. These served as signification of worker for hire. So did the look of fear and apprehension on youthful faces and the giveaway bundles of their working clothes. As in MacGill's case, farmers played on the young people's backwardness, inexperience and insecurity. It is well summed up in the words of one observer of the hiring fair:[29]

D'aithneodh na feirmeoirí na páistí bochta   The farmers would recognise by looking seo le féachant orthu gur as an Ghaeltacht iad – bhíodh said faiteach, critheaglach, cúthalta agus ar bheagán Béarla – agus bhéadh fhios ag na feirmeoirí seo.

at them that these poor children were from the Gaeltacht – they were fearful, terrified, shy and with very little English – and the farmers would know this.

The bargaining process took on the same pattern of haggling and banter associated with most fairs, often with parental interventions or those of onlookers. Reputations of good and bad farmers went well before them, with the latter sometimes immortalised in ballad or legend.[30] Hardship in alien worlds was to be the lot of many. As one worker put it pointedly of his hirers:[31]

Daoine Gallda. Gallda ina gcroidhe agus agus Gallda ina gcreidimh.

Foreign people. Foreign in their hearts and foreign in their belief.

Most of the farmers, the potential employees, were Protestant, which served to further cloud the perception of those with nothing but their labour to sell.

Luck money at fair to seal a bargain was often the last earnest to be received, as conditions were, in many cases, wretched for the workers. They made bitter complaints about states of loneliness, the long hours worked, and accommodation. Most especially, the dietary attracted their ire, spiced with humour. For example, the porridge of Indian meal distributed to some workers in the Lagan was itself given attribution of the 'runs':[32]

Brachán buí chomh lom go rachaidh sé de rása ón tine go dtí an doras.

Porridge so thin that it would run from the fire to the door.

They might never see butter or meat. Homesickness co-mingled with desperation. Many were driven to break away before their agreed term had expired. They included the writer, Séamus Ó Gríanna, who ran away from a farm at Guirtín on his first and only venture to the fat lands of the Lagan.[33]

There is no denying the pointedness and poignancy of the hiring fairs that served the Lagan. The hiring fair of Letterkenny was still being held in 1941, when it elicited a waft from memory:[34]

Bhí aonach fastóidh ariamh anseo in Leitir Ceanann; gcuimhne m'athara-móire, agus tá go dtí an lá inniu. Bhíodh páistí beaga ó ocht mbliadhna go dtí dhá bhliadhain déag agus ó sin go dtí ocht mbliadhain déag, cailíní agus buachaillí. B'fhéidir go mbéadh athair ag dul amach agus beirt nó triúr leis astoigh ins an na feadhnógaí ar dhruim na mbeathadhach go dtí go mbéadh sé amuigh I Leitir Ceanainn. Ní raibh said ábalta siubhal bhí said comh h-óg sin agus an turas comh fada. Tiochadh maighistir gallta aníos fhad leóbhtha annsan agus labhairfeadh sé i mBéarla, agus dheanfadh sé a bhfastódh b'fhéidir ar chúig scilling déag. Tá fhios agam bean annseo a bhí ar fastódh ar feadh sé mí ar deich scillinge, chualadh mé í a rádh go raibh sí 'na bean comh láidir ins an am sin agus a bhí sí nuair a pósadh í.

There was always a hiring fair in Letterkenny in my grandfather's time and there is still to-day. Young children from eight to twelve years and from that to eighteen years, boys and girls. Perhaps the father would be going out and two or three with him in the panniers on the back of the beast until they reached Letterkenny. They weren't able to walk, they were that young and the journey so long. A strange master would come up to them then and he would speak in English, and he would make the bargain for perhaps fifteen shillings. I know a woman here who was hired for ten shillings. I heard her saying she was as strong a woman then as when she married.

The years of dealing with the vagaries of the Lagan in childhood or young adulthood made them fit for the hard life. Letterkenny hiring fair still kept to its seasonal rhythms c. 1940, but by then things were better in every way. Wages and food had improved. So had esteem and respect for the hired help, features noticeable only by their absence in earlier days. Supply and demand had much to do with it. Servant boys and girls were scarcer and much better able to name their price and stake their claims.

V

In his first novel *A nest of simple folk* (1933), Sean O'Faolain draws out well, if sparingly, the contrast between fair and market day. His setting is the town of Rathkeale, Co. Limerick, and like Maurice Walsh in the case of Listowel, he rounds up the number of its public houses. These all pulsate with life of a fair day, the out-of-doors aura of which is penned with emanative force:[35]

> Outside the door the pent cattle thrust their tousled fur through the red bars and the blue bars of the creels under a drizzling rain, their mooing and bleating passing from cart-creel to cart-creel, and from dawn to noon, weaving in the wet air with the crying of men's voices, linking cry to cry in ceaseless lament. Only in rare moments did an astonishing silence fall, and then the deep moaning of beasts that had waked the town in the rainy dawn rose again and again over the dung-sodden streets. In that brief moment, while the beasts seemed to halt for breath, he heard the human voices, hoarse with passion, shouting in argument or dispute.

Then the writer seeks to catch snatches of the dialogue of the fair, the speech practices operative in this given society, at a given moment, in a given setting. In all the bustle, the idioms of different people from different classes, generations and locales competed for ascendancy. The heteroglossia[36] of the fair embraced worlds as diverse as Palatine and Gael, Anglo-Irish and Traveller, and at one time embraced the linguistic spread of Irish, English, German, and Cant or Gammon. Of a fair day before O'Faolain's time the claim that all Ireland was in and about Rathkeale took the guise of no empty boast.[37]

Market day Rathkeale provided an altogether more muted milieu.[38] Again there were rapt intervals, interrupted by the rattle of linch-pins and the bumping of wheels. There was the slow wind through the carts in main street to Madigan's grocery shop, and unlike the masculine ethos of the fair, femininity came to be cast clearly in the ascendant. There was the getting and packing of provisions, and the parting, with a kiss, of a mother bound again for the country and a daughter about to take her chance with the town. Then the slow amble of the donkey took the old woman away up the street, through the crowds, before rounding the corner of the hill road to the chapel.

For a much more dynamic and atmospherically charged impression of marketplace on market day, we may again revert to Co. Kerry and summon up the Listowel writer, Bryan MacMahon. Born in 1909, his entrée to the new and magical world of the market was facilitated by his grandfather, old Pat MacMahon, weighmaster of the marketplace of Listowel. It was his first-time country of the mind, through which he moved as a golden child:[39]

> The marketplace branded me for life. It was thronged with country-folk almost every day of the week. When it wasn't a calf market, it was a pig market or a butter market: on Fridays it was the country produce market – perhaps the most exciting day of all.

All aspects of country life came to be revealed to him through the glass of the market-place. Ancillary goods and produce were displayed for sale at its gates and archways – scallops or thatching withies, eelfry, cockles sold by the fluted pint glass, salmon, beef sold by the yard and hung on a steelyard or 'stiller' to be weighed, periwinkles and seagrass.

Women in shawls abounded at market. The wives of strong farmers wore biscuit-coloured woolen shawls, the amplitude of which was set off with a hem of tassels and ornamental thread-work. These served as a surrogate of wealth as affirming as the '*bán*'

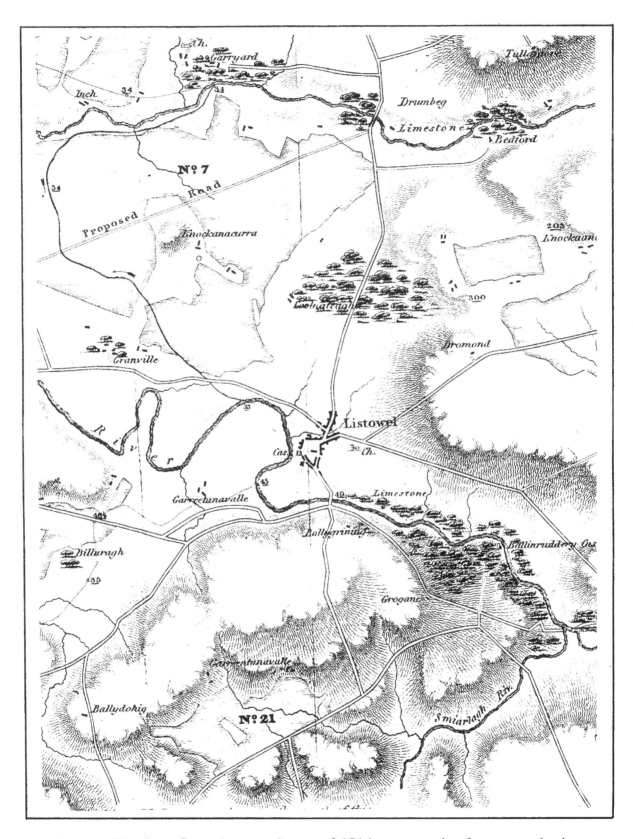

Fig. 5.2. The *Bog Commissioners"* map of 1814 suggests that from an early date, Listowel, Co. Kerry, exercised a magnetising power over its surrounding rural hinterland, a role still manifest in Bryan MacMahon's remembrance a century later

of cows on the home farm. Fisherwomen from Tralee sold cockles from their wicker baskets and had dark chocolate coloured shawls as identity markers. The women from the thatched cottages of the town wore plain black shawls. Most attractive of all was the green and black paisley shawl, which bedecked the women from over the Cashen, that is the area south of the River Feale and west to the Shannon mouth. It was known as 'Maghera' (*An Machaire*, 'the plain'), where the commitment to high tillage translated in equal measure to fidelity in sartorial splendour. The marketplace of Listowel was akin to a near-Eastern bazaar, full of beshawled women with faces just as inscrutable in their 'take' of the yashmak.

The marketplace too was full of carts, coloured a brilliant orange red with the shaft ends tipped with black, from all arts and parts within a radius of thirty miles. MacMahon's eye for detail appears exemplary:[40]

> The accessories for the carts were versatile – the creel or rail for bonnavs,[41] turf or turnips, the seat-and-guards for traveling to town or even to Mass, the low box for carrying sand or gravel while the bare cart itself was capable of being loaded with stable manure or a piled array of sacks of various kinds. The vehicles were locally called Scotchcarts as opposed to the 'tumbler from up the country' or even the 'slide' used in the Dingle area for bringing down turf saved on the mountain flank.

Indeed, for a boy with a mind for toponymy, the wonder was in the detail, as each cart had the name of its owner and his townland of origin print-painted black at the point where the right shaft met the body of the vehicle. From a perusal of such inscriptions, MacMahon could fashion a mental map of the names of people and places within the generous arc of the hinterland of Listowel. Moreover, his curiosity extended to ascertaining the meanings of the Irish versions of the townland names.

Flexible in its embrace, the marketplace was able to accommodate a butter market, a potato market, and a turf market, and a cast of characters that included ballad singers with their swatches of rebel songs, castclothesmen with their ready wit and repartee, trick-of-the-loop and three-card trick practitioners, delph sellers, a black doctor extracting a tooth with bloodied fingers and no anaesthetic, and a 'pick and win' merchant with the insignia of a grinning monkey perched on his shoulder. Also, at a time of heightened political sensitivity *c.* 1916-18, the overhang of bitter agrarian struggles still registered in dark mutterings about grabbed farms and rural boycotts, while British army recruiting officers, disported in busbies and scarlet jackets, sought to entice teenage boys to war. On a lighter note, pretty-pretty budgerigars helped to pick out fortunes for giggling country girls. Permeating almost everything MacMahon's sense of remembrance is Proustian, extending from the aromatic mutton pie shops of the market hall to the amoniac smell of horse droppings renting the open air.

VI

For a wide-ranging perspective on fair and market days in the 1920s and 30s, the Monaghan poet, Patrick Kavanagh, stakes strong claims in print as a participant observer from the small farm country of the drumlin edge. His was a life immersed in the daily grind of livelihood on a small farm with all its attendant chores and duties. From an early date, however, it is clear that attendance at fairs and markets in Carrickmacross and Dundalk (entailing round trips of twelve and eighteen miles respectively), furnished the main variation to the routine of his everyday life in thrall to the fields near the village of Inniskeen. Even in his autobiographical writing, he leavens the experience of accompanying seasoned dealers to fair with a frothy imagination. He certainly fictionalises the hiring fair of Carrickmacross in 1921 at the point where he offers himself for hire as a servant boy, and takes off with a farmer.[42]

Not that his scene setting loses the ring of authenticity. On the contrary, as with Walsh and MacMahon, it carries the stamp of accurate portraiture. A town of three streets and many nameless lanes, the town of Carrick is presented to best effect:[43]

> Every inch was crowded when we arrived. The horse-fair, ass-fair, pig fair, fowl market and hiring market were on this day ----- The 'stand' was that part of the sidewalk at the junction of Carrick's three streets where the hiring fair was held. Custom had sanctified or sanctioned it. On one side of the street the boys stood with their faces towards the workhouse, on the other side were the girls with their backs to the Bank of Ireland. 'You can be stiff with the bank to yer back', was a favourite phrase among the girls. 'There's nothin' in front of us but the workhouse', was the phrase among the boys.

Ass-dealers speaking an 'ancient language',[44] the tangler butting in with 'what's between yous?', castclothesmen, thimble players and roulette men all made the story of the day, while according to the well known ballad, the dalin' men from Crossmaglen put whiskey in the 'tay'.

Elsewhere, he expounds at some length on the ritual of deal-making at fair, having never seen a proper description of it in print himself.[45] Its conduct is formulaic, like the choreography of a dance. 'Here give me that hand?', marks commencement of the engagement between the seller and buyer of cattle or other animals. Compliments and courtesies (down to repeated mispronunciations of words, phrases and places) are exchanged. Qualities of lineage and honesty are extolled. The process becomes more dramatic, but the asking price remains obstinately high. Enter the tangler. He delivers his speech:[46]

> 'I know yous both and yous are both dacent people and yous'll both do as I say – divide what's atween yous.' Both principals remain mute, standing stiffly to attention. 'It's you that has the right pair of good-looking daughters that id keep a fella out of the gutter, and begod you might be buying more than a cow.' Sudden excitement again. Tangler grabs both parties hands and with a great struggle brings them into contact by the skin of the tips of the fingers. The deal is made.

Kavanagh makes allowance for duplicity such as the real seller masquerading as tangler, and he privileges the role of seller over buyer in deal-making. Most commentators would assign the greater initiative to the buyer.

Kavanagh was not averse either to letting himself be carried away by his poetic and literary proclivities. In a poem in memory of his mother, he offers an exquisite cameo of the aftermath of the fair [of Carrickmacross?]:[47]

> On a fair day by accident, after
> The bargains are all made and we can walk
> Together through the shops and stalls and markets
> Free in the oriental streets of thought.

At another time he contemplates the rapt interludes from market, with Carrickmacross again as likely venue:[48]

> I recollect moments of wonderful happiness. The market-places sometimes exuded the flavour of a primitive world where men were simple and childlike and close to God. The fresh wind of youth

Plates 5.3. and 5.4. The camera may not lie, but the captions attaching to each of the above Lawrence photographs appear transposed. No doubt, Patrick Kavanagh would have something acerbic to say about it

blew through the files of carts in the little town, and moments big as years were mine to squander while the clock on the Protestant church-tower counted out the miserly minutes of an adult world.

On another occasion, as drover, he alchemises the prosaic with magic the morning of the fair of Carrick:[49]

> Demand for all sorts of cattle was brisk, nearly every beast was bought and sold before we reached the town. We were very happy. What were we talking about? We were all poets, dreamers, and no man was old.

Kavanagh's imaginative fetch combined with a state of golden youth to transcend the mundane business of the local fair and market.

The pull of the fair of Carrick on Kavanagh's memory is tenacious, as another part of the business of the day illustrates:[50]

> I am back in a country town as I write this; it is Fair Day, late in the evening. There is a rumour going through the crowds that a match is being made in Donnelly's pub. It has been going on for hours and negotiations are in danger of breaking down. We wait tensely. Then a fat woman comes out of the pub with a smile on her face. There is a shaking of hands all round.
> Someone rushes up to the fat woman:
> 'Did you agree?'
> 'It's all settled.'
> Everyone is excited. We are in the midst of continuing life. The fair is alive with tomorrows.

Here, Kavanagh's optimism contrasts profoundly with another portrayal of a fair day match made at the fair of Galway.[51]

Attendance at the pig market and pork market of Carrick was a repetitive feature of Kavanagh's life, often with his mother in attendance. On one occasion he recounts being in the sucker pig market, seeking a few young pigs, and his mother arriving later by train.[52] He accounted his mother shrewd at business and himself one of the world's worst in fair or market. Preparations for the pork market were meticulous, once entailing the loan of a neighbour's ass and cart, loading the carcasses of four pigs, and taking a liberal sprinkling of holy water. Another time he picks up the memory of the turkey market:[53]

> Pulling a bag of hay for the mare and leaving it carefully in the body of the cart. Taking in the seat-board in case it should rain during the night. Everything is ready. I am as near contentment as any man could desire. Contented except for the worry that it might freeze during the night and that the road would be slippery.

Nor was it always selling that took Kavanagh off to Carrick. Once with expansive ideas to match his family's 'spreading dominions',[54] he headed for the fair of Carrick and successfully acquired a horse, cart and harness at auction.

Kavanagh's deal-making appears erratic. He registered success at the pork market:[55]

> I sold three times. The market rose sixpence after I had sold first time, so I rubbed out the pencil mark and sold again; the market rose another sixpence and I repeated the trick. Mother arrived then. I handed over the contract note to her and buried myself in the football results of the day's newspaper.

From the proceeds his mother paid all the bills and he got five shillings for his day. In contrast, the turkey market that he recounts during the Economic War was slow and sluggish, so that when his mother arrived by train he had failed to register a sale:[56]

> The only buyers in the market that day were smugglers – the cleavers from Crossmaglen. And though nobody has a higher opinion of the cleavers of Cross than I have, at the same time I could never recommend them as wholesale buyers of turkeys. Two of these amusing buyers were now examining my load of turkeys. One of them held a bird by the legs while he felt its breast. 'That's an oul' warrior,' he remarked to anybody who might be listening. 'He is not,' I answered back hotly. 'There's not an oul' turkey in that load.'

Eventually, his mother and himself disposed of all the birds for less than it would take to leave a man drunk.

Later, the farmer-poet might combine forays to Dublin during the week with going to the fowl market in Dundalk on a Monday, and hanging about for hours trying to match the sixpence a pound he got for one turkey, before settling for fivepence for a second.[57] He probably came home on the train that he once was constrained to write about:[58]

> The Monday train that carries the small farm folk to and from the Dundalk butter and egg market was returning with its load of open-mouthed but shrewd passengers. The compartment in which I sat was crowded with five people and about a dozen large baskets. On the seats and under them were plough parts and hampers holding potatoes, and in one corner were three pullets tied together by the legs. A woman was explaining that she had exchanged four cocks for the pullets and was pleased with the bargain.

Kavanagh, in contrast to his fellow passengers, may have been close to farewell to the life of farming, fairs and markets, as he sought to rise in an alternate world.

VII

The most enduring and best known of the Lammas fairs to mark harvest-time in Ireland have attracted some dedicated writing. These are the Lammas Fair of Ballycastle, Co. Antrim, and the Puck Fair of Killorglin, Co. Kerry. Both still survive mainly as pleasure fairs. The patents for each date back to the early seventeenth century, but there is speculation that the origins of the fairs may have pre-dated the towns by which they are known. Celebrity in song has long marked 'The Ould Lammas Fair at Ballycastle', while there is no dearth of rhyme to strike a resonant note to Killorglin's Puck Fair.

The distinguished geographer, E. Estyn Evans, expresses surprise at his first encounter with Lammas Fair soon after his arrival as a young lecturer in Queen's University, Belfast, in 1928. He thought it already a thing of the past, only to find it in full swing under steady rain one Tuesday morning towards the end of August. The main street is thronged and he avers that the fair is older than the town:[59]

> Tight knots of country folk take complete possession of the roadway, heads close together in earnest conclave as they exchange the gossip of many months. The air is thick with glottal-stops, the accent in this north-east corner of Ireland has a strong Scottish flavour. Greetings are shouted across the street, 'How are ye doing, Pat?', 'How's the form, Andy?', 'See you at Ned's Corner.' In many a coat lapel there is a sprig of white heather, in some a harvest knot of oat-straw cunningly twisted.

The tell-tale signs of harvest tended to be well represented in the gathering places of north east Ireland,[60] and the throngs on this occasion extended to the diamond or market square where yelling cheapjacks, apple women, castclothesmen and pedlars of the Lammas delicacies of dulse and yellow-man[61] all competed for attention.

Lending weight to all human life being at the fair, Evans eyes a harmonium mounted on an empty lorry across the square and gospellers lifting their voices in melodious song to the tune of 'Drink to me only'. It is a prescript that passes without notice by thirsty farmers moving in and out of a nearby pub. Clusters of livestock line a short steep street to the fair green: black cattle, donkeys and chestnut horses, the last having their tails tied with straw. The way is mired by a thick slime of animal droppings lubricated by rain and

Plate 5.5. 'King Puck', a male goat taken wild from the fastnesses of MacGillycuddy Reeks, holds court, and munches stolidly beneath his gleaming crown. Plate 5.6. is evocative of Puck fair getting into its stride

trampled upon by feet. A horse is put through its paces along a side street; the arguing and shouting of tangling and deal-making proceeds alongside a bunch of disinterested heifers. There is no mistaking the dealer at the centre:[62]

> Rotund, standing firmly on his highly polished brown boots. His sly piggy eyes are almost hidden in pouches of fat, his large mouth grotesquely extended with a handful of dulse from which long streamers hang down. The fancy moustaches are mysteriously sucked in and disappear as the dealer resumes his argument.

The crafty faces of countrymen, peering over the edge of the crowd, and tilting their caps back from heated brows, frame the scene. Nearby, a bargain is concluded with a mighty slap of the hand as giveaway.

In the highly sensate setting of the fair, sound leads Evans to the green where the sheep are penned:[63]

> Ballycastle lies among sheepy hills, and sheep and lambs play a large part in this ancient harvest festival. Business is brisker here, for the auctioneer comes between buyer and seller; he is a thin swarthy man in black boots and leggings. Yellow-backed ewes droop under the weight of their sodden fleeces, dabbed at the neck with red or blue dye. The sour smell of sheep hangs in the damp air. As I draw away a new smell takes its place, a smell not of animals but of rotting vegetation. It is the unforgettable whiff of the flax-dams drifting from nearby fields, pleasantly nostalgic in its urban dilution ----

This completes the writer's transect of the Lammas Fair, before he returns again to the Diamond at centre.

Here there are other smells and sights to assail the senses:[64]

> Gusts of Guiness or Bushmills as merry farmers, their bargains concluded, exude their joy, and the scent of turf as fires are set alight under kettles for the evening tea. As night falls the Diamond is lit up and shines brightly. Now the fun of the fair begins. An over-excited pair has come to blows, over a cow maybe, or a girl; the crowd parts a little to give them fist-room and opens a pathway as their momentum carries the fighting pair into a side-street. I watch them disappear, arms flying, as the crowd closes behind them.

Two amused policemen let them at it, because this is a seasonal saturnalia with leave for excess and indulgence. Lammas Fair wouldn't be the same without a fight at the end of the day.

Neither one suspects would Killorglin's Puck Fair, the setting for a great harvest gathering in southwest Ireland. However, it was the prelude rather than the afterlude which drew the topographer, Richard Hayward, to the famous fair so as to best savour the atmosphere. He was careful to arrive on the 9th of August, the day before the great concourse was in place, and on the way there overtook more and more bands of tinkers (or Travellers as they are now known) as they made for one of their prime places of annual assembly in Ireland.[65] Paying little attention to the possible invention of tradition, Hayward interpreted the spectacle as evidence of the survival an ancient pagan feast convened under the patronage of a male goat, known as a puck or *pocán*.

He positioned himself optimally to take in the spectacle by having a spacious room placed at his disposal when making a moving picture of Puck Fair in 1948, and again in 1964 when employing an artist to sketch proceedings:[66]

> Beneath us the pattern of the great festival started to evolve and to bring some kind of order to the wild disarray of the crowded streets. Killorglin, on this day of the *Gathering*, was literally jammed with people and beasts shoulder to shoulder, now a man jostling a cow to make his way into a pub, now a cow jostling a man to reach a bunch of grass growing from some old masonry. Before us a tall wooden structure rose in tawdry grandeur, beflagged and beribboned for the reception of *His*

Majesty King Puck, showmen stood at their stalls and crowded the small Square to bursting point and we were almost deafened by the bellows of frightened herds and the loud cries of men who sought to control them. Streets and pavements were already ankle-deep in cow dung and the savage spectacle of sound and colour and raw humanity was intensely exciting. This was, in short, *Puck Fair* getting into its stride.

Hayward then abandoned his bird's eye view of the fair to savour at first hand the sounding streets of a usually quiet little town.

Wherever he went, there was colour and movement and animation. No poet of any worth worth could fail to be infected with the immense energy of it all: horses and cattle; hounds and sporting dogs; pigs and sheep; foals crying for their mothers; cocks crowing; dealers shouting, laughing, gesturing; sightseers getting in the way; the attendant train of show people with their flashy attire and flashy language; then over the bridge at the foot of the town the caravans and encampments of the tinkers. Here too there was a great riot of colour, with swarms of children playing under the caravans, and buxom brightly shawled women reading fortunes in the upturned palms of laughing country boys and girls.

Back again in his eyrie overlooking the packed little square,[67] Hayward could feast on the activities of trick-of-the-loop men, three-card tricksters, and the wielder of a great handbell who peddled a miraculous cough mixture and a selection of knives with all sorts of ingenious attachments. A line of six fiddlers played 'The harvest home' with gusto, when the rhythm of their lively strings was lost to martial music. A roistering little band then appeared, leading a donkey and cart laden with vegetables, a motley crew of girls and boys gaily clad in coloured paper costumes, another band essaying 'The Kerry dance', and bringing up the rear, the royal coach itself, with its courtiers and the cynosure, King Puck, a dark-coated male goat taken wild from the fastnesses of the MacGillycuddy Reeks and sporting as fine a pair of horns as anyone had ever seen. This marked the climax of the *Gathering*, to which the crowd responded with a mighty roar that sent pigeons flying in terror high into the blue sky and shook the jackdaws out of every auditory ruin. King Puck in his crudely decorated crib was hoisted to the top of a scaffold-like tower, where he would reign for three days and three nights, munching stolidly under the gleaming crown set upon his horny head. Hayward notes the time: 6.20 p.m. on the 10th day of August. The *Gathering* was over. The fair had begun.

VIII

For a full-face portrait of fairs and markets at local level, few come better than Gallogly's depiction of old trading days in a Leitrim town.[68] Ballinamore furnishes the setting, and the fair, in particular, took a commanding grip of local life. By 1900 there were twelve fairs in the year, including the two 'old fairs' (12th May, 12th November). Later this was extended to fourteen – a monthly fair on the first Tuesday of the month, while continuing to uphold the dates of the two 'old fairs'. Every Tuesday the general market was much less of an occasion.

The fair was held on the Main Street, extending on to Cannaboe and into St. Brigid's Street (Chapel Lane) and Church Lane. As was often typically the case, a discrete use of

Plate 5.7. shows market day in Main Street, Ballinamore, Co. Leitrim, *circa* 1910. Plate 5.8. shows the assembled carts and their country owners in Market Place, Ballinamore, *circa* 1910

space came to be in vogue in conducting the business of the fair. Horses and asses were sold on the face of Cannaboe, following a resolution of 1909 that the horse fair be held there. The sheep, in contrast, were huddled against the 'preaching-house wall' close to the intersection of Main Street-Chapel Lane. Across the street the pig fair and pig market drifted up from the pig green and down to Church Lane corner. Pork and semi-fattened pigs known as 'runners' and in-pig gilts called *céasógs*[69] occupied the footpath from the bridge over the Fohera River to the Church Lane. Young pigs or banbhs were sold from carts with rails further up the street. Overriding all, cattle struck the note of broad ubiquity on Main Street, Cannaboe, Chapel Lane and Church Lane. Upon receipt once of a small legacy, a farmer's stated ambition from out Oughteragh way was 'to blacken the Church Lane with cattle'

The success of the fair was closely related to the number of buyers present, especially those from Northern Ireland. Disporting their familiar identity markers – red boots, cord trousers and cane sticks – these buyers purposefully patrolled the town picking out what they wanted. Bargains were driven with shouts and hand-slapping. The 'tangler' stepped in to split the difference between the price offered and asked, and often split diminishing differences. Tricks were played by the brokers of deals; cattle were sold and re-sold. The shrewd and discerning seller could also act as a buyer of the stock on offer, and with good luck on a good day was able to accumulate a handsome profit. Cattle sold for distant destinations were driven to the railway station at the top of the town, where they were loaded on the rail carriages for transfer to Dromod or Belturbet.

By about mid-day much of the buying and selling was over. On a good fair day business boomed in the town. Best of all was 8th December. The cantmen[70] set up from the bridge in the centre of town downwards on the left, selling secondhand clothes. Entertainment co-mingled with selling. Further down the street the delph-sellers set up their standings and peddled cutlery, ornaments and statues in addition to delph. They also competed with the cantmen for wit and banter. People moved around from delph standing to cant, to stalls selling light hardware, and whether they bought anything or not, they all enjoyed the *craic*. On the opposite side of the street at the bridge the products of local craftsmen stood clustered together for perusal and sale – creels, baskets, bundles of scollops for thatching, bundles of rods, butter tubs, loy-shafts, sléans and breast-spades. Local tinsmiths sold tin gallons, porringers and rattlers for children. Mongers dealt in fish – mostly salt herrings, while the hawkers of apples, oranges and Peggy's leg all joined in the eager quest for custom.

The fair was the social occasion *par excellence* where people met, mingled, and chatted over a drink or a treat. Women exchanged cordial greetings on the street and talked with animation over a cup of coffee in an improvised café or over a half-one of port wine or whiskey in the 'snug' of a public house. In a segmented world it was deemed socially unbecoming for a woman to stand at the counter in a bar or to drink porter. Outside in the open air democratic entertainment prevailed, and an array of side-shows added to the lustre of the day. Street musicians and street singers provided regular entertainment. Sheet music was sold at a penny a go to patrons who fancied themselves as singers. Thus songs and ballads were disseminated through the length and breadth of the country by diffusion from fair to fair. A stunt-man might occasionally perform his contorted rites of magic. The town crier on the other hand furnished an assured presence, ringing his hand-

Plates 5.9. and 5.10. offer views of Fair Day, The Square, Newcastle West, Co. Limerick, at the turn of the nineteenth century, when carts were replete with creels and everyone was apt to slip in the cowdung

bell and asking of all and sundry to 'Take notice! Take notice!', before the announcement of coming events. At the January fair a familiar selling voice would go through its regular routine: 'Almanac! *Old Moore's Almanac!* New Year's Almanac'.[71]

Routinely too, fair day had a court day sequel. As drink flowed flowed old scores, hurts, animosities and vendettas surfaced and for as long as the fairs prevailed, faction and friction were apt to marry. Blows were struck; rows ensued. The next court sitting always brought forth its crop of cases relating to assault, drunkenness and disorder. Feelings ran away with people:[72]

> Politics aroused the deepest and often bitterest emotions in what was a highly politicised society especially in the decade following the Parnell split when factions within the Ribbon society locally led to fighting between the Quinns and McGoverns at Fohera races and the local fairs. From the foundation of the State in 1922 until the 1950s election rallies on fair days in the town produced their own excitement and crop of scuffles. Cumann na nGael (later Fine Gael) held their fair-day election rally outside the northern Bank and Fianna Fáil further down the street outside B.A. Cryan's. Both sides fed their audiences on liberal doses of civil war politics, green nationalism and lavish promises.

A traverse of Main Street, Ballinamore on a fair day was like spanning a political spectrum, to judge from the representative presences emblazoned on colourful shopfronts.

In contrast, the Tuesday market was a much more subdued occasion. Potatoes, oats and hay were sold and weighed in the market house. A butter market lasted until 1930 and a pork market from 1903-31. The market immediately before Christmas was known as 'big market Tuesday'- the day turkeys and geese were sold:[73]

> Down to the early decades of this century [20th], the turkeys were walked to the market, their feet tied in such a way that they could walk but could not fly. It was known as the 'turkey step' ... Later the turkeys were taken to town by cart and on big market Tuesday the row of carts stretched from the Chapel Lane corner to the market house. This was also the day people began to enter into the Christmas spirit, exchanged Christmas greetings and good wishes., bought 'the Christmas things' i.e. a limited range of luxuries (food, clothes, shoes etc.).

The market, which had been struggling in the 1950s, died off in the mid 60s. It was joined by the fair, ailing since the closure of the Cavan & Leitrim Railway in 1959 and succumbing ultimately to the cattle marts of Carrigallen, Mohill and Drumshanbo.

IX

There are no half-measures in the remembrance of the fair. The fairs of my own hometown of Newcastle West, Co. Limerick, for instance, may be summoned up with facility and written about with power:[74]

> With the cow at the centre of affairs, I well remember the town pulsating on fair days, and Mikey 'Yalla' (O'Brien) swinging his tangler's stick with all the aplomb of a magician. Wooden guards lined up in serried rows outside the shops. Within, sawdust was liberally sprinkled. I recall the bustle of voices, of mooing and bleating, competing for ascendancy awake in bed in Church Street, before the faintest flicker of light of a winter's fair morning. And who can ever forget all those involuntary slips in the cowshit on a traverse of the town of a 10th December fair, the biggest of the year?

On a day off from school, it is all seared into the memory.

On that day:[75]

The town acted as a veritable catch-all, taking in the farmer, the jobber, the 'Corkie', the townie, the cute country mug; the broker, the chancer, the cantman, the trader, the 'toucher', the tinker; the man from the mountains with scallops for sale, the countrywoman with eggs, the boy with a rail of banbhs, the docile girl with her mother, and amid the surge of life and the cowshit knotted gatherings assembled and broke, money changed hands, bills got paid, and shopkeepers and publicans waxed rich for the day.

Such were the crowds at the biggest fairs that a newly appointed gárda coming off the Limerick-Tralee train once felt obliged to go around the back way to the barrack in the Square. Now only the Saturday market limps on in the Square of Newcastle. All the rest is lost to the rational capitalist order of another world – livestock fairs, hiring fairs, calf markets, butter markets, hay markets, turf markets and general Thursday markets.

CHAPTER SIX

Ends

From the 1850s onwards, the distribution of fairs and markets underwent contraction, as the newer, leaner bourgeois-led Ireland marched to the ruthless thrust of modernisation. The coming of the railways and later of motorised transport made a virtue of nodality, and heavily favoured the higher order urban centres. Concurrent with these developments, the improvement of shopping and banking facilities helped the concentrate fairs in the larger towns. Another significant factor which militated against smaller centres and countryside locations was the power granted to local authorities in 1872 to regulate fairs.[1] This too helped to increase the frequency of urban fairs, while accelerating the rate of loss elsewhere. Greater specialisation became evident in the most prestigious centres, with monthly pig fairs interspersed among general livestock fairs. Still a widespread pattern of fairs and markets prevailed throughout the island until the 1950s. Then in the 60s the demise of the fair was short, sharp and nearly ubiquitous, as the livestock marts rationalised and revolutionised the buying and selling of livestock. With straightforward efficiency, their auction format swept away the casualness, charm and glorious unpredictability of the fair.

I

In putting the contraction of livestock fair locations to the test, it is instructive to start with prevailing patterns in 1850 and 1900. Fortunately for the purposes of exemplification, Co. Limerick provides a ready-made test case,[2] and among its towns and villages we may note 1) a marked diminution in the overall number of locations and 2) a considerable re-focusing on to favoured centres of frequency. Fig. 6.1. shows a well strung out distribution pattern in 1850. It features a core of relatively high frequency through mid county at Dromcolliher, Newcastle, Rathkeale, Adare and Patrickswell, an intimate net in the east where small urban centres formed the central places set amid rich farmland, and conspicuous gaps in the west which reflected both the paucity of villages and the west to east movement of livestock. Even in the case of small villages the significance of fair day should not be underestimated. At Kilteely in east Limerick, for example, thrice-yearly fairs drew large numbers of victuallers from Co. Cork and from the various towns of Co. Limerick, and sufficient transactional activity was generated for the proceedings to last two days at a time.[3] The benefits were proportionately all the greater for the larger centres, among which Rathkeale, Newcastle, Adare and Dromcolliher boasted the highest frequency and the best attendances.

By 1900 the pattern of livestock fairs in the county had been radically re-cast (fig. 6.2.). The number of fairs remained static, but the number of centres at which these were held had been reduced from 42 to 24. Moreover, in accordance with the rapid progress of

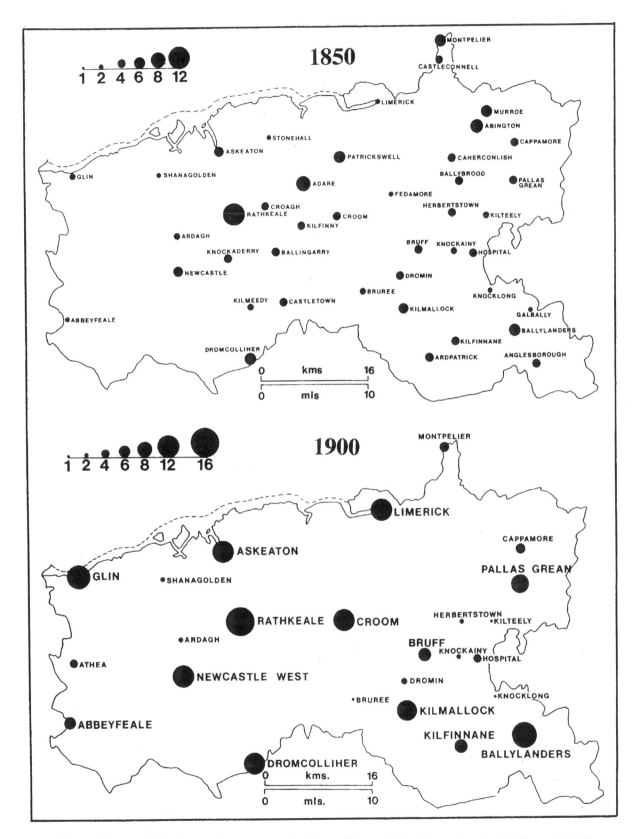

Figs. 6.1. and 6.2. show the town and village fairs of Co. Limerick in 1850 and 1900 respectively. Although the number of fairs remained static, the pattern had been radically re-cast by 1900

modernisation there was a marked re-focusing of rural centrality on to larger urban centres. In fifty years the broad dispersion of fair settings had yielded to a pattern of clear concentration. At one end of the spectrum the tiny village of Kilteely shrank to embrace only one fair in the year; at the other the town of Rathkeale graduated from 12 to 16 yearly fairs. Most outstandingly the major host towns of fairs exemplify well the theory of modern central places within the bounded setting of a county. By 1900 nodality and railhead location helped to give a crisper stamp to the pattern of fairs. Correspondingly, transactional activity burgeoned in the most progressive towns, and Newcastle West, for instance, which had risen to premier status among the towns of the county, saw over 90 wagons of cattle and sheep departing its railway station on August fair day 1916.[4]

II

Looking to the wider island setting, we may note a diminution in fair locations from 1297 in 1852-3 to 755 in 1950. This represents a reduction of 42 per cent, and while appreciable, the network of active fair locations still possessed a measure of resilience in 1950 (fig 6.3.). The big counties led out in their bold assemblages of venues, headed by Galway with 61. It was followed by Cork (58), Donegal (46), Mayo (45), Antrim (42), and Clare (39). In western Ireland the only conspicuous laggard was Kerry (27), which had undergone much re-location since 1850, but only a small net loss. Away from unproductive stretches, the pattern of fairs bore the stamp of broad ubiquity, with the exception of Cos. Waterford and Dublin, and an aureole around the latter.

To underscore the centralising trend already apparent at county level, 375 of the 755 venues countrywide hosted a full suite of monthly fairs (or more!) in 1950. The old Ulster hearthland in which monthly fairs had found earliest expression still commanded primacy for patterned frequency. In country where cattle and livestock rearing dominated the tempo of rural life, monthly fairs found best expression in Monaghan (7 out 8 locations), Armagh (11 out of 13), Derry (14 out of 17) and Tyrone (22 out of 27). The other counties to score heavily in this respect included Louth (9 out of 9), Leitrim (13 out of 16), Wexford (15 out of 21), Donegal (31 out of 46), Kildare (10 out of 15), Cork (an estimable 37 out of 58), and Down (15 out of 26). Individual towns too stamped a muscular profile for trade and the frequency of their fairs. Seven towns boasted of more than 30 fair days in the year: Ennis, Co. Clare; Charleville and Kanturk, Co. Cork; Newcastle West, Co. Limerick; Nenagh and Ballyporeen Co. Tipperary; and Castlerea, Co. Roscommon. A further 50 towns were able to claim yearly complements of 20 days or more, so that the counting pattern was a pattern of concentration among an aggregate of 7,384 fair days in the Ireland of 1950.[6]

Not that the old pattern of outright dispersion was dead. Indeed it still staked a place in the calendar and helped to draw a trading clientele to places of long favoured resort. Such would include the June and August fairs of Spancil Hill, Co. Clare; the July fair of Cahirmee and the September fair of Bartlemy, Co. Cork; the October fair of Croghan, Co. Roscommon; the May fair of Kilmainham Wood, Co. Meath; the June fair of Oldstone, Co. Antrim; the August fair of Muff, Co. Cavan, and the December fair of Rashedagh, Co. Donegal. Events at long deserted manorial centres still entered the calendar of

134

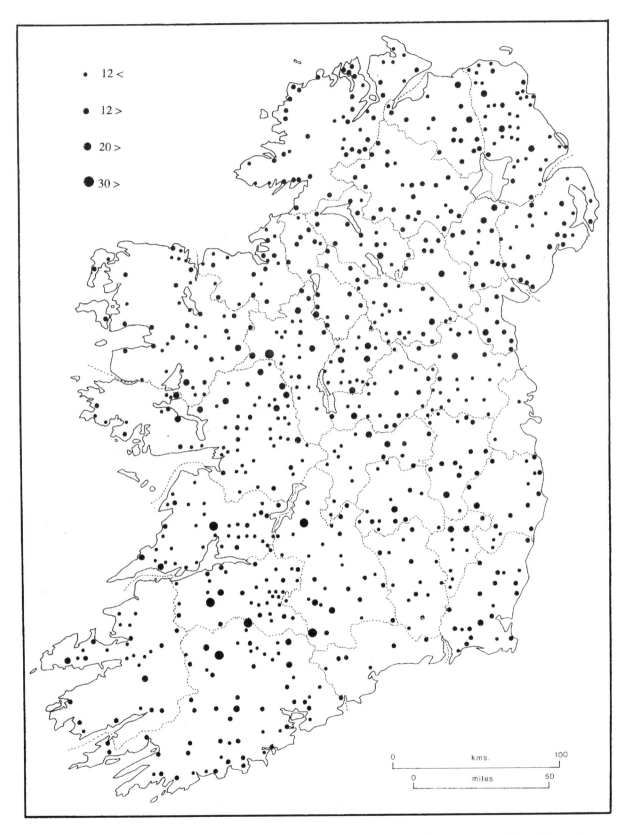

Fig. 6.3. The network of active fair locations still possessed a measure of resilience in 1950. According to *Old Moore's Almanac*, fig. 6.3. represented an aggregate of 7,384 fair days. The same source lists only 35 fair days for the year 2003

persistence, such as the May fairs of Glenogra, Co. Limerick, and Empor, Co. Westmeath. Neither were the hiring fairs altogether dead. The hiring fair in Antrim town in May remained a going concern, as did the May and November hiring fairs of Limavady, Co. Derry.

And yet within twenty years nearly everything represented on fig. 6.3. had succumbed to an order of formalised rationality. In the expansive decade of the 60s innovation swept the land; the past was consigned to another country.[7] The buying and selling of livestock was transformed. Individual bargaining between buyer and seller at fair ceded to an auction format at livestock mart. Once a seller was satisfied, each consignment of livestock was sold to the highest bidder. Moreover, open competition among prospective buyers offered the prospect of better prices for producers. Other factors exercised their own compelling force. The rail network contacted markedly; a motorised order claimed rapid ascendance. Car numbers doubled in the 60s, posing incongruity in streets of cattle mired by dung, and throbbing with the business of the fair. Dedicated space was sought at the town's edge where efficiency would rule and lorries could load and unload their cargoes with ease. The mart offered more comfortable conditions, protection from the weather, less disruption of traffic, and cleaner streets. Almost by stealth it appropriated the business of the fair,[8] and by 1970 the vast bulk of the 200 or so marts in Ireland proclaimed a fresh state of mind made concrete in the land.

Nowadays *Old Moore's Almanac* continues to advertise the fairs and marts of Ireland. The latter exercise the controlling influence. In contrast, only a small number of old style fairs are held, while others have continued as pleasure fairs. There are but 35 days of advertised fairs for the year 2003.[9] Go west for the preponderance, to Cos. Galway and Mayo. In Co. Galway, the renowned fair of Ballinasloe extends over no less than nine October days, while Leenane hosts three separate fairs for sheep and rams, Kilconnell hosts two for sheep, and Maam Cross and Turloghmore hold one each for horses. Co. Mayo furnishes the venues of Tourmakeady, Aughagower and Cuslogh for sheep, Westport for horses, and Newport for rams. Elsewhere the horse fairs of Listowel, Ballaghaderreen, Tullow, and Bartlemy, Co. Cork, all command patronage, and the last, in particular, is celebrated for drawing horses from 'everywhere'.[10] The Puck Fair of Killorglin promises pleasure as well as dealing in horses and cattle on successive days in August. Then ouside the remit of *Old Moore*, a small number of other fairs continue, including that northern setting for seasonal saturnalia – the Ould Lammas Fair of Ballycastle.

III

I remember the time well when the fairs had been swept clean off the face of most of Ireland. It was 1968, and over an immense catchment in Munster the only continuing fairs in the old style were those of Catlegregory and Dingle in the peninsular barony of *Corca Dhuibhne*, Co. Kerry. Fieldwork was my pretext, and to that end I inveigled my neighbour, the cattledealer, Lukie Doherty, to take me with him to the fair of Castle-gregory. It was the morning of 14th September, when we set out in the half-light aboard his truck, in the company of John Coleman, tangler. Coleman was then an inseparable companion of the dealer, as they plied a livelihood in cattle. They complemented each other. The one was pipe-smoking and laconic; the other instinct with energy. Steering with his elbows, our driver prepared his pipe in fastidious style, lit up, and filled the air with the aroma of his tobacco.

On the road to Castlegregory there were just a few clumps of cattle, each with a drover and a dog in attendance. Still sharpness was the order of the day, as my companions spotted the prospective seller of a lone tethered animal. They stopped to offer a lift to man and beast, with a view to brokering an early deal. Loading followed without a hitch. The owner then joined us in the cab. Once aboard, the deal went through with remarkable facility, considering that the seller claimed he was hard at hearing. A little later our man picked up the thread of conversation, only to draw an instant riposte from Coleman. 'I thought you were deaf, you fucker!,' he chided humorously.

It was a very small fair, and late getting under way. Mostly, it was young cattle for sale. The tangler stepped in with his stock of well-worn phrases: 'accept my ruling', 'divide a fiver', 'don't break my word', etc. Dealers were present from Tralee, Newcastle West, and Coen from Roscommon was 'as well known in Castlegregory as at home'. Taking no chances with a small fair day clientele, the three pubs of Castlegregory were presenting for business from about 8 o'clock. An early breakfast was had. Out-of-doors the dealing proved brisk, if lacklustre. Bullocks of 1-2 years mainly changed hands with the aid of a little tangling, and by 11 a.m. all transactions were over. We returned with a lorry load of cattle. There was talk of Castlegregory onions. 'No one wanted them', my companions averred; 'they were half-rotten and very badly saved.'

A week later we all set off again for the fair of Dingle. We took off in the dark of an early morning and passed droves of cattle destined for the fair from the Anascaul side at around 6.30-6.45 a.m. These were interspersed with ones and twos, and most often a solitary cow tethered by a rope. Lone cows found ready sale without reaching fair. Local particularity prevailed. The September fair in Dingle acted in lieu of an October one: 'Dingle was a month ahead', my companions said, to facilitate the sale of stock before winter. We made straight for the Fair Green – a rectilinear field, stone-walled and stolid off the Green Street of Dingle. Alongside a similar field kept sheep overnight, awaiting their separate morning fair at the bottom of Main Street. Fair Green was the preserve of cattle. It was a big fair, but there had been bigger. Business was brisk and almost complete by 10 a.m. From a welter of engagement, three bullocks of about 8 cwt. fetched £17 apiece. Doherty and Coleman gathered a lorry load of cattle, and checked with assiduity documentation and tagging.

Over breakfast cattle droves were recalled. During the Civil War, for instance, no trains ran for a time, and the long trek from Dingle to Abbeyfeale, Co. Limerick, was given an airing over the high road from Tralee to Knocknagoshel. Lukie Doherty too had his story as neophyte dealer at the fair of Dingle for being sent over the Conair Pass (1,354 feet O.D.) as short-cut, laden with a full consignment of cattle. As between the negotiation of corkscrews and switchbacks, not a single beast was standing by the time the road had straightened out, and Doherty accounted himself blessed that he did not lose a solitary animal, never mind the lot of them. The time he spent righting them would have taken him home by another route. He never went that crazy way again.

Then chatting to his fellow dealers, the business of the day was the grist of conversation. Good humour and banter abounded. There was talk of numbers bought and finishes achieved.[11] A question put by my neighbour to a ruddy-faced fellow was of the stuff of insiders. 'What did you finish that black polly cow at?' Once full of meaning, the answer is now immaterial. The past is a foreign country; they do things differently at the fairs and markets there.

Notes and References

CHAPTER 1

1. P.J. O'Connor, 'Markets and fairs in the eighteenth and nineteenth centuries', in J.S. Donnelly, Jr., et al. (eds.), *Encyclopaedia of Ireland*, Dublin and New York, 2003, no. 226.

2. D. A. Binchy, 'The passing of the old order', in B. Ó Cuív (ed.), *Proceedings of the International Congress of Celtic Studies*, Dublin, 1962, 122.

3. Tailtiu is the nominative form and Tailten the genitive.

4. D.A. Binchy, 'The fair of Tailtiu and the feast of Tara', *Ériu* 17, 1958, 113-38.

5. M. MacNeill, *The festival of Lughnasa*, Oxford, 1962, 328.

6. J.D. White, *Cashel of the kings*, Dublin, 1863, 5.

7. M. MacNeill, *op. cit.*, 1962, 305.

8. *Ibid.*, 339-40.

9. E.Gwynn, *The metrical dinnshenchas* (Royal Irish Academy, Todd Lecture Series X), Part III, 1913, 2-25.

10. M. MacNeill, 1962, *op. cit.*, 305-10.

11. S. MacGabhann, 'Landmarks of the people: Meath and Cavan places prominent in Lughnasa mythology and folklore', *Ríocht na Midhe*, 11, 2000, 223.

12. M. MacNeill, 1962, *op. cit.*, 306.

13. *Ibid.*, 348-9.

14. J. Gleeson. *History of the Ely O'Carroll territory of ancient Ormond*, Dublin, 1915, 98.

15. D. Ó Corráin, *Ireland before the Normans*, Dublin, 1972, 72.

16. K. Hughes, *The Church in early Irish society*, London, 1966, 167.

17. C. Doherty, 'Exchange and trade in early medieval Ireland', *Journal of the Royal Society of Antiquaries of Ireland* 110, 1980, 81.

18. *Ibid.*, 81.

19. *Ibid.*, 80; Ó Corráin, 1972, *op. cit*, 106.

20. This term is related to *sesra* from Latin *sexarius*: a measure of both fluids and corn, being about a pint and a half, but varying in magnitude according to time and place.

21. R.H.M. Dolley, *The Hiberno-Norse coins in the British Museum*, London, 1966, 119-41.

22. C. Doherty, 1980, *op. cit.*, 83.

23. C. Plummer (ed.), *Bethada Náem nÉrann*, 2 vols, Oxford, 1922, I, 144-5; II, 140-1.

24. M. Comber, 'Trade and communication networks in early historic Ireland', *Journal of Irish Archaeology* 10, 2001, 82.

CHAPTER 2

1. J.F. Lydon, *The lordship of Ireland in the Middle Ages*, Dublin, 1972, 90.

2. C. Dyer, 'Small places with large consequences: the importance of small towns in England, 1000-1540', *Historical Research* 75, 2002, 5-6.

3. K. Holton, 'From charters to carters: aspects of fairs and markets in medieval Leinster', in D.A. Cronin et al. (eds.), *Irish fairs and markets: studies in local history*, Dublin, 2001, 20, 43.

4. H.S. Sweetman (ed.), *Calendar of documents relating to Ireland* II, London, 1875-86, no. 672. Hereafter abbreviated as *Cal. Docs. Ire.*

5. J. T. Gilbert (ed.), *Historical and municipal documents of Ireland*, London, 1870, 61.

6. This may have been the fair held initially near the Hospital of St. John at the New Gate, Dublin, and was possibly continued at St. John's Well near Kilmainham in the form of a mid-summer festival until suppressed in 1834.

7. K. Holton, 2001, *op. cit.*, 20.

8. P.J. O'Connor, *Exploring Limerick's past: an historical geography of urban development in county and city*, Newcastle West, 1987, 15.

9. B.J. Graham, *Anglo-Norman settlement in Ireland*, Athlone, 1985, 28.

10. This, in effect, was a charter of incorporation, which conferred a significant measure of urban autonomy in terms of market, marketplace and the law within the feudal regime.

11. P. Aries, *The hour of our death*, trans. H. Weaver, London, 1981, 62.

12. S. Leigh Fry, *Burial in medieval Ireland, 900-1500*, Dublin, 1999, 48.

13. K. Holton, 2001, *op. cit.*, 22.

14. J. Bradley, 'The medieval boroughs of county Dublin', in C. Manning (ed.), *Dublin and beyond the pale*, Dublin, 1998, 138.

15. P. Logan, *Fair day: the story of Irish fairs and markets*, Belfast, 1986, 15.

16. *Ibid.*, 31.

17. K. Holton, 2001, *op. cit.*, 24.

18. *Cal. Docs. Ire., 1171-1252*, no.1401.

19. *Ibid.*, no. 2182.

20. *Ibid.*, nos. 2170, 2183.

21. A.F. O'Brien, 'Politics, economy and society: the development of Cork and the Irish south coast region *c.* 1170 to *c.* 1583', in P. O'Flanagan and C.G. Buttimer (eds.), *Cork: history and society*, Dublin, 1993, 93.

22. *Cal. Docs. Ire., 1171-1252*, no. 1429.

23. P. Logan, 1986, *op. cit.*, 32-3.

24. B.J. Graham, 'The towns of medieval Ireland', in R.A. Butlin (ed.), *The development of the Irish town*, London, 1977, 45.

25. H.P. Hore, *History of New Ross*, London, 1900, 115.

26. *Ibid.*, 160.

27. *Cal. Jus. Rolls*, ii, 348.

28. *Cal. Docs. Ire., 1285-92*, 109.

29. A. Thomas, 'Financing town walls', in C. Thomas (ed.), *Rural landscapes and communities*, Dublin, 1987, 72-4.

30. J. Bradley, 'The topography and layout of medieval Drogheda', *Journal of the Louth Archaeological and Historical Society* 19, 2, 1978, 118.

31. R.E. Glasscock, 'Land and people *c.* 1300' in A. Cosgrove (ed.), *A new history of Ireland II: medieval Ireland 1169-1534*, Oxford, 1987, 238.

32. M.D. O'Sullivan, *Italian merchant bankers in Ireland in the thirteenth century*, Dublin, 1962, 102.

33. *Cal. Jus. Rolls*, ii, 498.

34. *Ibid.*, 507.

35. K. Holton, 2001, *op. cit.*, 30.

36. T. O'Neill, *Merchants and mariners in medieval Ireland*, Dublin, 1987, 75.

37. *Ibid.*, 75.

38. National Library of Ireland, MS 2689, no.12.

39. J.F. Lydon, 1972, *op. cit.*, 90.

40. K. Holton, 2001, *op. cit.*, 31.

41. T. O'Neill, 1987, *op. cit.*, 61.

42. J.F. Lydon, 1972, *op. cit.*, 90.

43. H. Shields (ed.), 'The walling of New Ross: a thirteenth century poem in French', *Long Room* xii-xiii, 1975-6, 24-33.

44. B. Colfer, *Arrogant trespass: Anglo-Norman Wexford 1169-1400*, Enniscorthy, 2002, 171.

45. C. Dyer, 'Market towns and the countryside in late medieval England', *Canadian Journal of History* 31, 1996, 17-35.

46. *Cal. justic. rolls Ire., 1295-1303*, 265.

47. H.P. Hore, 1900, *op. cit.*, 214, 113.

48. *Cal. Jus. Rolls*, ii, 502.

49. *Ibid.*, iii, 461.

50. *Ibid.*, ii, 502.

51. *Ibid.*, 498.

52. *Ibid.*, 198.

53. *Liber Primus Kilkenniensis*, trans. A J. Otway-Ruthven, Kilkenny, 1961, 36.

54. *Statutes and ordinances and acts of Parliament of Ireland: King John to Henry V*, (ed.), Henry F. Berry, Dublin, 1907, 256.

55. J. Lydon, *Ireland in the later middle ages*, Dublin, 1973, iii.

56. H.P. Hore, 1900, *op. cit.*, 217.

57. *Statute rolls Ire., Henry VI*, (ed.), Henry F. Berry, Dublin, 1910, 43.

58. *Statute rolls Ire., 12 – 22 Edw. IV*, (ed.), J.F. Morrissey, Dublin, 1939, 818-21.

59. K. Nicholls, 'Gaelic society and economy in the high middle ages', in A. Cosgrove (ed.), 1987, *op. cit.*, 420.

60. Cited in P. Logan, 1986, *op. cit.*, 40.

61. *Sir Henry Sidney's memoir of service in Ireland 1556-78*, (ed.), C. Brady, Cork, 2002, 62-3.

62. *Ibid.*, 60.

63. M. MacCurtain, 'The fall of the house of Desmond', *Journal of the Kerry Archaeological and Historical Society* 8, 1975, 29.

64. *Extracts from the Desmond survey 1584-6*, M. 5038, 28, National Library of Ireland.

65. J.H. Andrews, 'Geography and government in Elizabethan Ireland', in N. Stephens and R.E. Glasscock (eds.), *Irish geographical studies*, Belfast, 1970, 178-91.

66. Most of the data in this section is based on *Report of the commissioners appointed to inquire into the state of the fairs and markets in Ireland*, Parliamentary Papers XLI, 1852-3, 48-149.

67. C. Gleeson, 'Carlingford', in A. Simms and J.H. Andrews (eds.), *More Irish country towns*, Dublin, 1995, 38-9.

68. P.J. O'Connor, *Atlas of Irish place-names*, Newcastle West, 2001, 148-9.

69. Fairs and markets report, 1853, *op. cit.*, 102.

70. The respective locations were Newcastle M'Cormicheap and Drumcormuck.

71. Fairs and markets report, 1853, *op. cit.*, 147.

72. K. Whelan, 'Enniscorthy', in A. Simms and J.H. Andrews (eds.), *Irish country towns*, Dublin, 1994, 73.

CHAPTER 3

1. D.W. Meinig, 'Geographical analysis of imperial expansion', in A.R.H. Baker and M. Billinge (eds.), *Period and place: research methods in historical geography*, Cambridge, 1982, 71.
2. L.M. Cullen, *The emergence of modern Ireland*, London, 1981, 25.
3. P.J. O'Connor, 'Markets and fairs in the eighteenth and nineteenth centuries', in J.S. Donnelly, Jr., et al. (eds.), *Encyclopaedia of Ireland*, Dublin and New York, 2003, no. 226.
4. *Report of the commissioners appointed to enquire into the state of fairs and markets in Ireland*, Parliamentary Papers XLI, 1852-3.
5. The procedure for acquiring a patent (in effect a long-term lease) for either a market or fair, or both, was as follows: The appellant(s) (of which the vast majority were landowners) made an application to the Lord Lieutenant stating the desired location for the market and/or fair, and the proposed day(s). Then the Lord Lieutenant referred such an application to the Attorney General for a report. Following this, the Lord Lieutenant issued a *fiant* for the granting of *letters patent*. Finally, it reached the office of the Great Seal to whom fell the last task of issuing the patent. The entire procedure was lengthy, bureaucratic, and expensive.
6. P. O'Flanagan, 'Markets and fairs in Ireland, 1600-1800: index of economic development and regional growth' *Journal of Historical Geography* 11, 4, 1985, 364-78.
7. *Calendar of the Irish patent rolls of James I*, Irish Manuscripts Commission, Dublin, 1966, x, 101.
8. *Ibid.*, xxxvi, 133.
9. *Ibid.*, lxiv, 155.
10. *Ibid.*, lxv, 161.
11. *Ibid.*, iv, 217.
12. *Ibid.*, xxx, 360.
13. L.M. Cullen, 1981, *op. cit.*, 61-8.
14. C. Coote, *General view of the agriculture and manufactures of the King's county*, Dublin, 1801, 138.
15. R. Gillespie, 'The transformation of the borderlands, 1600-1700', in R. Gillespie and H. O'Sullivan (eds.), *The borderlands: essays on the history of the Ulster-Leinster border*, Belfast, 1989, 83.
16. *Cal. Pat. Rolls Ire., James 1*, xlvi, 269.
17. R. Gillespie, 'The origins and development of an Ulster urban network, 1600-41', *Irish Historical Studies* 24, 1984, 18.
18. *Ibid.*, 19.
19. P. Robinson, 'British settlement in county Tyrone 1610-1666', *Irish Economic and Social History* 5, 1978, 10.
20. A. Clarke, 'The Irish economy, 1600-60', in T.W. Moody et al. (eds.). *A new history of Ireland III: early modern Ireland 1534-1691*, Oxford, 1978, 176.
21. *Cal. pat. Rolls Ire., Chas I*, ed., J. Morrin, Dublin, 1861-3, 452.
22. W.H. Crawford, 'The evolution of the urban network', in W. Nolan et al. (eds.), *Donegal: history and society*, Dublin, 1995, 383-4.

23. R.J. Hunter, 'Ulster plantation towns 1609-41', in D. Harkness and M. O'Dowd (eds.), *The town in Ireland*, Belfast, 1981, 55-80.

24. R. Gillespie, 'The O'Farrells and Longford in the seventeenth century', in R. Gillespie and G. Moran (eds.), *Longford: essays in county history*, Dublin, 1991, 18-19.

25. R. Gillespie, 'The small towns of Ulster, 1600-1700', *Ulster Folklife* 36, 1990, 18-26.

26. K. Whelan, 'Enniscorthy', in J.H. Andrews and A. Simms (eds.), *Irish country towns*, Dublin, 1994, 74.

27. *Ibid.*, 75.

28. *Cal. Docs. Ire., 1171-1252*, no. 1429.

29. Taking the entire aggregate for Co. Cork 1600-1650, it is asserted that more than 90 per cent of the patents confirmed were allocated to New English claimants. See P.O'Flanagan, ' Three-hundred years of urban life: villages and towns in county Cork *c.* 1600 to 1901', in P. O'Flanagan and C.G. Buttimer (eds.), *Cork; history and society*, Dublin, 1993, 401.

30. The fairs enjoyed long-term success in all locations. Only the markets of Moate and Finea survived until 1852-3.

31. B. Ó Dálaigh, 'The origins, rise and decline of the Ennis fairs and markets', in D.A. Cronin et al. (eds.), *Irish fairs and markets: studies in local history*, Dublin, 2001, 46-7.

32. W. Gacquin, 'A household account from county Roscommon, 1733-4', in *ibid.*, 112.

33. E. MacLysaght, *The surnames of Ireland*, Dublin, 1973, 122.

34. B. Ó Dálaigh, 2001, *op. cit.*, 48-9.

35. R.J. Hunter, 'Towns in the Ulster plantation', *Studia Hibernica* 6, 1971, 73-5

36. This was Dino Massari, dean of Ferno and secretary to the papal nuncio. For a record of his time in Cavan, see *Catholic Bulletin* 7, 1917, 112-14, 179-82 and 246-50.

37. R. Gillespie, 1984, *op. cit.*, 21.

38. *Cal. Pat. Rolls Ire., James 1*, iv, 477-9.

39. S. Lewis, *A topographical dictionary of Ireland*, London, 1837, s.v. Elphin, Co. Roscommon.

40. P. Logan, *Fair day: the story of Irish fairs and markets*, Belfast, 1986, 35.

41. D. Dickson, *New foundations: Ireland 1660-1800*, Dublin, 1987, 97.

42. I.D. Whyte, 'The growth of periodic markets in Scotland 1600-1707', *Scottish Geographical Magazine* 95, 1979, 13-26.

43. Examples of the three and four mile market area were given clear attestation in patent confirmations pertaining to the plantation of Ulster. See, *Cal. Pat. Rolls Ire., James 1*, v, 232 and *Cal. Pat. Rolls Ire., James 1*, iv, 217.

44. P. Muldoon, *Poems 1968-1998*, London, 2001, 10-11.

45. S. Lewis, 1837, *op. cit.*, s.v. Ballinahinch, Co. Down.

46. A. Rowan, *The buildings of Ireland: north west Ulster*, Harmondsworth, 1979, 433.

47. P.J. O'Connor, *Atlas of Irish place-names*, Newcastle West, 2001, 116-7.

48. P. Kavanagh, *The green fool*, Harmondsworth, 1975, 156.

49. T.C. Barnard, 'The political, material and mental culture of the Cork settlers, *c.* 1650-1700', in P. O'Flanagan and C.G. Buttimer (eds.), 1993, *op. cit.*, 337.

50. D. Dickson, 1987, *op. cit.*, 102.

51. T.C. Barnard, 'The worlds of a Galway squire: Robert French of Monivea, 1716-79', in G. Moran and R. Gillespie (eds.), *Galway: history and society*, Dublin, 1996, 275.

52. P. Cassidy, 'The markets and fairs of Cootehill, county Cavan', in D.A. Cronin et al. (eds.), 2001, *op. cit.*, 77.

53. Armagh Public Library, 'An account of Cootehill in 1740 by Revd. Dean Richardson' *Lodge MSS*, 1.

54. P. Cassidy, 2001, *op. cit.*, 79.

55. S. Lewis, 1837, *op. cit.*, s.v. Saintfield, Co. Down.

56. Ulster Architectural Heritage Society, *Historic buildings in the towns and villages of mid Down*, prepared by C.E. B. Brett, 1974, 48, 51.

57. P. O'Flanagan, 1993, *op. cit.*, 423.

58. *Ibid.*, 420.

59. P.J.O'Connor, *Hometown: a portrait of Newcastle West, Co. Limerick*, Newcastle West, 1998, 66-7.

60. D. Dickson, 'An economic history of the Cork region in the eighteenth century', unpublished Ph.D. thesis, T.C.D., 1977, 321, 373.

61. P.J. O'Connor, 1998, *op. cit.*, 62-3.

62. The fairs of Ballinasloe have existed immemorially. However, no patent for holding them appears on record before 8th June, 1757, when Richard Trench of Garbally, obtained a patent for holding two fairs annually, on 15th May and 15th July. This earlier patent appears to have been overlooked by the *Fairs and Market Commission* of 1852-3, which assigns a patent only in 1841. See, J. Hardiman, *The history of the town and county of the town of Galway*, Dublin, 1820, 287.

63. W. Crawford, 'The political economy of linen: Ulster in the eighteenth century', in C. Brady et al. (eds.), *Ulster: an illustrated history*, London, 1989, 134-57.

64. D.W. Miller, *Peep O'Day Boys and Defenders: selected documents on the county Armagh disturbances 1784-96*, Belfast, 1990, 46.

65. J.H. Andrews, 'Road planning in Ireland before the railway age', *Irish Geography* 5, 1, 1964, 32-4.

66. D. Dickson, 1987, *op. cit.*, 97.

67. 'The narrative of Captain George O'Malley', cited in L.M. Cullen, *An economic history of Ireland since 1660*, London, 1976, 81.

68. L.M. Cullen, *Irish towns and villages*, Dublin, 1979, no. 15.

69. S. Lewis, 1837, *op. cit.*, s.v. Banbridge, Co. Down.

70. K. Whelan, 'Towns and villages' in F.H.A. Aalen et al. (eds.), *Atlas of the Irish rural landscape*, Cork, 1997, 189.

71. P.J. O'Connor, 1998, *op. cit.*, 66.

72. P.J. O'Connor, *People, power, place*, Newcastle West, 2001, 24-5.

73. D.A. Cronin, 'The great Munster horse-fair of Cahirmee, county Cork' in D.A. Cronin et al. (eds.), 2001, *op. cit.*, 125.

74. P.J. O'Connor, *People make places; the story of the Irish Palatines*, Newcastle West, 1996, 59-65.

75. T.P. Power, *Land, politics, and society in eighteenth-century Tipperary*, Oxford, 1993, 35.

76. W. Crawford, 'Development of the county Mayo economy, 1700-1850', in R. Gillespie and G. Moran (eds.), *A various county: essays in Mayo history*,

Westport, 1987, 71; K. Harvey, 'Landlords and land usage in eighteenth century Galway' in G. Moran and R. Gillespie (eds.), 1996, *op. cit.*, 302-4.

77. P.J. O'Connor, 1996, *op. cit.*, 168.

78. W.H. Crawford, in W. Nolan et al. (eds.), 1995, *op. cit.*, 393.

79. *Post-chaise companion*, Dublin, 1786, 79.

80. L.M. Cullen, 1976, *op. cit.*, 101-22.

81. *Ordnance Survey Memoirs*, XXI, 65.

82. J. Healy, *The death of an Irish town*, 1968, 11-16.

83. *Sir Vere Hunt's diary 1811-1818*, Limerick City Library.

84. T. Jones Hughes, 'Landlordism in the Mullet of Mayo', *Irish Geography*, 4, 1, 1959, 23-4.

CHAPTER 4

1. T.W. Freeman, *Ireland: a general and regional geography*, London, 1960, 129.

2. J.H. Andrews, *A paper landscape: the Ordnance Survey in nineteenth-century Ireland*, (Oxford, 1975), Dublin, 2002.

3. Ordnance Survey Name Books, compiled 1827-35: original MSS, Ordnance Survey Office/ Library of the Royal Irish Academy, Dublin; Ordnance Survey Memoirs, compiled 1830-40, edited by A. Day and P. McWilliams and published in 40 volumes by the Institute of Irish Studies, Queen's University, Belfast, in association with the Royal Irish Academy, 1990-98.

4. *Report of the commissioners appointed to inquire into the state of the fairs and markets in Ireland*, Parliamentary Papers XLI, 1852-3, 4.

5. D. Dickson, *New foundations: Ireland 1660-1800*, Dublin, 1987, 97.

6. L.M. Cullen, *The emergence of modern Ireland 1600-1900*, London, 1981, 74.

7. *Ordnance Survey Memoirs* IV, 65. As to the measures, a puncheon is a large cask; a hank is a coil of yarn; and a gauge of turf is a car load. The linen on sale was the same as that in Enniskillen, i.e., a coarse kind of cloth fetching 8d. to 1s. per yard.

8. *Ibid.*, XIV, 79.

9. B. Friel, *Translations*, London, 1981.

10. W.E. Vaughan and A.J. Fitzpatrick (eds.), *Irish historical statistics: population 1821-1971. A new history of Ireland: ancillary publications II*, Dublin, 1978, 5-15.

11. L. Clarke, 'The rise and demise of the Dublin cattle market, 1863-1973', in D.A. Cronin et al. (eds.), *Irish fairs and markets: studies in local history*, Dublin, 2001, 180-1.

12. Thackeray, W.M., *The Irish sketch-book of 1842*, London, 1843, 96.

13. *Ibid.*, 122.

14. *Ibid.*, 329.

15. *Ordnance Survey Memoirs* XXXIII, 119.

16. *Ibid.*, 61.

17. L. Kennedy, 'The rural economy, 1829-1914', in L. Kennedy and P. Ollerenshaw (eds.), *An economic history of Ulster, 1820-1940*, Manchester, 1985, 5.

18. *Ordnance Survey Memoirs* VIII, 71.

19. A heifer is a young cow that has not had calf. A springer is a heifer, in-calf for the first time. A stripper is a cow, which fails to be put in-calf, and therefore yields little milk. 'That stripper will have to go the next fair day' was a

common prescript. See, T.P. Dolan, *A dictionary of Hiberno-English*, Dublin, 1999, 260.

20. These are hornless heifers or cows, adept in rock outcrop country at eating the grass between the rocks. See, *ibid.*, 179.

21. S. Lewis, *A topographical dictionary of Ireland*, London, 1837, s.v. Lurgan, Co. Armagh.

22. *Ibid.*, s.v. Tanderagee, Co. Armagh.

23. W.H. Crawford, *Domestic industry in Ireland – the experience of the linen industry*, Dublin, 1972, appendix.

24. S. Lewis, 1837, *op. cit.*, 1837, s.v. Bandon, Mallow, and Macroom.

25. W. Christaller, *Die zentralen orte in Suddeutschland*, Jena, 1933.

26. S. Lewis, 1837, *op. cit.*, s.v. Kenmare.

27. *Cín lae Amhlaoibh*, T. de Bhaldraithe (ed.), Baile Átha Cliath, 1970.

28. S. Lewis, 1837, *op. cit.*, s.v. Cloncare parish and Kiltyclogher.

29. *Ibid.*, s.v. Lanesborough, Co. Longford.

30. *Ibid.*, s.v. Strokestown, Boyle and Roscommon.

31. J.S. Donnelly Jr., 'Cork market: its role in the nineteenth century Irish butter trade', *Studia Hibernica* 11, 1971, 130.

32. *Ibid.*, 133; *Fairs and markets commission, op. cit.*, 1852-3, 27.

33. D. Dickson, 'Butter comes to market: the origins of commercial dairying in county Cork', in P. O'Flanagan and C.G. Buttimer (eds.), *Cork: history and society*, Dublin, 1993, 371.

34. J.S. Donnelly Jr., *op. cit.*, 1971, 133.

35. C. Rynne, *At the sign of the cow: the Cork butter market, 1770-1924*, Cork, 1998, 73.

36. *Report of the select committee on employment of the poor in Ireland*, H.C. 1823, VI (561), 23.

37. *Report on the roads made at the public expense in the southern district of Ireland*, H.C. 1823, X (249), 3-5.

38. *Report on the southern district in Ireland; containing a statement of the progress made on the several roads carried on at the public expense in that district*, H.C. 1829, XXII (153), 7.

39. C. Rynne, 1998, *op. cit.*, 90.

40. *Ibid.*, 86.

41. G. Ó Murchadha, 'Caoine Dhiarmad' 'Ic Eóghain', *Éigse* 1, part 1, 1939, 28.

42. *Ordnance Survey Memoirs* VI, 37; *Ibid.*, 31, 40.

43. *Ibid.*, XV, 25-6.

44. S. Lewis, 1837, *op. cit.*, s.v. named locations.

45. R. Gillespie, 'The reshaping of the borderlands, 1700-1840', in R. Gillespie and H. O'Sullivan (eds.), *The borderlands: essays on the history of the Ulster-Leinster border*, Belfast, 1989, 102.

46. S. Lewis, 1837, *op. cit.*, s.v. Ballinasloe.

47. *Parliamentary gazetteer of Ireland*, Dublin, 1846, s.v. Ballinasloe.

48. E.E. Evans, *Irish folk ways*, London, 1957, 257-8.

49. D.A. Cronin, 'The great Munster horse-fair of Cahirmee, county Cork', in D.A. Cronin et al. (eds.), 2001, *op. cit.*, 132.

50. *Cork Examiner*, 15th of July, 1846.

51. *Ordnance Survey Memoirs* XXXV, 60.

52. *Ibid.*, 61.

53. *Ibid.*, 61, 76.

54. In 1842, Thackeray saw a thimble-rigger at work in Killarney, Co. Kerry, and for subscribers to the game guessing which thimble a pea was under, had the invariable effect of parting them from their money. See, W. H. Thackeray, 1843, *op. cit.*, 133.

55. P.J. O'Connor, *All Ireland is in and about Rathkeale*, Newcastle West, 1996, 136.

56. *Ordnance Survey Memoirs* XXXV, 23.

57. See, for example, J. Bell, 'Hiring fairs in Ulster', *Ulster Folklife* 25, 1979, 67-78; and 'Farm servants in Ulster', *Ulster Folklife* 31,1985, 13-20.

58. P. Ó Canainn (ed.), *Filíocht na nGael*, Dublin, 1958, 161.

59. W.S. Mason, *A statistical account or parochial survey of Ireland*, Dublin, 1814, 125.

60. *Ordnance Survey Memoirs* I, 98.

61. In Co. Donegal at a later date hiring fairs in Ballybofey, Carndonagh, Raphoe and Letterkenny were known as the 'Rabbles'. The etymology is not clear, but it may refer to the throngs or 'rabble' converging on a town on the hiring day. See, A. O'Dowd, 'Seasonal migration to the Lagan and Scotland', in W. Nolan et al., (eds.), *Donegal: history and society*, Dublin, 1995, 631.

62. D. Fitzpatrick, 'The disappearance of the Irish agricultural labourer, 1841-1912', *Irish Economic and Social History* 7, 1980, 88.

63. *Second report by Mr. Wilson Fox on the wages and earnings of agricultural labourers in the UK*, P.P. 1905, xcvii, cd. 2376, 117.

64. See, footnote 8, and the text to which it refers.

65. *Ordnance Survey Memoirs* II, 63.

66. *Ibid.*, XIX, 30.

67. *Ibid.*, XVI, 47.

68. P. Logan, *Fair day: the story of Irish fairs and markets*, Belfast, 1986, 20.

69. *Ordnance Survey Memoirs* XIII, 46, 50.

70. S.J. Connolly, *Priests and people in pre-Famine Ireland 1780-1845*, Dublin, 1982, 167-70.

71. I. Weld, *Statistical survey of the county of Roscommon*, Dublin, 1832, 515-16.

72. E. Wakefield, *An account of Ireland, statistical and political*, London, 1812, II, 605.

73. W. M. Thackeray, 1843, *op. cit.*, 237-8.

74. W.R. Wilde, 'Glendalough pattern', *Journal of the Royal Society of Antiquaries of Ireland* 12, 1873, 449.

75. S. Ó Maitiú, *The humours of Donnybrook: Dublin's famous fair and its suppression*, Dublin, 1995, 12.

76. E.E. Evans, 1957, *op. cit.*, 256.

77. S. Ó Maitiú, 1995, *op. cit.*, 32.

78. *Saunder's newsletter*, 28th August, 1822.

79. S. Ó Maitiú, 'Changing images of Donnybrook fair', in D.A. Cronin et al. (eds.), 2001, *op. cit.*, 177.

80. D.W. Miller, *Peep O'Day Boys and Defenders: selected documents on the county Armagh disturbances 1784-96*, Belfast, 1990, 9-42.

81. P.E.W. Roberts, 'Caravats and Shanavests: Whiteboyism and faction fighting in east Munster, 1802-11', in S. Clark and J.S. Donnelly Jr. (eds.), *Irish peasants: violence and political unrest 1780-1914*, Dublin, 1983, 66.

82. *Ordnance Survey Memoirs* XXIII, 56-8.

83. *Ibid.*, XXXI, 3.

84. *Ibid.*, 32.

85. S. Lewis, 1837, *op. cit.*, s.v. Maguiresbridge, Co. Fermanagh.

86. P. Logan, 1986, *op. cit.*, 108-9.

87. Cited in S. Clark, *Social origins of the Irish land war*, Princeton, 1979, 77.

88. P.D. O'Donnell, *The Irish faction fighters of the nineteenth century*, Dublin, 1975, 63-75.

89. *Ibid.*, 84-5.

90. *Cín lae Amhlaoibh*, T. de Bhaldraite (ed.), 1970, *op. cit.*; *The diary of Humphrey O'Sullivan 1827-1835*, T de Bhaldraite (trans.), Cork, 1979.

91. *The Kilkenny Moderator*, 3rd September, 1834.

92. L.M. Cullen, 1981, *op. cit.*, 73-4.

93. *Ordnance Survey Memoirs* IX, 78.

94. *Ibid.*, 117.

95. J.H. Andrews, *History in the Ordnance Survey map*, Dublin, 1974, 18-19.

96. T. Jones Hughes, 'Village and town in mid nineteenth century Ireland', *Irish Geography* 14, 1981, 101-3.

97. *Cín lae Amhlaoibh*, 1970, *op. cit.*, 86-7.

98. *Ordnance Survey Memoirs* XXVIII, 21.

99. *Ibid.*, XXX, 27.

100. S. Lewis, 1837, *op. cit.*, s.v. Tralee, Co. Kerry.

101. *Ordnance Survey Memoirs* XL, 165.

102. S. Lewis, 1837, *op. cit.*, s.v. Edenderry, Co. Offaly.

103. *Ordnance Survey Memoirs* VIII, 42.

104. The American cultural geographer, Peirce Lewis, has used this term to signify historic leaps. See, P. Lewis, 'Axioms for reading the landscape', in D. Meinig (ed.), *The interpretation of ordinary landscapes*, New York, 1979, 13.

CHAPTER 5

1. R. White, *Remembering Ahanagran: storytelling in a family's past*, Cork, 1998, 17.

2. *Cín lae Amlaoibh*, T. de Bhaldraite (ed.), Baile Átha Cliath, 1970, 3; *The diary of Humphrey O'Sullivan 1827-1835*, T. de Bhaldraite (trans.), Cork, 1979, 17-18.

3. *Ibid.*, 115; *ibid.*, 135.

4. *Ibid.*, 116; *ibid.*, 136.

5. *Ibid.*, 73; *ibid.*, 91.

6. M. Silverman and P.H. Gulliver, *In the valley of the Nore: a social history of Thomastown, Co. Kilkenny 1840-1983*, Dublin, 1986, 4-7.

7. *The diary of Humphrey O'Sullivan*, 1979, *op. cit.*, 50.

8. These were known as *moileys* or *pollies*, adept in rocky terrain at eating the grass between the rocks. The proverb in full states: 'Don't buy a hornless cow, don't sell a hornless cow, and never be without a hornless cow'.

9. *Cín lae Amlaoibh*, 1970, *op. cit.*, 48; *ibid.*, 63.

10. T, O'Malley, 'Inscape: life and landscape in Callan and Co. Kilkenny', in W. Nolan and K. Whelan (eds.), *Kilkenny: history and society*, Dublin, 1990, 618.

11. W.M. Thackeray, *The Irish sketch book 1842*, London, 1843, 274-5.

12. *Ibid.*, 275.

13. *Ibid.*, 275.

14. S. Fenton, *It all happened*, Dublin, 1948, 68.

15. *Ibid.*, 77.

16. *Ibid.*, 78.

17. See, for example, M. Walsh, *Son of a tinker*, London, 1951, 167.

18. M. Walsh, *The road to nowhere*, London, 1934, 289.

19. *Ibid.*, 289-90.

20. *Ibid.*, 290-2.

21. Co. Kerry registered the lowest ratio of fairs to total population of any county in Ireland in 1851-3.

22. An Seabhac (P. Ó Siochfhradha), *Jimín Mháire Thaidhg*, Baile Átha Cliath, 1922, 24.

23. *Ibid.*, 25.

24. A. O'Dowd, 'Seasonal migration to the Lagan and Scotland', in W. Nolan et al. (eds.), *Donegal: history and society*, Dublin, 1995, 631-2.

25. P. MacGill, *Children of the dead end*, London, 1985, 26.

26. *Ibid.*, 28-9.

27. P. MacGill, *Glenmornan*, London, 1919, 137.

28. P. MacGill, 1985, *op. cit.*, 30-1.

29. Irish Folklore Commission, Q80/ Donegal 1, Meenmore, Inishkeel, Boylagh.

30. For legendary meanness the eponymous farmer from Hungersmother townland in Raymoghy parish, some 15 miles from Raphoe, could scarcely be matched in toponymy or life.

31. Irish Folklore Commission, MS 799: 412, Beltany, Tullaghobegley, 1941.

32. A. O'Dowd, *Spalpeens and tattie hookers: history and folklore of the Irish migratory worker in Ireland and Britain*, Dublin, 1991, 123.

33. S. Ó Grianna, *Nuair a bhi mé óg*, Baile Átha Cliath, 1942, 206-9.

34. Irish Folklore Commission, Ms 799: 407.

35. S. O'Faolain, *A nest of simple folk*, New York (1990 ed.), 215.

36. A set of conditions – social, historical, meteorological, physiological – that ensures that a word uttered in any given time, in any given place, will have a meaning different than it would have under any other conditions. Heteroglossia insures the primacy of context over text.

37. P.J. O'Connor, *All Ireland is in and about Rathkeale*, Newcastle West, 1996.

38. S. O'Faolain, 1990, *op. cit.*, 167.

39. B. MacMahon, 'Born in a market place', in G. Fitzmaurice (ed.), *Kerry through its writers*, Dublin, 1993, 89.

40. *Ibid.*, 92.

41. A small pig, a sucking pig, from the Irish *banbh*. Bonham is the more customary rendering in English.

42. As was the norm in rural Ireland, Kavanagh partook of the bartered labour system known as 'cooring', but he was never a hired labourer. See, A. Quinn, *Patrick Kavanagh: a biography*, Dublin, 2001, 31-43.

43. P. Kavanagh, *The green fool*, Harmondsworth, 1971, 111-3.

44. This may have been the social register of the tinkers known as Cant, Gammon or Shelta.

45. P. Kavanagh, 'I went to the fair', *Kavanagh's Weekly*, 1, no. 11, 21 June, 1952, 3.

46. *Ibid.*, 3.

47. P. Kavanagh, *Collected poems*, London, 1972, 163.

48. P. Kavanagh, 1971, *op. cit.*, 183-4.

49. *Ibid.*, 101.

50. P. Kavanagh, 'The marriage market', *Kavanagh's* Weekly, 1, no. 10, 14 June, 1952, 3.

51. M. Ó Cadhain, *The road to brightcity*, trans. Eoghan Ó Tuairisc, Dublin, 1981, 85.

52. P. Kavanagh, 1971, *op. cit.*, 157.

53. P. Kavanagh, *A poet's country: selected prose*, edited by A. Quinn, Dublin, 2003, 76.

54. P. Kavanagh, 1971, *op. cit.*, 209.

55. *Ibid.*, 183.

56. P. Kavanagh, 2003, *op. cit.*, 77.

57. A. Quinn, 2002, *op. cit.*, 73.

58. P. Kavanagh, 2003, *op. cit.*, 83.

59. E. Estyn Evans, *Ireland and the Atlantic heritage: selected writings*, Dublin, 1996, 133.

60. C. Ó Danachair, 'Distribution patterns in Irish folk tradition', *Béaloideas* 33, 1965, 104-6.

61. Dulse is an edible seaweed and yellow-man is a rock-like toffee with a golden colour. The signature song of the fair offers the chorus, 'Did you treat your Mary Anne to dulse and yellow-man?'

62. E. Estyn Evans, 1996, *op. cit.*, 134.

63. *Ibid.*, 134.

64. *Ibid.*, 134-5.

65. R. Hayward, *Munster and the city of Cork*, London, 1964, 286.

66. *Ibid.*, 288-90.

67. *Ibid.*, 290-1.

68. D. Gallogly, *Sliabh an Iarainn slopes: history of the town and parish of Ballinamore, Co. Leitrim*, Mullagh, 1991, 279-84.

69. A young sow. Typical usage would include the following: 'he had a *ceasóg* for sale' or 'he bought the makings of a *céasóg*'.

70. From *ceant*, the Irish word for an auction and adapted for selling downwards.

71. D. Gallogly, 1991, *op. cit.*, 283.

72. *Ibid.*, 283.

73. *Ibid.*, 284.

74. P.J. O'Connor, *Hometown: a portrait of Newcastle West, Co. Limerick*, Newcastle West, 1998, 66.

75. *Ibid.*, 66.

CHAPTER SIX

1. D.A. Cronin et al. (eds.), *Irish fairs and markets: studies in local history*, Dublin, 2001, 16.

2. P.J. O'Connor, *Exploring Limerick's past: an historical geography of urban development in county and city*, Newcastle West, 1987, 139-42.

3. *Ibid.*, 138-9.

4. P.J. O'Connor (ed.), *The Limerick* and Kerry *railway: inventory and prospect*, Newcastle West, 1986, 4.

5. Data for 1950 is based upon the painstaking aggregation of fair locations and numbers from *Old Moore's Almanac*, Dublin, 1950, 26-60. This source was compiled 'from the most authentic information that could be procured by the editor, neither pains nor expense being spared in its preparation.'

6. *Ibid*, 26-60.

7. F. Tobin, *The best of decades: Ireland in the 1960s*, Dublin, 1984, 95.

8. P. Logan, *Fair day: the story of Irish fairs and markets*, Belfast, 1986, 7.

9. *Old Moore's Almanac*, Dublin, 2003, 29-69.

10. P. Logan, 1986, *op. cit.*, 86.

11. This relates to the prices paid for certain designated animals.

Index

Index to Counties